ADDITIONAL ADVANCE PRAISE
UNDERSTANDING E-CARCERAT

"Essential reading. A powerful precautionary tale about how big data and technology can undermine the kind of society we want to build."

—Elizabeth Hinton, author of *From the War on Poverty to the War on Crime* and *America on Fire*

"Uncovers the truth behind the digital smokescreen, revealing how the intimate details of people's lives are devoured, digested, and used to deepen social control in the name of public safety and prison reform."

—Ruha Benjamin, professor of African American studies at Princeton University and founding director of the IDA B. WELLS Just Data Lab

"Kilgore warns us that the surveillance state is forever upgrading tech to expand its reach. He carefully explains the harms of carceral technology and invites us to work for an abolitionist future."

—Naomi Murakawa, associate professor of African American studies at Princeton University

"An incisive, thoroughly researched, and utterly frightening investigation into how technology, posing as reform, is expanding our prison nation into systems of hybrid punishment."

—Victoria Law, author of *Prison by Any Other Name* and *"Prisons Make Us Safer": And 20 Other Myths About Mass Incarceration*

James Kilgore is an activist, researcher, and writer based in Urbana, Illinois, where he has lived since paroling from prison in 2009. He is the director of the Challenging E-Carceration project at MediaJustice and the co-director of FirstFollowers Reentry Program in Champaign, Illinois. He is the author of five books, including the award-winning *Understanding Mass Incarceration*.

Also by James Kilgore

Understanding Mass Incarceration

We Are All Zimbabweans Now

Freedom Never Rests

Prudence Couldn't Swim

Sister Mercy's Revenge

UNDERSTANDING
E-CARCERATION

ELECTRONIC MONITORING,
THE SURVEILLANCE STATE, AND
THE FUTURE OF MASS INCARCERATION

JAMES KILGORE

THE
NEW
PRESS

NEW YORK
LONDON

Requests for permission to reproduce selections from this book
should be made through our website: https://thenewpress.com/contact.

Published in the United States by The New Press, New York, 2022
Distributed by Two Rivers Distribution

ISBN 978-1-62097-614-2 (hc)
ISBN 978-1-62097-615-9 (ebook)
CIP data is available

The New Press publishes books that promote and enrich public discussion and understanding of the issues vital to our democracy and to a more equitable world. These books are made possible by the enthusiasm of our readers; the support of a committed group of donors, large and small; the collaboration of our many partners in the independent media and the not-for-profit sector; booksellers, who often hand-sell New Press books; librarians; and above all by our authors.

www.thenewpress.com

Book design and composition by Bookbright Media
This book was set in Bembo and DIN

Printed in the United States of America

2 4 6 8 10 9 7 5 3 1

CONTENTS

UNDERSTANDING E-CARCERATION

PART ONE

INTRODUCING
E-CARCERATION

1

INTRODUCTION

I've spent the bulk of my adult life under state surveillance. Beginning in 1975, for twenty-seven years, I was a fugitive from justice. For the first two decades or so, that surveillance consisted of "wanted" posters with my picture on post office walls, periodic visits by the FBI to family members and friends, and the occasional "Where is he now?" story in the newspaper. For a white man not living with a disability, evading the law in those days was nothing like it is today.

Even getting a fake driver's license in those days wasn't much of a challenge. Many states didn't have pictures on licenses, let alone fingerprints or iris scans. I drove a car for most of that time and only got pulled over twice by the police. On one of those occasions, I accidentally drove down a one-way street directly at a cop car. Whiteness and an analog security system kept me out of harm's way.

By the turn of the century, things were changing. What criminology professor Susila Gurusami refers to as the "stickiness" of the internet began to set in. Everything in my past began to catch up to me via the digital world. My age-enhanced photos were starting to appear on the internet. John Walsh profiled me on *America's Most Wanted*.[1] The authorities hired a forensic sculptor to produce a three-dimensional plaster image designed to look like me after a quarter century of aging.[2] Eventually, they caught up to me in 2002 in Cape Town, South

Africa, though I am not totally sure how. It wasn't through that plaster thing, because it didn't look like me at all. Likely, it was through old-fashioned phone taps.

In prison, I encountered a different form of surveillance. The anonymity I craved as a fugitive was no longer possible. Everyone knew where I lived. My government name and prison number were on my cell door. Prison authorities read every one of the hundreds of letters that I sent and received. They gazed at pictures of my son's birthday parties, of holiday dinners at Grandma's house. At any given moment, the prison authorities knew my location. When I disappeared from direct vision the guards in the control tower had me on their screens. If they lost track for some reason, hundreds of other men knew my whereabouts. Just to be sure, though, the authorities sent me and everyone else in the institution back to our cells two or three times a day for body count. If one of us wasn't where we were supposed to be at count time, they would lock the whole prison down until they found out.

Privacy was a foreign concept. Though people did manage to smuggle in drugs and other contraband, we only really applied the notion of privacy at one moment, when we were using the "restroom" or, as we put it, "on the phone." Nature's call provided us with an opportunity to construct a cubicle of invisibility in our cell. We created a room divider with a hanging bedsheet. Paper clips embedded in the sheet served as hooks to attach the curtain to the bed and the wall. To complete the private space, we taped a piece of paper over the small window in our cell door so the guards couldn't see. Most guards respected that privacy curtain if you didn't keep it up for too long. Like most of the incarcerated population, they respected the unwritten homophobic code of "nobody wants to look at another man's ass." Defecation created our most formally recognized intimate moment.

Of course, those of us in the population found other ways to create our own moments and spaces of privacy. We read books together, shared legal papers, and built human relationships that were invisible to and beyond the reach of authorities. But we all knew that these relationships were vulnerable, capable of being snatched away by a transfer to another institution, a prolonged lockdown, a trip to the solitary confinement unit known as "the hole," or by the violence of our captors.

After six and a half years in federal and state prisons in California with shitting as my only official opportunity for privacy, they paroled me to Illinois where my family lived. I had one important condition on my parole: I had to wear an ankle monitor for a year. I was so happy to get out of prison that I didn't think much about that monitor. I didn't see how a plastic band could be a bother after all those years in cages and on wanted posters.

On my second day home, a cheery middle-aged white woman named Mary showed up and announced that she had come to install my device. She chatted about summer holidays and impending rains as she clipped the strap around my ankle. The ankle monitor somehow communicated with a box that looked like an iPod dock. The box connected to our landline phone. Immediately the box started to beep. It finally stopped after about a minute. Mary also gave me a tracker, a device about the size of a 1995 cellphone that I had to take with me when I left the house.

"If you're on the phone and the box starts beeping, you have to hang up immediately," she instructed us. "That means it's sending information to the office."

"Don't touch or move the box," she added, "you might lose the connection."

I was waiting for her to hand me the manual and rules of the road, but she kept talking about her impending vacations, how installing monitors was a side job to her full-time gig at the local prison. A Caribbean cruise was on her vacation horizon.

As she took her perky smile out the door, she told me, "Your parole agent will give you all the rules when he comes tomorrow. Until then, you are on lockdown."

After the woman closed the front door, my wife's voice came loud and clear from the kitchen. "I wanna punch that woman," she said. "She acts like she brought us a Christmas present." I laughed. What else could I do? Locked down in my own house. I had thought I would never hear the term "lockdown" again.

In prison, there is a rule for everything. When I landed in the California state system, they handed me a copy of Title 17, all the rules that apply to prison. Title 17 was eighty-five pages long and printed in seven-point font. This skinny volume laid out every detail imaginable— your daily entitlement of calories, how many pairs of socks and boxer shorts the laundry folks had to issue you, and all the bureaucratic details about penalties you would incur for violating the rules, whether you refused an order from a guard or got caught with an apple pilfered from the kitchen.

I expected the same for being on parole with an electronic monitor. There would be detailed rules and I would figure out how to live with them.

When my parole agent showed up the next day strapped with his 9-millimeter, he only had a few rules. No handbook, no Title 17. "You are allowed out of the house Monday to Friday, from 6 a.m. to 10 a.m.," he told me without looking anywhere near my eyes. "That should be enough time to take care of all your business." After another glance at his 9-millimeter and the handcuffs attached to his belt, I withheld my argument about how most stores didn't open until 10 a.m., that very few job interviews were going to happen before 10 a.m. and that all the soccer matches my sixteen-year-old son would be playing were going to happen well after 10 a.m.

As far as rules go, *he* was the rules. The only documentation I got was a piece of paper with a few phone numbers on it. In very large print appeared the 800 number for the call center, the folks who arranged what the parole people called "movement" every time I wanted to leave the house.

"You call them up and tell them if you have an appointment," he said. "They will let me know and I will authorize it. If I don't authorize it, you don't go." My eyes flashed to the 9-millimeter again. He handed me a few more pieces of paper with lists of phone numbers on them.

"Here's where you can look for a job," he said. I looked at the list. Kelly, Express, Worknet. Temporary employment agencies. Kelly was around before I got locked up, but we called it Kelly Girl back then. How times had changed.

"Will I be able to go and visit my mother?" I asked. She lived about ten minutes away.

"Let's see how it goes," he said and stood up to leave. I didn't try to prolong the conversation. He might have come armed to the teeth, but at least he skipped the part where he tore my house apart looking for drugs and had me peeing in a cup. White privilege again. I didn't bother escorting him to the door. My son was sitting on the couch pretending to watch TV. His face looked hollow. No armed stranger had ever entered our house before and my son knew what these people could do. He'd visited me in prison many times.

That night, as we got into bed, I felt the presence of a third person. I was certain my parole agent had sneaked into the house and was lying under the covers looking up at me and my partner from that device on my leg. It was a restless sleep. At one point I thought my toes touched the cold steel of his 9-millimeter.

For the first week, I got up at 5 a.m. every day, had a cup of tea, and went for a walk. I had to exhaust myself by 10 a.m. and prepare for the next twenty hours of lockdown. I had piles of books to keep me occupied and websites to explore on my laptop. I could cook teriyaki chicken and cape bean curry. These were things I had dreamed about while I was locked up, but what I dreamed about more was freedom, going where I wanted, when I wanted. That wasn't part of the bargain.

Just like I somehow adjusted to prison, I got used to the electronic monitor. Just like prison, I hated it but found ways to make the most of the structured time it provided. Gradually, my parole agent loosened his noose. If I gave him a schedule of all my movements two weeks in advance, he would simply hand them over to the call center folks who were supposed to program them into my weekly schedule. That worked most of the time. But trying to plan every time I left the house two weeks in advance was challenging. I would go grocery shopping and the line would be too long for me to get back home in time, so I would just abandon the shopping cart and go home.

Then there were the nights when they phoned and told me the satellite had lost connection with my device. They would tell me to go stand outside until the satellite re-connected. I would stand there looking up at the sky as if the satellite were going to cruise past the house, beam down a signal , and I would be re-connected to my electronic ball and chain. I never did quite figure out how my ankle communicated with the satellite, but after a few minutes, they let me go back in the house.

The biggest moral dilemma came the night my mother phoned at 2 a.m. and told me she had chest pains—she thought she was having a heart attack and had already called 911. My first instinct was to rush to her side. After all, she was ninety-six and had lived twenty-seven years without really knowing where her son was, then six and a half years knowing he was in prison. And she still loved me unconditionally. I owed it to her to be by her side if she passed. I phoned the number on the piece of paper. They told me I would need my parole agent's permission to leave the house and go to the hospital. I knew my parole agent wasn't going to pick up the phone at 2 a.m. unless there were dead bodies or boatloads of cocaine involved. I had to make a choice: rush to the hospital without permission and hope the parole agent would understand in the morning, or wait it out until 6 a.m. when I had movement and hope Mom didn't pass away in the night. Fortunately, my partner was able to go to the hospital to check on my mother's condition so I didn't have to take the risk. In the end, it wasn't a heart attack, and she didn't die. In fact, she lived another seven years, long enough to see my ankle without a monitor and my persona without parole.

The next morning, I phoned my parole agent and asked him if in the future I could go to the hospital in such a situation. He told me it was a "gray area." After six and a half years in prison, I knew to avoid gray areas. They had a way of perilously changing color very quickly.

When I found the time to step back, much of the electronic monitoring regime turned out to also be a clown show of ineptitude: the incompetent leading the apathetic, implementing a program with bad ideas and pointless, ineffective but punitive technology. The call center operators rarely answered the phone in under fifteen minutes. They could take up to an hour. Once they called me and told me to go back home at a time when I had movement. I argued, they insisted I go back, but I persuaded them to check. They put me on hold for ten minutes and told me I was good to go on my movement. My parole agent, no genius himself, referred to the call center operators as "the morons."

One time I had movement to go to the University of Illinois library. I had been wandering through the six floors of stacks looking for various books. I took a pile to the front desk to check them out and my cellphone rang. The morons were calling.

"Where's your tracker?" they asked. I reached for my belt where the tracker always hung. It wasn't there. "I just had it," I told them, "it must have fallen off. I'll trace my steps."

They located the tracker outside, on the street in the front of the library. I raced down the stairs to where they said it was and phoned them back. I couldn't see it anywhere. They told me it was at Sixth and Daniel, about four blocks away. I ran over there, keeping the moron on the phone. When I got to Sixth and Daniel, she told me it was at Fourth and Green. When I got to Fourth and Green, she told me it was at Wright and Daniel, about five blocks away.

My adrenaline kept me going as the sweat came pouring off. The sweat of running mixed with the sweat of worrying. Replacing a lost tracker was supposed to cost $1,000, but they could also hit me with a tampering charge or even attempted escape. I could be heading back to prison because of this shitty little tracker.

My low-speed chase for the elusive device went on for an hour and a half. The whole time I was on the phone with the woman from the morons' office. She turned out to be quite reasonable and calm, though she couldn't explain how the device could keep traveling in circles and eluding my clutches. I avoided saying the obvious—if this thing is supposed to be tracking me and you don't know where it is, how do you know where I am? This was not my moment to question the technology. This was a moment between me and my God of freedom. This was a moment that might drive me to prayer after more than three decades of abstinence. If this shitty little device was going to send me back to prison, I had no idea how I would cope.

I never found the tracker. Near the end of the chase, I was stopping people on the street and asking them if they'd seen a device that looked like a 1990s cellphone anywhere. I was convinced someone had picked it up and I'd probably see it on e-bay the next day.

I abandoned my search for library books as well and headed for home base. Two hours later my parole agent phoned. I explained what happened. He said I could still have the movement that was already approved and that someone would come the next day and bring me a new tracker. He never mentioned anything about the $1,000 or sending me back to prison.

The combination of white privilege and parole agent apathy had saved me at least a grand. More importantly, my wild goose chase for the tracker dispelled any doubts I might have had that this technology could do even what it claimed: keep an accurate, real-time record of where I was. The ankle monitor was all a techno-sham, a Y2K scare brought to the criminal legal sphere.

As my year on the ankle monitor wore on, I grew more curious about this technology. I was amazed no rules and regulations came with it, and that a parole agent along with their team of morons could basically make up the rules and regs that controlled your life and you had no avenues of appeal.

Not only were there no rules and regulations, there was also little or no research on the impact of these devices. I went through that huge library at the University of Illinois and found just a few articles. I read about something online called the *Journal of Offender Monitoring*. They didn't have the journal in our library, so I had to drive an hour and a half to Springfield, Illinois, to find the copies there.

The *Journal of Offender Monitoring*'s research wasn't really research. The articles were a combination of advertising and guides on how to make the devices punish more effectively. By this time, my curiosity about these devices had brought me into contact with a few other people who had been on a monitor. Virtually all of them said the same thing: no rules, no freedom. Some were even paying a daily fee to be monitored.

In the quiet of my house arrest, I began a quest to get to the bottom of electronic monitoring. I wanted to know who all was on this device, how it affected them, and who was making money from it. Most of all, I was determined to unravel where this technology was headed. At about the time I was on the monitor, fitness trackers began to emerge. The Fitbits were close cousins to the trackers law enforcement put on us. Though one was providing a service and the other punishment, they seemed to come from similar historical roots. As the power of Google, Amazon, Facebook, and Microsoft grew, I felt the importance of what was on my ankle begin to swell.

I shared my concerns about this with many people. Those who had been on the monitor understood my worries. But the policy wonks and the liberals kept hitting me with the same line: "At least it's better than prison." My friend Johnny Page, who spent over two decades in Illinois state prisons, complained about those who said he should be grateful to be out of prison, as I did. "I'm not out," was his reply, "it's just another form of incarceration."[3]

Ultimately, I realized the monitor was a trick they were playing on us. Like a carceral Grubhub, electronic monitoring had brought the prison to me, rather than taking me to the prison. My family had to live inside this techno-cell with me. Perhaps the one consolation to being separated from my family during incarceration was that they weren't around for the daily rounds of humiliation and degradation. I could tell them what I wanted them to hear and hope they would suppress their worst fears about the rest of it.

But with the monitor, my cell was in our collective living space. The intrusions of the carceral state, be they voice recognition phone calls asking for my name and number, or parole agents strutting through the house with 9-millimeter pistols strapped to their side, were right there in my family's face. Plus, the box beeped at unpredictable moments. To make matters worse, every time I went out with my family, there was the fear that traffic or a car breakdown would deliver us back home after my time of movement had expired. This meant parole could respond with its ugly side with my loved ones bearing witness. That could include house searches, cuffing me up facedown on the floor, or showing off their latest taser technology. If my partner or son protested, they too could be swooped into the net. The monitor came with many tripwires.

I did adjust and so did my family, but since that time I've been studying ankle monitoring. Most people call these monitors ankle "bracelets," but I've given up talking about them like they are jewelry. They are shackles. No need to confuse decoration with incarceration.

For the past ten years, I have been interviewing and talking with people who have been impacted by electronic monitoring. This includes not only those who have been strapped with the shackles, but their loved ones, their pastors, their employers, and those who provide programs and services to individuals who have been captured by this form of deprivation of liberty by means of technology—or what we now call "e-carceration."

This book aims to place electronic monitoring in the bigger picture, to grasp the importance of these little bands of plastic. We need to understand their complexity. Why are they tools of incarceration and punishment instead of vehicles for change? How do they connect to the structures of what Harvard professor and bestselling author Shoshana Zuboff calls "surveillance capitalism"?[4] Why do they contribute to what abolition theorist and activist Ruth Wilson Gilmore describes in the context of Black people as "premature death"?[5] How do they block our ability to imagine freedom?

The age of mass incarceration and the GPS tracker emerged in the midst of a neoliberal transformation of the global economy in which free market policies enhanced corporate power and increased inequality. In the United States, neoliberalism meant a Reagan-inspired set of policies aimed at diminishing the power of the state and organized labor in the economy. To maximize profits, the neoliberal agenda drove companies to shut down high-wage, unionized operations in industrial cities such as Detroit, Chicago, Cleveland, Milwaukee, Buffalo, Pittsburgh, and Camden, New Jersey. For the working classes of those cities, especially Black people, the elimination of manufacturing jobs meant large swaths of the population became surplus labor. The state had to make a choice about how to handle this surplus labor. It could either spend money on providing the surplus labor population with employment and economic supports, or create new ways to control them, to ensure they didn't organize and rebel like they had in the uprisings of the 1960s. The state opted for control, for policing, for creating a War on Drugs that provided enormous budgets to expand and militarize police. With this came prisons and jails to house those surplus workers, many of whose only economic options were the underground economy. This became mass incarceration, or the expansion of a prison-industrial complex, a set of institutions of punishment that generated revenue and power for certain privileged sectors of the population.

At the same time, major corporations and neoliberal policy makers were reorganizing at the top. According to Marxist sociologists Foster and McChesney, this meant an economy increasingly dominated by financial derivatives trading, the militarization of security systems, and digital surveillance.[6] This rise in power of the financial and surveillance sectors diluted the influence of political institutions and elected leaders. This historical context, where the power of democratic institutions steadily diminishes, is the framework within which e-carceration emerges.

The evolution of technology will certainly soon leave the ankle shackle in the barn with the horse and buggy. The question is, where is the arc of the technological universe taking us and what can we do to make it bend toward justice?

The complexity of this reality poses serious problems for those of us who argue for a new system. Many people, including me, have argued that abolition, rather than reform, holds the key to transformation. On one level, abolition refers to the elimination of carceral institutions such as prisons, jails, immigration detention centers, and lockup mental health facilities. But theoreticians of abolition such as Angela Davis and Ruth Wilson Gilmore make the case for abolition as a complete transformation of society, a form of democracy that displaces the dominance of the profit motive with a model that centers human needs, dignity, and respect for the planet.

But how do we create an agenda for abolition in an era of surveillance capitalism? How do we address the invasiveness of surveillance technology and corporate control? We may call for the abolition of prisons and jails, but what about the technology of surveillance? Do we compromise and fight for watered-down versions of surveillance devices and regulation of data collection? Or do we fight for the abolition of data-mining companies that thrive by extracting our data and turning it into dollars or Bitcoin? If abolition is the correct course, what kind of organization and organizers do we require to make this a reality? The abolition road is not always clear. To make matters worse, most of us who ardently fight for freedom carry our cellphones in our pockets or handbags. We have enormous digital footprints and a huge presence in the databases that seem to be creating algorithms of doom. But we still rely on this technology. In fact, many of us love it, are even addicted to it. I am.

The advent of the coronavirus pandemic in 2020 threw all of this into a new light. The virus brought both mass death and crisis. The crisis was multidimensional—social, political, and economic. Crisis often makes the impossible possible and the normal abnormal. The "impossible" of the crisis was a Congress that constantly proclaims to be cash-strapped raising trillions of dollars of relief money in a few days. Empty streets in places like New York City and Beijing became normal. But in the world of policing and surveillance, suddenly, gathering data became an imperative to ensure the nation's health. Overnight, the repressive surveillance state apparatus of China became a model to emulate in the name of ensuring safety. Surprisingly, even the notion of releasing people from prisons and jails, although often on electronic monitors, became a reasonable policy measure to consider, once again in the interest of community safety. In this context, new surveillance devices stepped to the fore— apps that could take temperature remotely, software to measure the collective physical daily movement of the entire population, drones that could surveil houses looking for quarantined individuals who were violating lockdown orders. All of these vaulted into the ranks of the "new normal," a category that continues to evolve.

While crisis facilitates repression and the technologies of e-carceration, it also sparks creative, revolutionary thinking. Technology not only has the power to control, it also contains the potential to bring people together, to carry out mutual aid, to share stories and experiences, to build communications systems free of the control of corporate capital, to reverse climate change and eliminate imperialist wars.

I grew into the world of liberation politics in the 1960s and 1970s. In many ways, the battle lines during that period felt much clearer than they are today. From the perspective of the global Left, we saw imperialist wars taking place in Southeast Asia, southern Africa, Central America, and Palestine. Many of us saw liberation movements in those regions as the harbingers of new, human-centered societies that put people before profits and fought for racial and gender justice. We drew inspiration from the heroic Vietnamese constructing hundreds of miles of underground tunnels to transport the goods they needed to wage war against the imperialist machine, from the Chinese and their Long March to Fidel and the guerrillas taking over Cuba village by village. In our most optimistic moments, we looked to the vision of Mao Tse-tung, which predicted a future where the liberation forces of the Third World would surround the industrialized countries, much as the Chinese Red Army in the 1940s had built up power in the rural areas and then taken over the cities. Black Panther Party cofounder Huey P. Newton summed up how we viewed the dynamics of these victorious liberation wars: "The spirit of the people is greater than the man's technology."[7]

Yet these historical icons ultimately have not shaped the world we envisioned. Once they took over the state, the revolutionary movements we idolized all too often abandoned their ideas of popular power. Instead of becoming champions of the working class and rural poor, these movements frequently caved into the neoliberal revolution of British prime minister Margaret Thatcher and President Ronald Reagan. Promises of land to the tiller and power to the people morphed into privatization, tax holidays for foreign investors, and the production of cash crops for the consumers in the global North.

By comparison, any search today for global revolutionary models and heroes yields sparse results. We have only a few icons and even fewer nations or liberation movements to stand as examples of a world we want to make. The architects of the new global technology order continue to move ahead with all the aggression and ruthlessness that imperialist war machines have demonstrated over the centuries. Those of us ready to contest the power of Google and Amazon are still learning what it looks like to constitute a movement of resistance, a force of power and healing. We cannot fight fire with fire or fight algorithms with algorithms, but we can ignite our own flame and develop our own formulas for change.

Nonprofit organizations such as the Algorithmic Justice League and Data 4 Black Lives have used research to highlight the issues of racial and gender injustice that emerge within the world of algorithms and artificial intelligence. MediaJustice, where I have directed the Challenging E-Carceration project since 2017, fights against the advance of Amazon and other Big Tech players while opposing the spread of ankle shackles and other forms of e-carceration. The work of these organizations asks the question: How can we subject this technology to popular control?[8]

As the COVID-19 moment has reminded us, where there is deprivation of liberty, the potential for imagining freedom inevitably surfaces. How do we alter the narratives of liberty deprivation? How do we reimagine technological power and creativity in the image of freedom? How do we transform society by contrasting the drive for data and surveillance with a vision of technology informed by popular knowledge? This book will explore these questions as we walk down the e-carceration road, from the simple analog-like ankle shackle to the great corporate data clouds in the sky. No data point is an island.

Undoubtedly, from the time you began reading this chapter, a new app or even new technology has been born. Even more, the internet of things—the configuration that connects devices, appliances, and other objects via sensors, monitors, interfaces, and networks—will have widened its reach. Given the pace of technological change, we can't keep up with every new development, but we can develop a critique and a plan of action to prevent this technology from becoming a form of all-enveloping mass e-carceration.

2

WHAT IS E-CARCERATION?

Many of the current reform efforts contain the seeds of the next generation of racial and social control, a system of "e-carceration" that may prove more dangerous and more difficult to challenge than the one we hope to leave behind. . . . Some insist that [this system] is "a step in the right direction." But where are we going with this?

—*Michelle Alexander, author of* The New Jim Crow[1]

Black liberation organizer and media justice visionary Malkia Devich-Cyril introduced the term "e-carceration" in 2015. Devich-Cyril defines e-carceration as mass incarceration blended with the technology of electronic surveillance and punishment.[2] Since Devich-Cyril introduced this term, three important things have happened. First, e-carceration has become equated largely with only electronic ankle monitors, narrowing our vision and capacity to assess the challenges we face from these technologies of oppression. Second, the emergence of new technologies and rapid expansion of what existed in 2015 has dramatically changed the scale of the e-carceration Devich-Cyril first defined. Third, the technologies of e-carceration are becoming normalized within our contemporary political economy. The term "racial capitalism" best depicts that political economy by reminding us of the presence

Racial Capitalism

The term *racial capitalism* was first popularized in the United States in Black Studies professor Cedric Robinson's book *Black Marxism*. Robinson, who drew extensively on the work of South African writers such as Martin Legassick and Neville Alexander in elaborating this term,[3] emphasized that race and racism have been key components of capitalism at every stage, even before the enslavement of people from the African continent.[4] Contemporary Black historian Robin D.G. Kelley maintains there is "no such thing as a non-racial capitalism." In examining the historical roots of capitalism, Kelley contends that from the outset, capitalism expanded by creating "segmented populations" that were unequal. He links this process to imperialism and settler colonialism, citing not only the conquests of Africa and Asia but the colonization of Ireland and the introduction of people from the Arab world into British society.[5] Activists in the prison abolition movement such as Ruth Wilson Gilmore also use this term.

of racism at every stage of capitalist development, even before the enslavement of African people.

Today we can think of e-carceration more broadly as the application of a network of punitive technologies to social problems. Ultimately, these technologies deprive people of their liberty. They do this through confinement, tracking, and recording a range of movements, activities, and even bodily functions. Sometimes, this extends to entire communities or social movements. The most well known form of e-carceration is house arrest with an ankle monitor, but new technologies of e-carceration are emerging every day. They include facial recognition software, license plate readers, closed-circuit TV (CCTV) cameras, drones, and social media monitors. Of central importance among these technologies are risk assessment tools, which are mathematically based formulas often used by the criminal legal system and other government agencies to determine whether or not a person should be incarcerated or surveilled.[6] Although many of these technologies at first glance may appear to be neutral and not punitive or harmful, when applied in conjunction with criminal legal and repressive immigration policies within a neoliberal economic framework, they inevitably contribute to deprivation of liberty.

HOW E-CARCERATION IS DIFFERENT

E-carceration deprives people of their freedom but not through physical confinement as applied in places like prisons, jails, immigration detention "centers," and lockup mental health facilities. Four main differences distinguish e-carceration.

First, e-carceration often may deprive a person of their liberty by denying them access to resources such as employment, housing, medical treatment, therapy, or the opportunity to spend time with their loved ones. This deprivation of liberty often occurs through the weaponization of data. This involves using a range of information stored in various databases to create a profile that rates a person's eligibility to access certain social services. These ratings can even determine whether or not a person should be imprisoned. The eligibility rating may be deeply influenced by a number of factors including a person's race, age, gender/gender identity, disability, religion, immigration status, and national origin.

Second, the punishment of e-carceration is not always time bound by a sentence or period of carceral control such as parole or probation. If it involves the collection and storage of data, the punishment or harm done by this technology may have no time boundaries. This particularly applies when e-carceration involves medical interventions such as what researcher Erick Fabris refers to as "tranquil prisons" that involve forced treatment orders and mandatory medication.[7] Fabris, who is a survivor of the psychiatric punishment system and a co-founder of Psychiatric Survivor Pride Day, emphasizes how medications may deprive people of their liberty by reducing their cognition or ability to communicate.

Third, in some instances, the technology of e-carceration is administered without a person's explicit knowledge or permission. While an individual definitely knows if they are in a jail cell or on an ankle monitor, they may not be aware when they are subject to e-carceration technologies such as facial recognition and drones. Among other things, these technologies have the capacity to select and target individuals in a crowd. For example, during the early days of the coronavirus pandemic in 2020, Chinese authorities introduced drones with facial recognition capacity to identify people who weren't wearing masks. Police in U.S. cities have used facial recognition to identify and arrest protesters who they allege have broken the law. One of the most publicized incidents occurred in 2020 when Donald Trump cleared the streets to stage a photo op of him holding a Bible in front of St. John's Episcopal Church in Washington, DC. Michael Peterson, who was taking part in a Black Lives Matter protest near the church at the time, was later arrested after being photographed in a scuffle with police during the street clearing. To match Peterson's face, police used a national database called National Capital Region Facial Recognition Investigative Leads System, then scoured Twitter to track him down.[8] New York BLM leader Derrick Ingram was arrested on an assault charge after facial recognition supposedly identified him as the person who shouted into the ear of a police officer with a bullhorn.[9] Facial recognition also featured in the identification of those involved in the coup attempt of January 6, 2021.[10]

Fourth, people may be directly complicit in the intensification of their e-carceration. They may do this by adding data and information to databases used to predict behavior and authorize official responses or by not protecting themselves from such data captures. The simple act of providing personal details for an online purchase or downloading the many apps that have location tracking capacity exemplify this sort of unconscious complicity. The popular Weather Channel app, which informs users they are gathering location data, has faced lawsuits for selling that data to private companies. Even Muslim prayer apps such as Salaat First (which has more than 10 million downloads) and Muslim Pro have been discovered to be tracking location.[11]

THE EXPANSION OF E-CARCERATION

The expansion of e-carceration is the result of two forces in tension: popular mobilization against mass incarceration and the drive for profitability. The late 2000s saw the emergence of a wide range of critiques of and organized opposition to mass incarceration. Much of this focused on the War on Drugs. Civil rights lawyer Michelle Alexander's 2010 book, *The New*

Jim Crow: Mass Incarceration in the Age of Colorblindness, spent more than 250 weeks on the *New York Times* bestseller list. This work highlighted measures that led to the rise of the prison population, including drug policies that disproportionately impacted Black people, and the enduring consequences that a prison sentence levies on people once they are released.[12] Her writings, along with pressure from national advocacy organizations such as the Drug Policy Alliance to moderate drug sentencing laws, ultimately reached the highest levels of government. In 2015, Barack Obama became the first president to ever visit a prison and used the opportunity to commute the sentences of forty-six people who had spent many years in prison, many for nonviolent drug offenses. His criminal justice platform stressed the racial inequities in the system and the need for more effective reentry programs.[13] His attorney general, Eric Holder, condemned "widespread incarceration" as "both ineffective and unsustainable," and ordered a rollback in enforcement of some federal drug laws.[14]

At the state and local level, community-based activism blossomed, targeting the excessive expenditure of prisons and jails, racialized police violence, and the need for bail reform. In many of these struggles, radical voices led the way, often from people who were survivors of incarceration themselves. Activist-philosopher Angela Davis, a political prisoner in the 1970s, was among the leaders calling for a more radical agenda, including the abolition of prisons. This growing mobilization against mass incarceration overlapped with the meteoric rise of nationwide protests against the police murders of unarmed Black people such as Michael Brown, Eric Garner, and Sandra Bland. The newly emerging formation, Black Lives Matter, founded by three Black women, Patrisse Cullors, Opal Tometi, and Alicia Garza, became the largest organized voice for racial and gender justice in decades.

The growth of these social justice movements forced many people in the law-and-order camp to moderate their views. Former speaker of the House of Representatives Newt Gingrich, a Republican and long a staunch supporter of the "lock 'em up and throw away the key" approach, formed the conservative, reform-minded campaign Right on Crime. Gingrich and his cohort spoke of an "urgent need" to reduce the prison population and argued that "conservatives must lead the way [in] fixing the system." Gingrich's change of heart apparently reflected a deep-rooted soul-searching: "Once you decide everybody in prison is also an American then you gotta really reach into your own heart and ask, is this the best we can do?"[15]

These shifts in viewpoint among both Democrats and Republicans sparked debates about measures to reduce the prison population. The economic crisis of 2008 put further pressure on lawmakers to reduce expenditure on the criminal legal system. One result was an exploration of "alternatives to incarceration," ways to handle people who broke the law without resorting to prison or jail. These alternatives, which included forms of e-carceration such as electronic monitoring, reflect what I have labeled "carceral humanism," the re-packaging of methods of social control and punishment as the delivery of caregiving services.[16] This reform process had economic ripple effects, prompting those who had financially benefited from mass incarceration to explore new avenues of gaining revenue through punishment. At a time when the technology sector as a whole was taking off, e-carceration suited the moment.

The discussion about alternatives to incarceration overlapped with the development of heightened GPS capacity, and investors began to eye electronic monitoring as a ticket to the future. BI Incorporated, the Boulder, Colorado, firm that bought out electronic monitoring originator Michael Goss in the 1980s, was the leader from the outset, first cornering the market for radio-frequency devices, then pioneering the expansion of GPS tracking. The GEO Group, then the world's second-largest private prison operator (it has since become number one), seeing the opportunity in e-carceration, jumped into the fray, buying out BI in 2009 for $415 million.[17] Corporations including the GEO Group recognized that the addition of GPS capacity to ankle monitors didn't just enhance authorities' capacity to track location. As these devices got "connected," they blended location-tracking information with data housed on the rapidly expanding mega-storage sites that became known as "clouds." Rather than remaining solely a tool of criminal legal policy, this foundational technology of e-carceration was becoming part of the surveillance state, a politicized system to aggregate and store data for transmission, retrieval, comparison, mining, trading, and, of course, intelligence gathering.

The technologies of e-carceration, especially under the surveillance state, dehumanize in a unique way, transforming us from human beings to a collection of data points. In this world of e-carceration, we are no longer living, breathing beings or spiritual entities. Nor are we simply a case file or registration number as in the pre-computer, pre-internet days. We become data points rendered on a screen, in an algorithmic formula, living not on the street or in a house but in databases or computer renderings of reality. We acquire a digital life of our own. In the words of Shoshana Zuboff, author of *The Age of Surveillance Capitalism*, "both the world and our lives are pervasively rendered as information." But the power dynamics of this relationship often remain hidden. Zuboff provides us with an important wake-up call: "We think we're searching Google. Google is actually searching us."[18] Or as surveillance scholar Ruha Benjamin puts it, "what we have access to has access to us."[19]

THE KEY FORMS OF E-CARCERATION

E-carceration takes four major forms, which often overlap and intersect.

1. RISK ASSESSMENT AND PREDICTION

The technology of contemporary risk assessment emerged alongside the heightened computational capacity to create complex mathematical formulas known as algorithms. Largely drawing on historical trends and patterns, algorithms allow for the calculation of the chances, or the "risk," that a certain event will happen or a certain person will act in a certain way. Once the risk is calculated, it can be converted into a score or assessment for prediction.

Commercial usage of scientifically based risk emerged in the eighteenth century in the life insurance industry when British mathematician James Dodson combined mortality tables and probability studies to calculate premiums.[20] Today, corporations and government departments calculate risk in many spheres of social, political, and economic life—from the likelihood that someone will contract cancer to the possibilities of nuclear war to the chances of a hurricane striking the coast of Florida. Perhaps the most familiar risk assessment tool (RAT) is the credit score, which lets a business owner or financial institution know how risky it would be to lend money to a particular person. More recently, sports betting entrepreneurs have developed mathematical formulas for determining the likelihood of certain outcomes of a football or baseball game.

RATs are surfacing in the worlds of health care, education, social welfare, and policing to chart "appropriate" responses to anticipated situations and inform policy and budget considerations. In the criminal legal system, decision-makers most frequently use RATs to assess the pros and cons of releasing someone from prison or jail. In nearly all these instances, RATs contain massive bias. Because authorities typically base their algorithms on historical data from a society in which race, class, gender, and ableist biases abound, the algorithms offer biased assessments.[21] Researcher Ruha Benjamin gives particular emphasis to the anti-Black bias in these algorithms, referring to such formulas as part of a "New Jim Code."[22]

This dynamic is perhaps most obvious in the criminal legal system, where predicting a person's future relies on examining data from their past record. For example, a RAT may assess whether authorities should release a certain person awaiting trial on a burglary charge without having to pay a cash bond to the court. A typical RAT will use metrics such as a person's past criminal history and their employment status as variables in the risk calculation.[23] In such instances, the RAT gives the person a point score that suggests incarceration or release.

RATs may also lead to social deprivation of liberty, which occurs when a person's ability to access services is limited because of their risk assessment score. For example, property managers frequently use RATs with deep-seated bias to evaluate rental applications. RentPrep.com, judged the best tenant screening tool of 2021 in a national survey, includes criteria such as criminal background, evictions, and credit scores, all of which contain considerable racial bias.[24] But while a person on parole typically has a human being like a parole officer to negotiate with (however imperfect that negotiation process might be), when it comes to RATs, the algorithm is the final word. Transparency doesn't exist. In most instances, what data goes into the algorithm or how it is calculated is not revealed. A 2019 study of pretrial RATs by the nonprofit Electronic Privacy Information Center noted that "one of the primary criticisms of these RATs is that they are proprietary tools, developed by technology companies that refuse to disclose their inner workings. COMPAS is one of the most widely used of these tools, and Northpointe, the company that owns COMPAS, holds that the RAT formula is their intellectual property that they have a right to protect."[25] The 2017 case of *Loomis v. Wisconsin* challenged Northpointe's right to keep their formula secret. The plaintiff, Eric Loomis, argued that the secrecy of the formula limited his access to due process, since he couldn't challenge the actual calculation of his risk assessment score. Although the court ruled against Loomis, it did recommend that companies at least disclose what data they are keeping from the public.[26]

2. IDENTIFIERS/AUTHENTICATORS

Government bodies have used fingerprints to identify suspects in police investigations for over a century. But whereas fingerprints were once analog, in the twenty-first century they are digitized, as are many additional unique identifiers, or "authenticators." These have upstaged the traditional stalwarts of forensics: hair samples, bodily fluids, and DNA. Increasingly, identifiers are also linked to biological functions. Our voice cadence, gait, heartbeats, and brain waves may have unique, measurable qualities. These identifiers can be used to open a door for us, boot up our laptop, and allow us to remotely turn on the heat in our house. While these uses may not be explicitly carceral (and some may be convenient), identifiers can be key tools in criminalizing people or collectives, placing them as players in criminal conspiracies or political resistance activities.

3. LOCATION TRACKING

In 2003, only about 5 percent of electronic ankle monitors had GPS capacity.[27] Today, the overwhelming majority of ankle monitors have GPS tracking that records a person's movements in real or near-real time. Like biometrics, this location data has the potential to digitally report a person's behavior in ways that can implicate them in criminal activity, pair them with those of known criminal background, place them in illicit places such as known drug houses or gambling establishments, or label them as carriers of a virus.

Moreover, GPS devices have the capacity to designate exclusion and inclusion zones into their programs. These zones are geographic areas that define where a person can or cannot go. If a person has an exclusion zone programmed into their GPS, an alarm or voice recording will sound if they enter the neighborhood or block of that exclusion zone. Entering an exclusion zone may even trigger a 911 call and summon the police. Ultimately, these e-carceration zones can reconstruct our cities, keeping some people "in" and some people "out" of selected places. These have the potential to reinforce processes of gentrification, using technology to segregate populations by race, class, and other categories. I refer to this as e-gentrification.[28]

Biometrics, Algorithms, and Predicting Behavior

As the data-grabbing capacity of devices grows, scientists are developing algorithms to attempt to predict behavior. One key part of this process is biometrics, which are the unique measurements and calculations derived from our bodies, including fingerprints, the iris of our eyes, our earlobes, our face, and our DNA. Researchers record these biometrics and use artificial intelligence to make conclusions and suggest decisions. For example, the National Institute of Justice, the research, development, and evaluation agency of the U.S. Department of Justice, is funding a set of research projects that will use data from people who are on parole to predict their behavior.[29] The data will be gathered via ankle monitors and smartphones and will measure biometrics such as blood pressure, heart rate, cortisol levels, and body temperature. In one of the projects, a group of researchers from an Indiana college, Purdue Polytechnic Institute, will monitor 125 people who have been paroled from Indiana state prisons with an ankle monitor that records those biometrics.[30] Using artificial intelligence, the researchers will then attempt to predict what physiological metrics correspond to risky behavior and recommend appropriate responses by authorities. Their responses will be compared with those of a control group of 125 people on parole without the monitor.

More specialized areas, such as "Femtech," are also expanding through artificial intelligence.[31] "Femtech" generally refers to technology specifically targeted at what they labeled "women's" medical and health needs. This technology originally focused on monitoring pregnancy, sexual health, and menopause. The introduction of artificial intelligence aims to do things such as blend metrics for mucus quality and menstrual bleeding into algorithms used to predict behavior.[32] Industry insiders estimate this could become a $50 billion market by 2025.[33]

A key issue for the future of location tracking is the evolution of the devices. For the past three decades, the criminal legal system has relied on bulky ankle shackles, often connected to a landline telephone. But more recently, many other options have surfaced, the most prominent among them being the cellphone. Since most phones already have GPS tracking capacity, many law enforcement agencies have switched to more compact, less visible cellphone-based trackers. These phones offer parole and probation officers, as well as other court officials, a range of options beyond tracking and personal communication. Applications on these phones can send reminders of court dates, provide lists of resources and service agencies, and offer direct reporting methods for checking in with a department of corrections. But devices linked to the criminal legal system are not the only ones that are tracking location. A wide range of apps—from weather predictors to platforms for hedge fund management—include location tracking. In many cases, when the apps are downloaded, the location tracking runs in the background permanently unless the user blocks it.

For authorities, the next iteration of these devices may be Fitbit-style watches that track location and biometrics, or even computer chips embedded under the skin. Although several states have banned such chip implants, one employer in Wisconsin, vending machine distributor Three Square Market, enlisted fifty volunteers to have chips implanted under their skin that could be scanned like a credit card to buy things in the store.[34] Such examples raise the question of "the cellphone paradox," the unfortunate reality in which people seek out enjoyment, enrichment, convenience, or even protection via the same technology that deprives us of our liberty. The cellphone paradox reveals that the very device that most people are glued to 24/7, the device that they rely on to communicate with loved ones, to carry out business affairs, to research anything and everything, the device that they sleep next to at night is also the device that locks them into an e-carceral cage for which they are the keyholder. By tracking their every move, grabbing and handing over every detail of their personal data to corporate and government bodies, cellphones—and their extended family of tablets, laptops, and Fitbits—are key vehicles for profiteering, surveilling, and damaging people's lives. Yet we still can't live without them, and in many cases, we spend far more time holding them than any loved one.

4. THE OMNIPOTENT EYE

Cameras are a key vehicle for capturing data. In recent years, these cameras have proliferated, appearing on city streets, transport hubs, and on the bodies of police officers as well as in private businesses and homes. By 2018, the United States had one camera for every 4.6 people.[35] The real dynamic force in this marketplace is not state or police cameras but smart home surveillance cameras. Unit sales for these devices reached 54 million in 2018, with analysts predicting that figure would more than double by 2023.[36] Like cellphones, surveillance cameras are governed by a paradox. They intrude in our lives yet provide a service, and help us to feel safe and in control. In millions of instances, we have chosen to surveil ourselves. Smart home surveillance systems are not typically stand-alone items. Like cellphones, these networks offer convenience while sacrificing privacy and opening the door to surveillance.

While dedicated surveillance cameras have spread rapidly, our own cellphones have become the most common photo-capture devices. They are the main vehicle for sharing visual information and experiences, giving them a social function that runs in parallel to their surveillance function. For instance, any video or still picture posted to Facebook can be surveilled, analyzed, and run through algorithms without the knowledge of the owner or subject of the photo. In some instances, distribution of these photos can do harm, such as facilitating the trolling or public sharing of personal data (known as doxing) of targeted persons.

Surveillance cameras in public spaces are yet another form of visual documentation that has become the norm. According to one survey, in London, surveillance cameras can capture an individual's image up to two hundred times a day, whether they are walking down the street, riding the subway, or sitting on a park bench.[37] And no cameras exist without an agenda—they target specific populations, directly or indirectly. For instance, when surveillance cameras focus on targets, such as "porch pirates," who snatch packages that don't belong to them from the front of residential buildings and run, they typically are the technology of the better off wielded against the poor.

BIG DATA AND THE CLOUD

In the 1990s, now-obsolete computer hardware and software companies like Compaq and Netscape began talking about cloud computing, but the real public splash came in 2006 when then Google CEO Eric Schmidt told the world, "There is an emergent new model. . . . It starts with the premise that the data services and architecture should be on servers. We call it cloud computing—they should be in a 'cloud' somewhere."[38] The cloud has since become the central mega-storage space used by everyone from the U.S. government and transnational corporations to individual users who log on to Microsoft 365 or Google Docs.

The cloud is central to the advance of e-carceration. Like all investors, the owners of data are constantly looking for new buyers and new markets. The power of calculation and its link to profit-making mean this data must be processed, used to predict and analyze, and in some cases, condemn. This is Big Data, a hallmark of our age—data on a scale beyond the processing capacity of analog or simple calculation programs. This digital force attempts to reach into every nook and cranny of life that can be subject to calculation. By 2020, cloud computing had become a $266 billion industry, with Amazon's cloud service, known as AWS (Amazon Web Services), dominating the sector with about 39 percent of the market. AWS and major competitors Microsoft, IBM, and Google control more than 50 percent of the cloud.[39] The monopolization of the cloud will continue to increase. As its monopoly power expands—in the absence of resistance—accountability and transparency will decrease.

The cloud enables increased surveillance, prediction, and profitability. It illustrates how the complexities of e-carceration play out. Location tracking can show a person at a particular place, facial recognition can pick out their face from the crowd, a survey of nearby car license plates can further verify their presence in the area, as can a scan for credit card purchases made in nearby stores or a selfie taken there and posted to Instagram. The data can make much more complex connections, linking an individual to family members or grade school associates who live in other cities or even other countries. These connections can also include profiling more complicated networks and organizations. For example, after the rise of Black Lives Matter, the FBI created a category of Black Identity Extremists (BIE).[40] To be placed in that category, a person allegedly had to "use force or violence in violation of criminal law in response to perceived racism and injustice in American society."[41] Following a process much like the creation of the federal no-fly list post-9/11, the FBI constructed a set of filters to determine who might qualify as a BIE, then ran those filters through its massive databases to determine who actually fell under this category. The BIE label could have kept a person from acquiring a passport or being hired for a government job, but they would never be privy to the data that fed the algorithm that made that determination. The BIE category drew so much protest that the FBI ultimately claimed to have abandoned it. However, in the midst of the June 2020 uprising, a Freedom of Information Act request filed by MediaJustice and the ACLU revealed thousands of pages were still being devoted to investigations of Black people as "domestic terrorist" threats for potential "Black identity activities."[42]

The cloud also plays a powerful role in surveilling and regulating the distribution of social services. Activist sociologist Dorothy Roberts, whose work focuses on racial and gender justice, has detailed how surveillance in the social welfare space masquerades "under the guise of fraud prevention and quality control."[43] In the name of crime prevention, this dragnet approach may demand that welfare recipients identify all sexual partners, submit to blood and urine tests, and become subject to warrantless visits from social service investigators, euphemistically called "home invasions" by those on the receiving end. Roberts concludes, "Systems that ostensibly exist to serve people's needs . . . public assistance and child welfare . . . have become behavior modification programs that regulate the people who rely on them."[44]

E-CARCERATION: THE CRIMINALIZED SECTOR OF THE WORKING CLASS

The revelations of former NSA contractor Edward Snowden, among others, have made large cross sections of the population aware that the NSA and other security agencies are tracking all of us, capturing our emails, our phone conversations, our Facebook postings.[45] Former Google CEO Eric Schmidt's views about such revelations are clear: "If you have something that you don't want anyone to know, maybe you shouldn't be doing it in the first place."[46] Snowden offered a clear-cut response to Schmidt: "Arguing that you don't care about the

Big Data, Artificial Intelligence, and Machine Learning

Big Data represents the computerized systems that have the power to perform complex calculations on huge data sets. Increasingly, Big Data is being used to feed algorithms, the mathematical formulas that predict events and human behavior. Big Data provides the raw material for artificial intelligence (AI), a type of computing that processes data in order to perform tasks, such as decision-making, in ways similar to humans. AI was popularized in the 1999 movie *The Matrix*, in which humans fought machines driven by computerized artificial intelligence. To maximize effectiveness, AI combines with machine learning, a mechanism by which the computer learns from and corrects its own mistakes. Perhaps the most widely known examples of AI and machine learning working in tandem are online personal assistants, such as Apple's Siri and Amazon's Alexa, which are able to refine searches by "learning" from previous searches.

right to privacy because you have nothing to hide is no different than saying you don't care about free speech because you have nothing to say."[47] Other privacy advocates have pushed back against Schmidt by arguing that if you don't know what data the government or corporations have or what they plan to do with the data, you can't really determine if there is something to fear.[48]

Malkia Devich-Cyril reminds us that, just as with incarceration in physical cages, e-carceration has a distinct impact on working-class people of color. For households or communities with low incomes, the repressive power of e-carceration, especially in the form of massive data sets we call Big Data, goes well beyond privacy. In the era of mass incarceration, the working-class poor constitute a criminalized sector of the population. They are disproportionately Black, Latinx, Indigenous, undocumented, disabled, and LGBTQ+. Their precarious economic and social situation criminalizes their daily survival activities. These may include sleeping in a public place, asking people for money, having sex for pay, getting high, selling loosies, resisting gender-based or transphobic violence, or living in a car. Here, criminalization refers not only to indictments or convictions but also to having a presence in databases of law enforcement, immigration authorities, school disciplinary structures, or the foster care system; being on the rolls of public benefit providers or in the files of mental health or substance abuse treatment providers; or being tagged as part of the LGBTQ+ population. Data lands there via surveillance devices of e-carceration such as cameras and license plate readers or simply by the person in question voluntarily surrendering the data to access an app or apply for a credit card. As abolitionist researcher Dorothy Roberts emphasizes, "All institutions in the United States increasingly address social inequality by punishing the communities that are most marginalized by it."[49]

Ultimately, the data collected on the criminalized population constitute key weapons in the arsenal of a racialized class warfare blocking people from access to employment, housing, education, travel, credit, health care, and many other resources. Data are not dead facts or raw material for future calculation but live artillery of punishment and denial. They keep people in what Virginia Eubanks, author of the award-winning book *Automating Inequality*, calls the "digital poorhouse."[50] Dorothy Roberts emphasizes that Big Data "targets marginalized groups for tracking and containment in order to exclude them from full democratic participation."[51]

Winifred Poster, who researches feminist labor theory and digital globalization, has described the complex dynamics of the weapons of e-carceration as a system of "multi-surveillance," in which a person's data may land in many databases depending on their "race, gender, sexuality, class and so on." Poster notes that a single individual can be both surveilled and surveilling others. For example, a small business owner might be surveilled by tax authorities or because of past criminal convictions at the same time they are surveilling their employees via cameras or criminal background checks.[52]

HISTORY OF TRACKING

While e-carceration may be new, the use of technology to track, monitor, confine, and criminalize is not. The use of data to criminalize has been part of U.S. history since the first days of the formation of the settler-colonial state in what today is the United States. Tracking and monitoring were essential to the creation of Native American reservations, the implementation of pass laws requiring Native people to have a travel document in their possession any time they wanted to leave the reservation, and to holding Native children captive in boarding schools.[53] Similarly, the history of chattel slavery in the U.S. reveals incredibly detailed systems of tracking and monitoring Black bodies. Slave patrols were the first real police in the United States. As Simone Browne, renowned chronicler of the surveillance of Blackness, reminds us, slave owners used the technology of the day to monitor people.[54] They burned the name or icon of the owner into the skin of enslaved men and women. Just as the Swoosh appears on all Nike gear, so too did slave owners proudly display their "logo" on the bodies of the enslaved Black people they "owned." In New York, authorities passed "lantern laws," which forced Black and Indigenous people to carry a lantern at all times if they moved about after dark.[55] Historian James Loewen has spent decades uncovering the presence of hundreds of "Sundown Towns" across the United States, places where local authorities tracked Black people by banning their presence inside the city limits after dark.[56]

Data and surveillance have also been used to target and criminalize immigrants and political activists. From mass deportation to anti–immigrant laws like the Chinese Exclusion Act of 1882, monitoring the flow of populations across borders has always been essential to ensuring a sufficient labor supply while keeping a limit on the presence of people of color.

At various moments when popular movements have resisted the inequities of U.S. capitalism, the state has cracked down on revolutionaries and other political dissidents. The Palmer Raids, named after then attorney general A. Mitchell Palmer, led to the deportation of over five hundred mostly European immigrants who were deemed sympathizers of the 1917 Russian Revolution. At the height of the Cold War in the 1950s, the FBI targeted members of the Communist Party. In 1948 eleven leaders of the party were charged under the Smith Act of conspiring to teach and advocate the overthrow of the U.S. government by force and violence."[57] Julius and Ethel Rosenberg, suspected of connections to the Communist Party, were executed in 1953 after being convicted for sending secret documents to the Soviet Union. In the 1970s, the FBI's Counterintelligence Program (COINTELPRO) focused on revolutionary organizations such as the Black Panther Party and the American Indian Movement, and in 1969, carried out the assassination of Illinois Black Panther Party chairman Fred Hampton, which was depicted in the Academy Award–winning 2021 film *Judas and the Black Messiah*.

Although much of the population delights in the use of cellphones and eagerly awaits the next app or social media platform, in the ambit of government and companies, these technologies are ultimately about control, punishment, and destruction. Everyone over fifty who has a cellphone or laptop is acutely aware of how far and how rapidly things have moved since the days of rotary dial phones, manual typewriters, and telegrams. Most of us from that age group, especially those who live in the industrialized world, revel in amazement as each new development unfolds. As this technology progresses, we find ourselves living in a technological universe we never could have imagined even two or three decades ago. The benefits of this technology are obvious—our ability to communicate and access information instantaneously, the opportunity to play a game, watch a movie, or find out about a disease that may be troubling us or a loved one. The sinister parts of this technology are far less visible. They are not on our dashboard; we can't pin them to our desktop—but those of us fighting to transform racial capitalism must resist these expanding powers of surveillance and control. These technologies of e-carceration are evolving at the speed of light, but may remain largely obscured from us unless we dive deep into the past, remain aware in the present, and apply our imaginations to the future.

In the criminal legal system, such a deep dive should necessarily focus initially on the development of the first real device of e-carceration, the electronic ankle monitor. We will turn to an examination of the origins of this device in the next chapter.

3

MONITORING:
BORN IN THE PUNISHMENT PARADIGM

If, and when, electronic monitoring taps into this reservoir of human aspiration, positive transformative social interactions will emerge that can enhance the long-term safety and welfare of the community at-large.

—*Robert Gable, inventor of the first electronic monitor*[1]

The small body of literature depicting the history of electronic monitoring (EM) casts the inventors, the Gable brothers, as noble reformers.[2] In this narrative, the Gables are idealistic, somewhat quirky technologists striving to develop a monitoring device to ease the punishment of those caught up in the criminal legal system. That dominant narrative demands a rethink, taking into account that the electronic monitor emerged in the midst of critical debates about the destiny of the criminal legal system. Far from being near the cutting edge of progressive change, the Schwitzgebel twins, Robert and Ralph (who would change their last name to Gable in 1983), were acolytes of renowned psychologist B.F. Skinner, the father of behavior modification. The experiments carried out by Skinner with rats pushing bars in cages to get food rewards had already etched their way into the memories of Psychology 101 students. More importantly, they inspired an entire school of thought that cast humans as simply a product of their environment, rather than conscious beings who shape and respond to their environment, capable of collective efforts to change that environment.

Touched by the apparent poverty and misery of the youthful "street people" who hung out in the area around their lab, the Gables applied this Skinnerian reward-and-punish approach to the juvenile justice world. As graduate students at Harvard in the early 1960s, the brothers framed their project in the language of psychology and human needs. In their view, EM would act in "synchrony with basic human desires—the desire to be happy, to be free of pain and to be socially valued." They believed some form of monitoring device could "suppress unwanted behavior . . . by applying mild punishment for every transgression."[3] Ultimately they aimed to create a form of "therapist-controlled positive reinforcement for juvenile delinquents in natural settings."[4] Central to this approach was the notion of "positive punishment" with the addition of "unpleasant stimuli" administered in response to a certain type of behavior.

To this end, they designed a transceiver that could receive tactile signals. These early monitors were to be mounted on the user's belt with a button in the center that could send signals. Incoming communication precipitated a vibration, much like a cellphone. The signals could only transmit within a given neighborhood, and actual communication between devices required a small FCC-licensed radio station. With fellow researcher William S. Hurd, Ralph Gable obtained patent #3,478,344 for this technology in 1964, after procuring the required FCC license to operate such a system.[5]

In a project they named "Streetcorner Research," the researchers set up their testing site in an office in a low-rent area of Cambridge and employed youth from the local neighborhood to wear the devices. Most of the brothers' equipment consisted of electronic gear cast off by the military. It included a screen that was set up inside the office to map the location of everyone wearing one of the monitors. Some monitors even recorded heart rate. At one point, police became suspicious of this high-tech operation in a run-down part of town and questioned the Gables as if they were possible enemy agents. Eventually the brothers convinced the authorities they were just students doing an experiment.[6] The Gables viewed the monitor as a temporary measure "similar to a walker that is down-graded to a crutch, then to a cane and finally abandoned." The brothers conducted periodic interviews with those on the monitor to mine their experiences of the device.

The Gables were reformers of a particular stripe at a particular moment, a moment that is hard to comprehend from the distant locus of the twenty-first century. Peering into the brothers' story from a contemporary prism of mass incarceration, visions of gentle technological taps against the abdomen appear almost harmless. However, much of the Gables' theoretical considerations focused on the details of the technology itself. Their deepest theorizing considered possibilities like running wire antennas from a person's foot to their waist or sewing a metal strip into the back of their shirt.[7] The Gables believed they could curb the errant individual of bad behavior through a technologically based mixture of punishment and reward. Their instrumentation linked to the simplistic explanation that people end up in prison because of "bad behavior" and "bad choices." The cure was the correct technology to stimulate behavior change rather than re-shaping consciousness or restructuring the social environment where "bad behavior" took place. The Gables' approach implied that essentially, human beings were like the rats in the cage: if mechanically rewarded often enough, they would see and do things differently.

Yet the balance the Gables sought to strike between reward and punishment vanished with the advance of mass incarceration and the punishment paradigm. Their laboratory experiment mode of operation offered little resistance to the carceral winds of change that were gusting across the criminal legal system. The brothers were experimental scientists who thought their technology could create "positive social groups" from "juvenile delinquents." For these romantic idealists, the journey of their devices was ultimately heartbreaking. Writing in 2011, Robert Gable said he didn't regret the "naive enthusiasm of our early experiments" but was saddened by the fact that contemporary monitoring "has turned homes into prisons instead of making public spaces into areas of positive excitement." That some solitary confinement sections of several California prisons are called "Behavior Modification Units" is further testament to how corrections authorities twisted the Skinnerian principles invoked by the Gables to inspire the most punitive sites inside their institutions, sites where notions of reward and positive reinforcement were totally absent.[8] In the end, we can view the Gable brothers as precursors of the carceral humanists of today, people who repackage punitive and controlling devices such as electronic monitors in the language of caring and concern. However, the Gables never went quite that far. They continued through the 1980s trying to sell the notions of reward to corrections officials who were increasingly uninterested. In Robert Gable's words, the officials accused him "of giving cookies to gang members."[9] The punitive, controlling elements of EM were what appealed to policy makers and prison operatives wanting to get tough on crime and criminals. Reward had little or no place at this moment in history.

THE LIBERATION MOVEMENT INSIDE PRISONS

Moderate reformers like the Gables represented one pillar of the criminal legal debates of the day. As in the twenty-first century, the early monitors were framed as an "alternative" to incarceration. In the policy space, the devices offered a way to give the appearance of reform while deepening an increasingly complex paradigm of punishment. Ultimately, the framework of behavior change, by stressing individual actions, stimuli, and decision-making, offered a strategy for reform that landed far from a critique of the system of prisons and punishment. A brief history of the social movements of the 1960s, particularly the efforts of criminal justice reformers and prison revolutionaries, is crucial to placing the early EM devices in historical context, as well as for understanding the evolution of the monitor and e-carceration more broadly.

THE RADICAL PRISON MOVEMENT OF THE 1960S AND 1970S

The mid-1960s, the period when the Gables were conducting their experiments, was the germinating moment for the radical movements of that decade and the next. The most famous of these were the antiwar movement, the civil rights movement, and the Black Liberation Movement. But out of that period also came the women's liberation movement, the gay liberation movement, and Latinx organizations like the Young Lords Party and the Brown Berets, along with the American Indian Movement. These organizations and movements shared a common systemic critique of U.S. society, the notion that the system "could not be fixed."

Less well known were the organizations dedicated to reforming prisons, largely influenced first by the Nation of Islam and then by civil rights movement and Black Power organizations.[10] At the same time that the Gables were tinkering with communications devices, rebellions and cries for change were erupting inside prisons. Incarcerated people were becoming folk heroes of the struggle for justice. The most prominent was Black revolutionary and author George Jackson, who first hit the headlines as part of the Soledad Brothers, a trio accused of the 1970 killing of a guard in California's Soledad State Prison. Jackson gained further fame with the publication of a collection of his letters, *Soledad Brother*. The book, which sold over four hundred thousand copies despite the fact that Jackson was in prison at the time of its publication, played a major role in awakening public consciousness to the abuses and systemic racism of the prison system. In rich prose, *Soledad Brother* brought to readers the harsh reality of life for young Black men like Jackson who, in his words, were "born a slave in a captive society" and "conditioned to accept the inevitability of prison." Jackson's writings not only revealed how his youth made him "prepared for prison"; they also offered an inspirational call to arms for readers to "discover your humanity and your love in revolution."[11]

The drama and attention around Jackson's case and publications rose dramatically when his younger brother, seventeen-year-old Jonathan Jackson, stormed a courtroom in Marin County, California, on August 7, 1970, to take the judge and bailiffs hostage and demand freedom for his brother. Armed deputies thwarted the action before Jonathan could even exit the courthouse parking lot. They shot the young man to death, and in the process, killed two other incarcerated men, James McClain and William Christmas, who were in court to testify, and the judge, Harold Haley. Authorities accused former Black Panther Angela Davis of supplying Jonathan Jackson with weapons in the incident. Davis had been fired from her professorial post at UCLA because of her radical views. The State of California charged Davis with a capital crime. She spent three months as a high-profile fugitive before her capture, then more than a year fighting a murder case before winning acquittal. A year later, prison guards at San Quentin shot and killed George Jackson during an alleged escape attempt. These episodes reverberated in popular culture, inspiring songs by Bob Dylan, the Rolling Stones, and reggae band Steel Pulse as well as a jazz ode by Archie Shepp. George Jackson's second book, *Blood in My Eye*, was published posthumously to considerable critical acclaim.[12]

In the literary history of mass incarceration, the Jackson volumes were to the 1970s what Michelle Alexander's *The New Jim Crow* has been to the 2000s. These works shifted the mindset of millions of people about what was going on inside prisons. In the words of literary scholar H. Bruce Franklin, "George Jackson was both an internationally acclaimed author and the central figure in the burgeoning resistance movement among American prisoners."[13] To draw a contemporary parallel, Jackson maintained a profile much like that of present-day political prisoner and self-identified Black Panther Mumia Abu-Jamal, who has been in Pennsylvania prisons since 1982 on charges of killing a police officer.[14] Jackson became an iconic symbol of Black resistance to systemic oppression, his legacy extending beyond the readership of his books. He was also the inspiration behind the most momentous prison rebellion of the twentieth century, the Attica uprising.

Some three weeks after Jackson's murder in San Quentin, incarcerated men in New York's Attica prison seized control of the institution's D Yard and issued a set of thirty-one demands. They called for improving conditions inside the prison, pressing for better food, more education, and less censorship of reading material. Their requests raised issues that revealed a more radical critique of U.S. society, particularly their request for amnesty for participants in the Attica rebellion and their "speedy and safe transportation out of confinement, to a non-imperialistic country."[15] The men who carried out this action, known subsequently as the Attica Brothers, believed salvation rested with a face-to-face meeting with then governor Nelson Rockefeller. To facilitate that encounter, the Brothers called on Bobby Seale, cofounder and national chairman of the Black Panther Party, plus lawyer William Kunstler, who had defended dozens of political prisoners, to negotiate on their behalf. Both Seale and Kunstler responded by coming to the prison; Kunstler managed to go inside and speak with the rebellion's leaders. Ultimately, negotiations failed and Rockefeller, rather than coming to the negotiating table, ordered a state trooper takeover of the prison. The attack left thirty-one people dead, including ten prison guards. While reformers like the Gables were working in their labs, a revolutionary upsurge in the world of criminal justice was taking place.

Unlike the opposition to mass incarceration that arose in the 2000s, the core impetus for the movement in this period emerged from incarcerated people themselves. However, also unlike the twenty-first-century campaigns, these actions were closely connected to the broader social movements of the day. As radical criminologist Tony Platt has noted,

> The prison movement of the 1960s–1970s was actually several movements: liberal campaigns to humanize conditions inside and implement the post–World War II "rehabilitative ideal"; civil rights activism and civil disobedience practiced in Southern jails and prisons; left campaigns to "tear down the walls," drastically reduce the prison population, and expose the malevolent abuses of rehabilitation policies; the revolutionary politics of prisoners incarcerated for non-political crimes who followed Malcolm X's example as he transformed himself from a "ghetto-created Negro" to a leader who offered the "black man something worthwhile"; and feminist organizing in women's prisons, carving out a space in the hyper-masculinist world of the struggle inside.[16]

Heather Thompson, who wrote a prize-winning history of the Attica uprising, also emphasized the connections between the mobilizations of incarcerated people and the broader social movement: "Their demands very much mirrored those of activists on city streets—they spoke out against racism, against the violence directed at them by officers of the state, for better living and working conditions, for greater access to education, and for better medical care. On the other hand, as people under the full control of the state, their demands often and most pointedly focused on fundamental human rights—they demanded time and again to be treated like people."[17]

While Attica was the most high-profile of the prison rebellions, similar actions would take place in Illinois and Massachusetts facilities. In another strain of the movement, a California group calling themselves the United Prisoners Union (UPU) put forward a manifesto in 1970 in which they identified themselves as the "convicted class," declaring "before the world . . . that Basic Human Rights are systematically withheld from our class."[18] The platform of the UPU and the actions of the Attica Brothers exemplified how, in the words of historian Alan Eladio Gómez, "imprisoned people imagined new worlds, different social institutions and economic policies, and a transformation of people's relationship to the state. The prison rebellion years were a total re-imagination of what was possible in society."[19] Their vision did not include notions of EM or e-carceration in any form.

Even within mainstream politics, serious critiques of prisons and the criminal legal system were emerging. In 1972, Justice James E. Doyle, father of a future governor of Wisconsin, stated in a response to a court petition contesting prison authorities' confiscation of mail, "I am persuaded that the institution of the prison probably must end. In many respects it is as intolerable within the United States as was the institution of slavery, equally brutalizing to all involved, equally toxic to the social system, equally subversive to the brotherhood of man, even more costly by some standards, and probably less rational."[20] State-level reports in Wisconsin (1972) and Minnesota (1974) recommended replacement of prisons with a "community-based, non-institutional system."[21]

The radical prison movement ultimately confronted two counterforces: the reactionary advocates of law and order who would eventually drive the War on Drugs and mass incarceration, and reformers who tried to keep notions of rehabilitation on the agenda.

The Gables, though fairly isolated in the confines of their laboratories and operant-conditioning protocols, were with those reformers. Efforts like theirs were part of a trend to reshape the carceral system in the United States without making fundamental change, whether inside the institutions themselves or in the broader society. While George Jackson preached Marxist-Leninist revolution and extoled the virtues of Che Guevara, the behavioral school technologists tweaked their inventions, meticulously recording changes in behavior. As the Gables' technology evolved, its essence and purpose went through changes that coincided with the process of right-wing transformation that eventually engulfed every element of a system inappropriately labeled criminal "justice." Even if the Gables were reformers and believers in the power of technology to rehabilitate, their ankle monitor ultimately became subsumed by those who thought solely in terms of control and punishment.

Hence, by the late 1970s, rehabilitation was on the wane. Criminologists and policy makers plunged into intense debates concerning what measures could effectively transform those coming out of prison into useful citizens. One of the most important contributions to this debate came from sociologist Robert Martinson in 1974. Martinson concluded that "the present array of correctional treatments has no appreciable effects—positive or negative—on rates of recidivism of convicted offenders."[22] His views became known among criminologists and prison officials as the "nothing works" approach.[23] In the 1970s and 1980s, "nothing works" inspired attacks against prison programs such as higher education, vocational training, and therapy that aimed at "rehabilitating" incarcerated people. Instead, efforts at "restoring fear to prisons" combined a political backlash against the social movements of the 1960s and 1970s with a drive for retribution.[24] The spirit of revenge was occasioned by both increased crime rates and a less frequently noted event in 1979, what the media called "the Iran hostage crisis." This "crisis" was precipitated by Iranian militants' capture of fifty-two U.S. diplomats and citizens in Tehran.

In that retributive environment, interventions like EM were shunted to the side as part of a "soft on crime" approach. Moreover, the official pendulum swung away from giving any priority of place to voices of the incarcerated. Instead, stricter prison regimes concerning visiting and communications further silenced people behind bars and deepened their isolation.

At the same time, by the mid-1970s social justice and revolutionary movements went into decline. The COINTELPRO agenda of assassinations, surveillance, infiltration, and disinformation undermined the organizational cohesion of groups like the Black Panther Party, the American Indian Movement, the Communist Party USA, and factions of the antiwar movements. Internal divisions over race, class, gender, and ideology further fractured the movements. The end of the wars in Southeast Asia in 1975 removed one of the most compelling issues that inspired activism.

The 1979 capture of U.S. citizens inside the embassy in Tehran, which kicked off 442 days of "American held hostages," sparked a revival of faith in military solutions to global problems, an impulse that had been tempered by the antiwar movement and the failure of the United States to secure a military victory in Vietnam and Cambodia. The resurgence of imperialist consciousness delivered a decisive blow to both mass social justice movements and notions of rehabilitation.

The revival of U.S. xenophobia came with a broad-based spirit of retribution. In that environment, national campaigns like those to free Angela Davis and the Soledad Brothers became a thing of the past. Law and order took center stage. This right-wing hegemony widened its net when, in the midst of escalating crime rates and the spread of crack cocaine, even some high-profile Black leaders clamored for authorities to expand policing and deliver harsher sentences to youth and drug dealers from their communities. As James Forman Jr. pointed out in his Pulitzer Prize–winning volume, *Locking Up Our Own*, many Black elected officials were under pressure from their own constituencies to push for a more hard-line approach.[25]

ENTER THE GABLES

Although the Gables provided much philosophical flourish for EM, in the end, they were unable to convince authorities to use their technology in real-life situations. By the mid-1970s, their approach to reform had fallen off the table. By this point, the Gables had extended their vision way beyond ankle monitors, into realms that perhaps appeared a bit quirky to the staid bureaucrats of the corrections world. In addition to transceivers, they were also exploring possibilities of an "electronic parole system," which could alert the wearer to undesirable physical responses or those that might be associated with anxiety such as nervous gestures or physical activity. In the Gables' view, such signals could help prepare the wearer to address an impending mental health crisis or urge to commit a crime. Their technological explorations also delved into methods for connecting users of the transceivers—an early network that could allow twenty people to share information and provide "encouragement to other members by facilitating planned and unplanned beneficial social interactions while preserving public safety."[26]

Like technologist visionaries of the twenty-first century, the Gables extrapolated, charting new universes that presented their inventions as resolutions to the central challenges of their time. At a time when astronauts like Alan Shepard and John Glenn were among the country's most prominent heroes, the twin brothers connected the interplanetary dots, suggesting that EM devices were on a path to a time when "men transport themselves across the solar system by radio-telegraph and life spans are measured in radiation count rather than by the speed at which the Earth revolves around its sun."[27] The Gable brothers' techno-fantasies never reached far beyond the laboratory stage. Neither the criminal legal system nor NASA was quite prepared for their ideas. Over the years, the Gables' interplanetary, humanitarian aims stood on the sidelines as their invention wandered down an alternative pathway of punishment, becoming, in the words of brother Robert, "basically a misdirected technology that falsely promises long-term public safety by increasing surveillance and punishment."[28] They did, however, plant seeds that would sprout nearly two decades later as reforming judges looked for alternatives to jail for people with low-level felonies. There was nothing intergalactic about what law enforcement came to call the "ankle bracelet."

THE RISE OF EM IN THE CRIMINAL LEGAL SYSTEM

A decade after the Gables stepped aside, the task of bringing EM into mainstream law enforcement fell to New Mexican judge Jack Love. Love drew his inspiration from two newspaper items he read in the late 1970s: an article about the implantation of a radio transmitter under the skin of a cow, and a Spider-Man cartoon in which a villain clamped a device on the superhero's wrist to track his movement. These images apparently stewed in Judge Love's mind until 1983, when three young men charged with minor drug offenses came into his court. Love didn't want to send them to prison or let them off without penalty. His solution was an electronic monitor. He approached several tech entrepreneurs, finally corralling Michael Goss, a former sales rep at transnational technology giant Honeywell. Goss bit on the

EM idea and got a $10,000 bank loan to form a company, National Incarceration Monitoring and Control Services (NIMCOS). Goss built several cigarette pack–sized transmitters that could be strapped to a person's ankle. The device limited the wearer's movement to a radius of 150 feet. Any movement beyond that distance would trigger an alarm.[29]

In April 1983, unencumbered by legislation or regulations surrounding electronic surveillance, Love put three of his defendants on this "ankle bracelet" for thirty days. All three successfully got through their month. A few months later, another prototype emerged when a Monroe County, Florida, judge sentenced a young carpenter to a weekend of home detention for driving without a license. The court fitted the young man with a radio transmitter that would verify he was at home. The following year, a sheriff in Palm Beach County, Florida, partnered with a private probation company, Pride Integrated, to run a pilot project that included the first example of defendants paying to be on the monitor.[30] The wearer paid $250 for the privilege of spending nights and weekends at home on a monitor instead of in jail.

Despite the devices' emergence in Love's court and adoption in parts of Florida, EM fever was not yet ready to spread. After a few months, Goss ran out of money. He approached Colorado-based Boulder Industries, a producer of radio-frequency identity tags for livestock, and interested its proprietors in the device. After lengthy negotiations, Boulder bought all rights and assets of NIMCOS for $250,000, and what would become the nation's largest electronic monitoring company, BI Incorporated, was born.[31]

EM, THE DIGITAL AGE, AND THE RISE OF MASS INCARCERATION

Over the course of the next few years, the technology spread, albeit very gradually. By 1988, there were an estimated 2,277 users, rising to an estimated 12,000 in 1990.[32]

For policy makers with an appetite for punitive justice, the interest they might have had for electronic monitors was captured by prison building and fighting the War on Drugs. From 1980 to 1987, the number of people incarcerated in the United States grew from 329,000 to 581,000.[33] For those who were beginning to see the prison-industrial complex as a fattening cash cow, building and operating prisons appeared a far more lucrative enterprise than ped-dling ankle monitors.

Another reason for the slow uptick of EM was that it was technologically ahead of its time. By 1987, the digital world was just beginning to develop. Cellphones were only three years old and had the dimensions of a size 13 men's shoe. The first mobile computer, which was far too large for a lap, had hit the markets in 1983. Only 15 percent of U.S. homes even had a computer in 1987, leading one commentator to conclude: "There is a general feeling that the home computer was a fad and that there is really no practical purpose for a computer in the home."[34] Mass infatuation with technological solutions and acceptance of mass surveillance were yet to come. EM remained an oddball sci-fi idea, hardly a frontline weapon in the war against drugs.

Nonetheless, electronic monitoring did acquire a fan base. In 1987, EM devotees birthed their own publication, the *Offender Monitoring* newsletter, renamed the *Journal of Offender Monitoring* (*JOM*) in 1989. Still in operation after nearly three decades, this publication has become one of the few sources of non-company information on EM.

It was only in the 1990s that EM usage began to accelerate. From a technological stand-point, EM had become more in sync with the advance of information technology. Law en-forcement authorities searching for ways to stem the overflow of prison and jail populations turned to tech. As Tonry and Will, two important commentators of the day, observed, "In a field that is so human capital intensive as corrections, the idea that a 'technological fix' could reduce the workload in dealing with the problem of crime is almost irresistible."[35] By the end of the 1990s, a *JOM* survey of EM manufacturers turned up sixteen firms. BI was by far the largest with about 49,000 units in use. Its nearest competitor, Pennsylvania's Tracking Sys-tems Corporation, had just 10,000 devices in operation.[36]

Two important technological advances in the late 1990s propelled further EM growth: GPS tracking and alcohol monitoring technology. The first GPS-enabled devices came on-line in 1998. Up to that time, monitors had relied on radio frequency technology, or RF, which only informed supervisors if a person was in their home. By contrast, though accuracy was not always perfect, the GPS could send location information to a monitoring center. The upgrade to location tracking offered a more convincing public safety argument for proponents who could legitimately claim that those on a monitor were under the watchful eye of law enforcement twenty-four hours a day.

Alcohol monitoring technology was popularized under its commercial name: Secure Continuous Remote Alcohol Monitoring, or SCRAM. The spread of SCRAM was a result of national campaigning by groups like Mothers Against Drunk Driving (MADD) that began in the early 1980s. The group's agitation about deaths from drunk driving sparked experimentation with devices that could measure blood alcohol through bodily fluid emissions. Anti–drunk driving crusader-turned-inventor Jeff Hawthorne, who lost a close friend in an accident involving a habitual drunk driver, led the development of an ankle monitor capable of recording the presence of alcohol in perspiration. Although Hawthorne and his team first applied for a patent in 1993, it took many years of testing various prototypes via drinking sessions in Hawthorne's house until a functioning device made it to the market in 2003.[37]

These developments brought EM in step with the digital age and systems of surveillance. With GPS and SCRAM, monitors gained the capacity not only to control movement and behavior but to convert human activity into data and use that data to punish (or in rare instances, reward) the wearer. The GPS-enabled devices not only generated tracking data but introduced the capacity of monitors to reconfigure urban space. By incorporating exclusion and inclusion zones, GPS devices claimed a crime-fighting component by producing an alert when a monitored individual entered a high-crime area or a neighborhood where they had been previously involved in illegal activity.

The SCRAM device, often worn in tandem with a second GPS-enabled ankle band, predated the Fitbit and other "wearables" in recording biometric data. But unlike personal fitness technologies, SCRAM and subsequent biometric-based surveillance devices focused on delivering data for purposes of punishment. Farther down the road, they would also gain the capacity to convert that data into a product to be sold to marketers, compilers of credit scores, and other agencies and corporations. Something akin to the innocent transceiver communications device of the Gables would become an implement in the toolkit of data mining and the surveillance state. At one point, Robert Gable had suggested that the core function of the device was to provide some sort of positive response to positive behavior. As an example of his reinforcement approach, he proposed a scenario where a local citizen volunteer would take a person on EM out for a pizza when they exhibited positive behavior. However, by the early 2000s, after two decades of mass incarceration, the notion that a local citizen volunteer would take a person on EM out for pizza as a reward for good behavior seemed as far-fetched as the Gables' vision of intergalactic communication via their transceiver. The reform had lost its rehabilitative vision and become yet another tool of punishment, a point of convergence between mass incarceration in cages and the e-carceration of the rising surveillance state, a convergence to which we will now turn.

4

BUILDING THE MYTH OF ELECTRONIC MONITORING: NOT A "SHRED OF DATA"

> There is no serious, rigorously executed research providing significant evidence that electronic monitoring has a positive impact on the person being monitored. However, there are a handful of research works, all with major flaws, which are used to justify EM.
>
> —*Challenging E-Carceration Project*[1]

Electronic monitoring (EM) first gained traction in the 1980s when, as criminal justice professor Betsy Matthews proclaimed, "rehabilitation formed the basis of correctional practice."[2] At that time, authorities like Judge Love frequently reserved electronic monitoring as a sentence for people convicted of relatively minor offenses. EM typically put a curfew in place—confining a person to home in the nighttime hours, when law enforcement figured most criminal activity occurred. Since then, the terrain of electronic monitors has vastly expanded. Today, monitors appear in all sectors of the criminal legal system—pretrial, post-prison, youth justice—and as part of a sentence for driving while intoxicated. Thousands of migrants awaiting adjudication for asylum or residence permits are captured by what Spanish speakers call *el grillete*, the shackle.

EM MYTHOLOGY

As noted, the impetus to widen EM's net sprang from the 2008 economic crisis coupled with a growing critique of mass incarceration. These developments combined to pressure authorities to examine the potential of EM devices as a "solution" to the problems of criminal justice. This narrative drew on earlier work such as the 2002 reiterations of the behaviorist mantra of Robert Gable by the late Peggy Conway. A high-profile consultant and the editor of the *Journal of Offender Monitoring*, Conway told a *New York Times* reporter, "We want to create a jail without walls in the community—a virtual jail. You can reinforce positive community behavior."[3] In 2014, Ann Toyer of the Oklahoma Department of Corrections offered a more practical version of Conway's vision: "We get them back into the community where they can work, they pay taxes, they have access to community services . . . and they can pay for those services."[4]

Many supporters noted the potential of EM for systemic impact. Professor Barry Latzer of City University of New York's John Jay College of Criminal Justice saw the monitor as a quick-fix solution. "Used more widely," Latzer proclaimed, "electronic monitoring can reduce incarceration rates while minimizing the risks to public safety—a win-win proposition." Journalist Dylan Matthews, writing for *Vox* in 2014, further mythologized the powers of EM as a vehicle that could "reduce [prison] admissions by at least half, probably much more."[5] Matthews drew largely on research from Switzerland and Sweden, countries where rehabilitation remains the dominant ethos in criminal justice circles, to reach his conclusion. The very limited studies cited by Matthews showed low rearrest rates for those on electronic monitoring compared to those not on EM. In drafting a strategy for a vast increase in the use of EM across the spectrum of the criminal legal system, University of Minnesota professor Stuart Yeh went several steps beyond Latzer and Matthews, presenting EM as the centerpiece of change, contending that electronic monitoring was "arguably more effective, efficient, humane and ethical than any alternative strategy."[6]

Predictably, the companies in the electronic monitoring industry joined efforts to hype the power of their product. Referring to EM as "the solution," leading ankle monitor producer

Omnilink suggested these devices would have a transformative effect on carceral workplaces, providing "information that helps personnel make smarter, more effective decisions so that law enforcement teams can spend less time monitoring offenders and more on preventing and solving crimes." Omnilink declared that EM "reduces recidivism rates, incarceration rates and therefore the need for additional prison capacity."[7]

Arie Trabelsi, leading executive for Israel-based EM producer SuperCom, echoed the philosophical bent of Omnilink, maintaining in 2020 that increased use of electronic monitoring "reflects a greater overall shift to a more modernized, effective approach towards alternatives to incarceration and an emphasis on offenders' successful re-entry into society."[8] Investigative reporter Rachel Swan summed up the logic of the EM myth most succinctly in a 2014 *SF Weekly* op-ed, "Why lock people in cells when their whole prison experience could be condensed into one piece of wearable gadgetry?"[9] For these promoters of electronic monitoring, the key to the transformation of the criminal legal system rested with the fate of this "wearable gadgetry."

While this mythmaking certainly contributed to the increased adoption of electronic monitors, the myths do not rest on any foundation of proven success or even supporting data. Authorities and providers have rarely demonstrated any proclivity for documenting the usage or impact of EM. Take the simple issue of how many electronic monitoring devices are in use. Prisons and jails count and record their populations several times a day, and the Bureau of Justice, along with most state departments of corrections, issues annual statistical reports. By contrast, few authorities gather such data on EM. Though federal, state, and local governments spend millions on electronic monitoring annually (a precise aggregate figure remains unknown), there are no structures in place compelling any accountability for these funds. We simply don't know how many people are on electronic monitors across the country.

In the absence of government data gathering, at least two private sources have made efforts to carry out a national EM census. Their efforts highlight the absolute chaos that pervades the world of information gathering on electronic monitoring. From 1999 to 2009, Peggy Conway, a staunch advocate of EM, did annual surveys of monitors for the *Journal of Offender Monitoring*, relying largely on figures that electronic monitoring companies shared

Electronic Monitoring: The Technology

Most EM systems consist of an ankle band linked to an electronic box. The band must remain on the person's ankle twenty-four hours a day. There are two main kinds of devices: radio frequency (RF) and GPS. RF merely records whether a person is at home. GPS-based monitors track location through satellite, Wi-Fi, or Bluetooth technology. The devices send tracking data to the monitoring authority through either a landline or a cellphone connection to the ankle box. Many monitors have additional features. Some can detect alcohol in a person's perspiration. Others include audio and video recording as well as features that enable supervisors to send text and voice messages. Most EM systems are battery powered. Like cellphones, they need to be recharged through connection to a wall plug, in many cases for two consecutive hours. Some require recharging as often as every four or five hours. This usually means the wearer must sit next to a wall plug for substantial periods of time throughout each day. Though it looks sturdy, the traditional ankle monitor can be removed with a pair of household scissors (though some producers have recently changed from plastic to steel bands). The bands on the monitor contain sensors, so removal or tampering will trigger an alarm. In some jurisdictions, removing or tampering with the device can result in a felony escape charge. In Georgia the penalty for such an offense can be up to five years in prison.[10]

Typically, a monitoring sentence means a person is under house arrest and only permitted to leave home if granted "movement" by their supervising authority, usually a probation or parole officer or other official of the court. In most cases, movement is to a specific place and for a specific period of time. Going to an unapproved location or returning late can lead to a restriction of movement or reincarceration. People on monitors typically cannot communicate directly with their supervisors. In most cases they have to connect with a call center, which relays messages to a parole or probation officer or a court official.

In cases of domestic or gender violence, the technology slightly differs. Instead of a single monitor there are two, with one monitor on the person who has committed the abuse and the other in the house of the survivor of the abuse. The survivor's device may also include a pendant with an alarm button. The monitor of the person who has done the harm is programmed with an exclusion zone that requires them to keep a certain distance from the survivor. This effectively serves as a digital restraining order. The survivor's device has a mirror program with an alarm that goes off if the person who committed the abuse violates the exclusion zone.[11] The aim of this "bilateral" monitor is to trigger a police response if the person who committed the abuse violates the exclusion zone.

with her.[12] Since then, the only attempt at an EM census was a 2015 survey of providers by the Pew Trust. Unfortunately, the data generated by Conway and Pew create as much confusion as clarity. Conway's survey showed a steady rise for each year of a decade-long span of work. By the end of her study in 2009, she arrived at a final census of just over 200,000 devices. By 2015 Pew's team counted 125,000 devices (excluding those used by Immigration and Customs Enforcement), up from its estimate of 53,000 in 2005 (Conway reported 95,000 devices in 2005).[13] The enormous decrease as indicated between Conway's 2009 count and the Pew results six years later seems highly unlikely.[14] In her reports, Conway did provide a global figure of the number of devices claimed by each company, but gave no specifics about where they were deployed or the type of program that used them. Pew has never revealed the statistics for individual companies, merely releasing a global total.[15] Apart from these public studies, off-the-record interviews with industry insiders estimate about 350,000 devices are in use in the United States as of late 2020.[16]

EM AND ACCOUNTABILITY: "NOT A SHRED OF DATA"

The absence of even basic statistics for EM highlights the fundamental reality that purveyors and implementers of electronic monitoring have rarely been called to account for the outcomes or cost of their product. On April 9, 2019, one such rare moment took place in

an Illinois state legislature hearing on EM. State representative Will Guzzardi asked Craig
Findley, director of the state's Prisoner Review Board (a structure similar to a parole board),
if he could produce one "single shred of data" to establish that individuals placed on electronic monitoring had better outcomes than those who were not. Findley, whose board had
been authorizing electronic monitors for people coming out of Illinois prisons for more than
a quarter of a century, responded by saying that EM was a "good thing" in many instances.
When Guzzardi repeatedly pressed Findley for data, the director ultimately admitted that he
had none and expressed the hope that the hearing and whatever legislation might emerge
would generate that data. Several months later, HB 386 was signed into Illinois law, mandating the state's department of corrections to file an annual report of data on its electronic
monitoring program. The legislation was the first of its kind anywhere in the United States.[*]
Essentially, EM providers and officials across the country who oversee monitoring programs,
like Findley, have been getting a free pass on their funding—they are not accountable for
outcomes nor required to be transparent about their operations.

Backers of EM have attempted to use research to justify this technology in terms of public
safety, recidivism, and cost-saving. As the main arena for the EM debate has shifted to using
monitors in the pretrial setting, supposedly as a flight deterrent, purveyors of EM have tried to
promote the device's effectiveness in reducing the rate of people failing to show up for court
appearances. However, the body of research that has emerged on this topic has been extremely
limited, contradictory, and often poorly conceptualized. Overall, this literature does little to
support the efficacy or cost benefits of electronic monitors in any situation. Like the efforts
at carrying out a census of EM devices, the research output has only added to the confusion.

PUBLIC SAFETY

No body of evidence has surfaced to support claims about the contribution of EM to public
safety. In fact, the very attempt to statistically isolate its impact on public safety poses a daunt-

---

[*] As of this writing, the Illinois Department of Corrections had not filed the data specified in HB 386.

ing task, typically not acknowledged by EM's supporters. Rather than taking up this challenge, law enforcement agencies and their allies have resorted to profiling individual cases where a person cuts off an ankle monitor and commits a crime or an incident where the GPS tracking of the device has placed a person on the monitor near a crime scene. For example, Confederate flag waver Bryan Betancur was located on the grounds of the US Capitol during the insurrection on January 6, 2020, because of his ankle monitor. While such commentaries grab headlines and contribute to sustaining the flow of taxpayer dollars for policing and jails, they don't actually provide the type of data required to prove the effectiveness of electronic monitoring. Such data would compare the impact of electronic monitoring with that of other interventions over some period of time.

Publicity surrounding a pretrial electronic monitoring case in Charlotte-Mecklenburg, North Carolina, illustrates how law enforcement typically assesses EM's efficacy. In early 2020, a local news story broadcast on a Charlotte station reported that many people were repeatedly being let out of the local jail on electronic monitoring, only to be rearrested in a few days. The focal point of the story was a twenty-three-year-old Black man who had allegedly been arrested more than sixty times, many of them while on the monitor. While the sheriff's response was to question continued participation in the electronic monitoring program, local defense attorney Jeff Thompson noted, "The fact that he was on electronic monitoring when he was charged doesn't mean that electronic monitoring doesn't work."

This case shines a bright light on the failure of the criminal legal system to analyze evidence and reach conclusions consistent with that evidence. Obviously, if a person is arrested more than sixty times, many of them while on a monitor, something fundamental needs to change in both the life of this individual and how the system responds to his repeated encounters with the law. The keys to solving any problem rest with defining the underlying cause, posing a solution, testing that solution, and modifying it if it fails. As long as authorities follow the Charlotte-Mecklenburg approach of applying the same toxic medicine to a wound that is not healing, nothing will change. This is precisely the blinkered, punitive mindset that drove a process of mass incarceration in which the population of prisons and jails increased sevenfold between 1980 and 2010.

Moreover, whatever case authorities might make for EM as a means for improving public safety disintegrates under close scrutiny of the performance of this technology. The devices have a long history of failures and glitches. In 2014, a *Los Angeles Times* report alleged that deputies supervising people on monitors received twenty thousand "meaningless or mundane alerts a month."[17] These alerts could have been triggered by anything from the wearer scratching their leg under the band of the device to the user entering a concrete building where the signal could not penetrate. In 2013, journalist Mario Koran of the Wisconsin Center for Investigative Journalism reported on a number of cases where people were sent back to prison because of false alarms triggered by their ankle monitor.[18] The report sparked an investigation and some recommendations for improvement by the state legislature. Yet five years later, a reporter from the Center did a follow-up story on EM and found that during the month of May 2017, the state monitoring center had lost cell connection with 895 people on monitors a total of 56,893 times.[19] Little seemed to have changed. In July 2016 the state of Massachusetts announced it was replacing all three thousand of its ankle monitors because of what the probation department called "poor cell coverage." One judge refused to place anyone on a monitor due to the technical faults.[20] The scale and frequency of these errors cast serious doubts on EM as a "solution."

At the individual level, the two biggest technical glitches in electronic monitoring are dead batteries and loss of signal. Most programs require a person to plug their device into an electrical power source for two or more consecutive hours each day. But many people report the charge doesn't last a full day. They have to find a public place like a fast-food restaurant where they can plug it in. If they fail to recharge their device, police may come looking for them. For example, in 2018, Daehaun White enrolled in a job training course at a local college in St. Louis. One day a police officer showed up in his class and ordered him to leave and go home because his battery had gone dead.[21] The challenge becomes even more difficult for people who are housing insecure. Ali Sentwali, for instance, was living in his car in 2018 while on parole and found the most convenient place for him to charge his device was at an outdoor plug at Sproul Plaza at the University of California at Berkeley. A photo in *The Guardian* captured him sitting among the students with his monitor connected to a plug in a concrete wall.[22] Sentwali's problem is not unique. A 2018 report by Riley Vetterkind stated that 10 percent of people on GPS monitors in Wisconsin under the state's department of corrections were without housing. One person told Vetterkind his only housing option was a $10-a-night trailer park where he plugged his ankle monitor into the outlets designed for trailers.[23]

Researcher Shubha Bala spent years at the Center for Court Innovation testing electronic monitoring devices. They concluded that the "one-size-fits-all" approach to monitors fails to take into account how these technologies can have "life-altering consequences on freedom, employment, housing and family and community." Bala emphasizes that different technologies have different capacities for failure, ranging from losing signal to the challenges of charging batteries. They propose developing regulations and protocols for various devices and contexts. In Bala's view, regulators "would look not only at whether a technology achieves its stated goals but also at what cost (in terms of time, money and resources), what the risks and consequences might be, and how easy it is to use, both in perfect and real-world conditions."[24] Bala's proposals extend far beyond the existing cursory evaluations and research that currently informs decision-making.

EM AND THE SHELL GAME OF RECIDIVISM

Criminologists seem to view a decreasing rate of recidivism (return to custody) as the "gold standard" for measuring the effectiveness of parole or probation. But choosing recidivism rate as the key outcome has inherent limitations, since it only reveals whether a person on EM was rearrested or incarcerated. Recidivism does not in any way take into account the circumstances of a rearrest. In the case of EM, this would need to include the often arbitrary and pointless restrictions that accompany being on a monitor. In the end, whether a person under some form of carceral control is re-incarcerated depends far more on enforcement of rules governing supervision and the strictness of the individual parole or probation agent enforcing those rules, than whether a person is on EM. For example, in some jurisdictions, authorities might return a person to custody for a positive drug test or getting home five minutes after EM curfew. By contrast, other jurisdictions may give several warnings before arresting. Ultimately, these discrepancies have far more bearing on someone landing back in jail than the presence of an EM device. Also, authorities can easily manipulate results depending on whether they want recidivism rates to rise or fall. A rise in recidivism may be useful to policy makers seeking more money for parole enforcement, while a fall in recidivism could help demonstrate that existing policies are working. As the late award-winning criminologist Joan Petersilia of Stanford University noted about recidivism: "That's just a shell game. . . . Let's just decide we are going to let people fail three or four times and not violate [rearrest] them. I can get your arrest rates down. . . . But have we really changed behavior? And so that's a much different thing."[25]

In terms of linking recidivism to EM, research in the United States has been very limited and problematic. By far the most significant overview on recidivism and EM was a 2017 project conducted by Jyoti Belur's team of researchers from the University College London's Department of Security and Crime Science. Their goal was to "systematically review the evidence of the effectiveness of electronic monitoring of offenders." The team scoured the globe for every English-language publication on EM since 1999 and came up with 372 books, journal articles, and research reports. Seventeen of these attempted to quantitatively measure EM's impact on recidivism. Belur's team concluded that EM "does not have a statistically significant effect on reducing re-offending."[26] An earlier, smaller-scale literature review by Washington State Institute for Public Policy researchers Steve Aos, Marna Miller, and Elizabeth Drake also reported a statistically non-significant effect of EM on recidivism rates. Their review of nine studies concluded that "although there is no current evidence that electronic monitoring reduces recidivism rates, it can be a cost-effective resource" when offset against jail time.[27]

The largest and most frequently cited EM study conducted in the United States on recidivism to date is a 2010 National Institute of Justice–funded project headed by Florida State professor William Bales. Incorporating data on almost three hundred thousand people paroled from Florida prisons in the 2000s, Bales's team attempted to compare the recidivism rates for those on EM with those without the monitor. Their conclusion, which is often cited by justice authorities and EM companies, held that monitors reduced recidivism by 31 percent. However, Bales's methodology, in which he created a control group by adjusting for a totally excessive number of variables, 122 in all, renders the isolation of any factor such as EM virtually impossible.[28]

Apart from the problematic work of Bales, the remainder of the research on EM and recidivism presents contradictory results. Two studies by criminal justice researcher Stephen Gies in California suggest a correlation between EM use and lower recidivism for people who are "high-risk" and categorized as "sex offenders" or "gang members." One of those studies suffers from control group design flaws similar to that of the Bales work; the other concludes that "gang members" on EM show a decrease in arrests for criminal activity but an increase in rearrest for violating the rules of parole. However, Gies failed to recognize that the state database of alleged gang members, CalGang, has a long history of inaccurate classifications, often based on racial profiling.[29] A group of studies from around the turn of the twenty-first century examining both pretrial and post-adjudication programs show "no significant difference in recidivism between offenders under electronic monitoring and under close manual supervision." In addition, much earlier research that was reviewed "suffered from poor research designs, a lack of program integrity, and an exclusive use of low-risk adult offenders."[30]

In 2017 and 2018, a small body of research surfaced on the impact of pretrial EM on people's failure to make court appearances. This more recent work also presented contradictory results. In the two most cited studies, those of Karla Sainju and Kevin Wolff, one correlated EM with a decrease in failures to appear and the other showed no change.[31] However, in both studies, people on monitors had a high level of technical violations of their pretrial release. In neither case did the researchers examine the actual impact of these violations, in particular, whether a violation led to a return to custody and what impact such a violation might have had on the final result of the case. Race was also omitted from consideration in the researcher's protocol. Once again, we find the research on electronic monitoring failing to sufficiently account for the broader context within which electronic monitoring is applied.

Similarly, studies of "failure to appear" in migration cases show no positive impact from electronic monitoring. A collaborative study by several immigrant rights groups in 2019 showed that the highest rate of compliance with Immigration and Customs Enforcement (ICE) regulations was achieved with programs that provided case management and personal support without the use of a monitor. One such initiative, the Family Case Management Program, achieved a 99 percent compliance rate with check-in appointments and court appearances in 2016–17.[32]

Despite this body of highly inconclusive evidence, the notion persists that people with a sex offense history constitute a unique danger to public safety and therefore warrant prolonged and intensive punishment under electronic monitoring. A 2019 Bureau of Justice Statistics report exemplifies this dishonest portrayal.[33] While the data in the report actually showed that people who had been incarcerated for sexually related offenses had distinctly lower recidivism rates than almost any other group, the report implied just the opposite. Wendy Sawyer, a researcher at the Prison Policy Initiative, a Massachusetts-based think tank, noted that the framing of the report is a "good example of how our perception of sex offenses is distorted by alarmist framing, which in turn contributes to bad policy."[34]

Such alarmism is central to building the myth of electronic monitoring in regard to people with convictions for sexually related offenses. The "bad policy" of which Sawyer writes has been institutionalized in at least two forms: "sex offender" registries and lifetime GPS monitoring for people with certain such offenses. Lifetime GPS exists in twelve states. In Wisconsin, lifetime GPS often comes with a monthly fee of $240. As with so much of electronic monitoring, no research exists to demonstrate that lifetime GPS has any positive impact on either the person on the monitor or any of those classified by authorities as the person's past and/or potential "victims." Moreover, in most states, no evaluation process exists to monitor the outcome of lifetime GPS monitoring. In fact, in Wisconsin, according to interviews with a number of people on lifetime GPS, they do not even report to a parole officer or any official of the state department of corrections. They simply pay any required monthly fees, and if they are the victim of one of the state's thousands of false alarms, they must be prepared to see the police at their front door.[35]

All fifty states plus the District of Columbia have some sort of mandatory sex offender registry for people with certain categories of sexually related offenses. Failure to register or inform authorities of a change of address can result in a felony charge. In 2018, the National Center for Missing and Exploited Children estimated there were more than nine hundred thousand people on state sex offender registries.[36] Nearly every state has an online searchable database of individuals on the registry that enables people to research their neighborhood to see if anyone on the registry lives nearby. Like everything in the criminal legal system, the sex offender registry is racialized. A study by University of Washington criminologist Alissa Ackerman found that Black people were more than twice as likely as white people to be on the registry. Research into the conditions for people on the registry showed that they tended to be harsher and more long-lasting for Black people than for their white counterparts.[37]

COST SAVINGS

In many instances, electronic monitoring may save money for law enforcement. Yet the presentation and calculation of these savings often misleads, hiding actual costs and failing to acknowledge that EM is rarely a substitute for incarceration but instead a condition of a person's release.

Three points are relevant when considering the actual calculation of cost savings. First, the typical metric to estimate cost savings involves comparing the daily costs of electronic monitoring (somewhere between $3 and $10 a day) with the daily costs of incarceration (somewhere between $60 and $164 a day).[38] This method of comparing costs totally neglects the enormous share that fixed costs such as salaries, power bills, and maintenance represent for carceral institutions.[39] While, in theory, removing a certain percentage of people from a prison or jail should reduce daily costs, this becomes a reality only if the institution reduces all operating expenditures, including fixed costs, by an equal percentage. This is rarely the case. The inclusion of EM also creates additional costs of supervision, since the workload for a probation or parole agent increases when a client has a monitor, largely owing to the need to constantly review tracking data and handle requests for movement.

Second, the comparison of the costs of electronic monitoring and incarceration ignores the cheapest option: not doing either one. Researcher Emmett Sanders,[40] who spent over two decades in Illinois prisons and ninety days on EM, argues that the "better than prison" scenario poses a "false binary," as if the only two options are a cell or an ankle shackle, and points out that "often, people put on EM would be free if it didn't exist." He also notes that before EM existed, people were released pretrial and on parole without these devices—and no electronic monitoring costs.[41]

Third, perhaps the most sinister aspect about the myth of electronic monitoring is that it can be "cost-effective." This alleged cost-effectiveness comes from forcing people on the monitor to pay fees for their own e-carceration. Heralded as a great triumph of fiscal discipline, the reality is quite the opposite. In a broad overview of the cost of EM programs, ProPublica journalist Ava Kofman concluded that "states and cities, which incur around 90% of the expenditures for jails and prisons, are increasingly passing the financial burden of the devices onto those who wear them."[42] A 2019 Brennan Center for Justice report highlighted the punitive impact of such fines and fees, arguing that such measures "can create perverse incentives with the potential to distort the fair administration of justice" since so many law enforcement departments and courts rely on this revenue to finance their operations.[43]

A 2014 investigation by NPR revealed that every state except Hawaii charged fees for electronic monitoring.[44] Celebrated as a success by policy makers and much of law enforcement, daily user fees and other EM charges contribute to the further impoverishment of the criminalized sector of the population. Daily fees range from $5 a day to $40 a day, with additional charges like setup fees of up to $300 and, if a device is lost or damaged, replacement costs that can exceed $1,000. For those who are unemployed or underemployed, these fees mean resources for EM payments must compete with covering basic household needs such as rent, food, power, phone bills, medical expenses, and transportation.

THE HUMAN PRICE OF COST-SAVING

A 2018 lawsuit filed in California provides evidence of the impact of these fees. This suit also indicates that people are increasingly finding ways to resist the imposition of EM. Each of the suit's plaintiffs was under contract to EM provider LCA in Alameda County. After one of the plaintiffs, Robert Jackson, served just three days of a 120-day sentence in the county jail, his wife suddenly died of meningitis. She was the sole caregiver for their three children. The court granted Jackson a compassionate release but put him on an LCA monitor with a start-up charge of $150 and a daily fee of $25.50, more than half his earnings. Jackson was forced to prioritize paying the EM fees or run the risk of going back to jail and losing his children to the foster care system. As a result, he fell behind in all his other financial obligations. He lost his car and his house, and had to send his children to live with relatives. He spent four months without a consistent place to live. James Brooks, another plaintiff in the case, faced similar circumstances. He received a compassionate release to look after his disabled mother. LCA placed two monitors on Brooks, one a location tracker and another unit that measured blood alcohol. Although LCA told him his daily fee would be $13, when he received the bill it came out to $28 a day. He was told that if he didn't pay the full amount he could go back to jail. Catherine Sevcenko, a lawyer who handled the case at the time, maintained that LCA was "taking advantage of people at their most vulnerable . . . you're basically forcing someone to play Russian roulette because they don't have enough money."[45]

EM AND THE LAW

The shoddy research methodology applied to EM is also often reflected in the murkiness of legislation dealing with electronic monitoring. Even the lack of clear-cut legal definitions is astounding.

In a 2008 piece for the *Duke Law Journal*, legal scholar Erin Murphy framed much of this debate:

> Physical incapacitation of dangerous persons has always invoked . . . constitutional scrutiny, [but] virtually no legal constraints circumscribe the use of its technological counterpart . . . courts erroneously treat physical deprivations as the archetypal "paradigm of restraint" and . . . largely overlook the significant threat to liberty posed by technological measures.[46]

Activist legal scholar and George Washington University law professor Kate Weisburd re-iterates Murphy's characterization. She argues that the practice of EM "exists in a legal and policy netherworld: wielded and expanded with almost no limits."[47]

The central practical question that emerges from Murphy and Weisburd is whether time spent on house arrest on an ankle monitor should be considered credit for time served, particularly in a pretrial setting. Drawing from a menu of terms that includes "home detention," "electronic home detention," "house arrest," "home confinement," "quasi-incarceration," and "electronic home monitoring," courts have wrestled repeatedly over the question of whether a person locked in their house via technology is actually incarcerated. No legal consensus has been reached.

The debate over pretrial credit has been a ball of confusion virtually since the early days of electronic monitoring. In a 1998 *New Mexico Law Review* article, Ben Feuchter noted that there were three general patterns of state policies on credit for pretrial EM.[48] The first held that only confinement in a jail or prison would qualify as "official confinement." The second pattern gave credit for confinement defined more broadly, to include electronic monitoring as well as substance abuse treatment programs "provided there are sufficient restrictions on a person's liberty." The third pattern was less stringent, allowing some credit for lockup programs that are not in prison or jail, but excluding credit for house arrest. These patterns remain today, though now with two additional decades' worth of twists and turns of legal jargon to further obfuscate clear definitions. For example, Iowa courts apply the term "quasi-incarceration" to electronic monitoring and residential treatment programs and grant them credit toward prison or jail sentences.[49]

The most obvious expression of this inconsistency in awarding credit for EM was the Cook County pretrial courts. The jurisdiction ran two electronic monitoring programs, one under the authority of the sheriff, the other under the auspices of the chief judge. Though not spelled out anywhere in policy, for many years the practice was that those on pretrial electronic monitoring under the sheriff had the time spent on EM applied to their sentence, whereas those in the chief judge's program did not. This contradiction was ultimately resolved in 2021 with the passage of HB 3653, which stipulated that all instances of electronic home detention and even house arrest without a monitor, as long as they were for a duration of at least twelve hours a day, would count as time served.

The confusion over credit for time served on EM remains in many states and local jurisdictions. Federal appellate courts have labeled time on EM as a form of pretrial release rather than "official detention" and therefore not eligible for credit.[50] Pennsylvania shared that conclusion in the 2017 ruling in the case of *Commonwealth v. Dixon*, holding that electronic monitoring at home is not viewed as in "custody" for purposes of credit toward one's sentence. "Time spent in custody" included confinement to a rehabilitation and treatment facility as a condition of bail.[51] Another court case in Pennsylvania allocated credit for time served based on whether a person was on a program run by prison authorities, which was deemed as worthy of credit; or one run by a private company, for which no credit was awarded. The court went on to rule that electronic monitoring did not contain enough restraints to be considered a form of custody since the defendant was "allowed to live in his own home . . . was free to watch television, interact with his wife and children, sleep in his own bed, eat whatever and whenever he wanted whether the food was in the refrigerator or he called for delivery."[52] In New Mexico, EM is deemed "official confinement" and thus credit is awarded under two conditions: (1) if a court has entered an order releasing the defendant from a facility but has imposed limitations on the defendant's freedom of movement, or the defendant is in the actual or constructive custody of state or local law enforcement or correctional officers; (2) if the defendant is punishable for a crime of escape if there is an unauthorized departure from the place of confinement or other noncompliance with the court's order.[53]

Though debate around credit for pretrial EM has been the focus of most debate on this topic, a "netherworld" still exists in some instances for EM post-prison. According to an Illinois statute, individuals serving time in prison can spend the last six months of their sentence on electronic monitoring. Hence the law defines this as incarceration. Yet, up until 2019, those who completed a prison sentence and were placed on EM as a condition of their Mandatory Supervised Release (MSR) were subjected to virtually the same punishment, but in terms of the law were no longer incarcerated. While on MSR, the typical policy for those on EM under the authority of the Illinois Department of Corrections typically only allowed movement out of the house on Monday, Wednesday, and Friday for four to six hours a day.[54]

In 2019, the severity of post-prison EM regimes in Illinois prompted a group of activists, including me, to form the Coalition to Challenge Electronic Monitoring to mount legislative action. We joined with State Representative Carol Ammons to propose HB 1115, the first bill anywhere in the United States to ban the use of electronic monitors for people coming home from prison. The Illinois Department of Corrections had been using ankle monitors for more than two decades as a condition of post-release. At the time the bill was proposed, about 2,500 people were on post-prison monitors across the state.

A coalition of seven reentry programs across the state signed onto a letter in support of the bill. The letter read in part:

> In our experience, these devices serve no constructive purpose in our participants' lives or in the broader efforts of reentry. We encourage policy makers and budgetary authorities to carefully re-think the use of electronic monitoring and GPS and consider redirecting the funds spent on these devices to supportive programs.[55]

The state legislature held two committee hearings on EM, with lawyers and other advocates giving testimony. However, the voice of people who had been on the monitor dominated. Chris Harrison, who had spent eighteen years in prison, then a year on EM, called the device a catch-22: "I think they want you to fail on electronic monitoring . . . it doesn't help you get employment. It doesn't help you get mental health treatment if you need it . . . it's just invasive."[56]

Two lawyers, Patrice James of the Shriver Center on Poverty Law and Sarah Staudt of the Chicago Appleseed Fund for Justice, also testified in the hearings, noting the obstacles EM posed for reentry. In a subsequent commentary, James stressed that "electronic monitoring is incarceration by another name," and it "extends the carceral state to our communities and into our homes. It does not serve returning citizens, a majority of whom are Black, and instead has proven to be a poor use of Illinois taxpayer dollars."[57]

Despite intense opposition from law enforcement, the bill passed the House in the spring of 2019. It needed to get through the Senate to become law, but COVID-19 restrictions shut down the legislature for most of 2020, thus closing the time window for the bill to go through the Senate.

However, the political ripples from the public debate sparked reform from the Prisoner Review Board (PRB). During intensive questioning by legislators in a House committee hearing on HB 1115, PRB director Craig Findley mentioned that the board would be willing to grant people on electronic monitoring movement for a minimum of twelve hours a day. In July of that year, Findley issued a memo to the Department of Corrections mandating twelve hours of daily movement for all individuals on EM under the PRB's authority.[58] A few weeks later parole agents began to grant individuals their mandated twelve hours a day of movement.[59]

IS EM PUNISHMENT?

Another key legal debate over EM—though astonishing that it's a matter of debate—concerns whether it falls under the heading of "punishment." This issue has emerged most frequently in cases involving lifetime GPS monitoring. As noted, twelve states have instituted lifetime GPS monitoring for people convicted of certain sexually related offenses.[60] The landmark decision came from Wisconsin in 2018, when the state Supreme Court decided 7–0 that being on a GPS for life did not constitute punishment but was a "minimal intrusion" in the interest of public safety. The decision came in response to litigation brought by DeAnthony Muldrow, who wanted to withdraw his guilty plea, since lifetime GPS was not mentioned among the conditions of his sentence when they were originally pronounced in court.[61]

Legal experts have also attempted to argue against the constitutionality of electronic monitoring on a number of other grounds. Kate Weisburd has been at the forefront of these critiques of EM. Weisburd, who has represented dozens of youth on EM in juvenile courts, has raised Fourth Amendment issues of illegal search in regard to EM, contending, among other things, the courts have framed EM as a situation where defendants "choose" surveillance instead of incarceration. Weisburd contends there is no consent involved, that since EM amounts to unconstitutional surveillance, consent is not a possibility. She argues that electronic monitoring gets a sort of "free constitutional pass." In her view, with highly restrictive limitations on movement, many EM regimes amount to a denial of First Amendment rights as well as denial of access to legal counsel. She notes, for example, the debate over whether former lawyer for President Donald Trump, Michael Cohen, should be allowed to write a book while on pretrial electronic monitoring highlighted the lack of clarity on this issue. Cohen was rearrested while on EM because he refused to accept conditions of his monitoring supervision, which banned him from writing a book and speaking to the media. Though in the end Cohen was released and allowed to publish the book, his situation raised constitutional questions that led Weisburd to ask, "Where does the Constitution say people have their rights diminished because they are being subjected to punishment?"[62]

Legal scholar Chaz Arnett makes note of additional Fourth Amendment concerns about EM that relate to the "massive amounts of data being captured and stored," often by private companies. Arnett goes on to pinpoint specific instances of electronic monitors increasingly capturing biometric data such as voice prints.[63] As the capacity of this technology expands and promoters of e-carceration advance new myths to justify the increasing invasiveness of their technology, more complexity will emerge in terms of its privacy implications. States such as Massachusetts have already anticipated potential lawsuits concerning data capture. The contract between the state and EM company ELMO required people on the monitor to sign the following statement: "I understand that the data generated by the GPS assigned to me is not private and confidential."[64]

DUE PROCESS

Although Fourth Amendment rights are the most obvious constitutional issue that emerges with EM, the question of due process also surfaces. Much like pretrial detention, the pressures resulting from a prolonged period of electronic monitoring often influence a person's response to negotiating a settlement of their case. One interviewee referred to EM as a "pry bar" that prosecutors use to coerce people into accepting plea bargains.[65] Lavette Mayes, who spent 121 days on a pretrial monitor, claims, "If EM had given me more movement, I probably would have fought the case. . . . [But] my kids were not getting the healing that they needed." She went on to explain, "You're not even able to provide or do anything in your community let alone your family. It's not a solution." Mayes had a seven-year-old child with learning challenges, which created additional complications. "Because my son is autistic, he had impulsive behaviors where he would run off and I wouldn't be able to chase him." Her daughter, who was fifteen at the time, noted "it was just really hard and stressful because knowing that if she stepped outside without calling the sheriff or letting someone know, then the sheriff would arrest her. It felt like we were being punished."[66]

Tyshontae Williams, who spent six months on EM awaiting trial in New Haven, Connecticut, presented a similar narrative: "It was depressing. . . . It had a lot to do with my mental stableness, and that pushed me more toward taking a plea deal." He was only allowed out of the house to go to work. He recalled, "I couldn't even take out the garbage; my mother actually made a point about that." Williams referred to electronic monitoring as a set of "tripwires" put in place to send you back to jail. He managed to get his rules changed slightly: "I got that little bit of freedom from my back porch to my trash can. It was annoying. . . . My home was like a prison."[67]

In still other instances, the financial pressure of having to pay daily user fees without any clear understanding of when the pretrial phase might end forces people to take the financially expedient path. Chicago attorney Emmanuel Andre laments that sometimes the electronic monitor "makes a liar out of me. I have to go into court and plead guilty for a client who I know is innocent."[68]

HUMAN RIGHTS AND ELECTRONIC MONITORS

While rights for people on EM in the United States have never attracted much attention from policy makers, the European Union (EU) has a lengthy history of debate on this topic. In 2014, after several years of discussion, the EU Committee of Ministers adopted a set of recommendations on electronic monitoring to member states. These recommendations called for the regulation of data gathered via monitoring, the consideration of the "overall impact on former prisoners, their families and third parties" when considering the duration and "intrusiveness" of EM, a ban on any devices that might do physical harm, and avoiding "as far as possible" the punitive practice of 24-hour-a-day house arrest. The ministers also proposed that EM should be "combined with interventions designed to bring about rehabilitation and to support desistance."[69] The recommendations were formulated by the Confederation of European Probation (CEP), which organizes annual conferences on electronic monitoring. According to renowned global expert on EM Mike Nellis, a professor at Scotland's University of Strathclyde and the leading driver of the process that led to the recommendations, the CEP is an association of probation officers who, unlike their counterparts in the United States, are largely "social work–based" rather than oriented toward law enforcement.[70] In 2017, the Challenging E-Carceration project developed a "Guidelines for Respecting the Rights of Individuals on Electronic Monitoring," which were based on the recommendations of the CEP. Over sixty organizations endorsed the guidelines, including the national offices of the ACLU, the National Association of Criminal Defense Lawyers, and Human Rights Watch. The guidelines opposed the imposition of fees for monitoring, promoted the granting of credit for time served on EM, and encouraged transparency in the implementation of electronic monitoring programs.[71]

The spread of EM has been driven by the myth of a cheap device that is efficient, is used judiciously, and has the capacity to effectively monitor and modify behavior while keeping the public safe. The purveyors of this myth have typically relied on unsubstantiated claims buttressed by dubious research and scant amounts of often irrelevant data posing as "evidence" of the technology's efficacy. Yet even now, as we have seen, the 2005 assessment of high-profile EM researchers Marc Renzema and Evan Mayo-Wilson still holds true:

 After 20 years of EM, we have only a few clues as to its impact. . . . Money spent on EM could be spent on empirically-tested programs that demonstrably protect our communities.[72]

However, this does not mean there is no legitimate evidence concerning the growth and impact of electronic monitoring. That evidence exists in abundance, in the lived experience of those impacted by EM, which we turn to in the next chapter. This evidence will offer a very different perspective of the realities of electronic monitoring.

5

THE "WAYWARD TECHNOLOGY": BUSTING THE MYTH OF ELECTRONIC MONITORING

GPS tracking is an example of public fear that has been augmented by politicians who want to be tough on crime. It's a wayward technology that has become warped into a punishment routine.

—*Robert Gable, co-inventor of electronic monitoring*[1]

When you think about it, it's nothing but twenty-first-century control and slavery, electronic style.

—*Jean-Pierre Shackelford, after nearly three years on EM in Ohio*[2]

In the absence of data from official sources and EM companies, busting the myth of electronic monitoring demands a multifaceted research approach that centers the experience of people directly impacted by EM. Though such evidence is often derisively labeled "anecdotal" or "informal," as Yeshimabeit Milner, founder of Data 4 Black Lives, reminds us: "The most powerful data is often our own lived experience."[3] Such evidence shows how anyone saddled with an EM device inevitably bears extra burdens in daily life that can have serious negative consequences. The renowned chronicler of Black history and culture, author and professor Saidiya Hartman, stresses that focusing on the nooks and crannies of daily life that emerge in people's own stories helps to "illuminate the terror of the mundane and quotidian" and may convey that experience more effectively than exploiting "the shocking spectacle."[4] In fact, while the mundane and quotidian aspects of electronic monitoring do at time strike terror into the hearts of those targeted by these devices, some of the egregious abuses of EM programs also fall into the category of the shocking spectacle. Legal scholar Chaz Arnett accurately identifies the shortcomings of EM as part of a decarceration strategy. In his view, "the pursuit of decarceration through electronic surveillance only perpetuates the role that the criminal justice system plays in entrenching a marginalized second-class citizenship, as the technology often acts as an additional barrier to successful rehabilitation and reentry." He goes on to stress that e-carceration acts "to further one of the greatest harms of mass incarceration, the entrenchment of race and class subordination, and abandons genuine attempts at rehabilitation and reintegration."[5]

In 2017, MediaJustice, a nonprofit organization that focuses on racial justice in the realms of media and surveillance, established the Challenging E-Carceration project, for which I serve as the director. The work of Challenging E-Carceration informs much of this chapter. I began this project by capturing the stories of people who had been on the monitor in various contexts.[6] I visited reentry programs in California, Michigan, Wisconsin, Connecticut, New York, and Illinois. I went to trailer parks that housed dozens of undocumented workers and set up focus groups with youth programs in Los Angeles where many participants had experienced EM. I also attended conferences and meetings of organizations of the formerly incarcerated such as All of Us or None and the National Council for Incarcerated and Formerly Incarcerated Women and Girls and spoke with individuals impacted by electronic monitors. Working in partnership with project researcher Emmett Sanders, I traveled to Chicago, where we interviewed people who had been on the monitor or had loved ones on EM, visited reentry programs and youth support groups, and attended Cook County court appearances of those dealing with EM.

Our aim was to fill in the blanks left by officials' near-total abdication of their responsibility to account for funds and for the people they were supposedly serving. To fulfill this part of the research mission, we sent Freedom of Information Act requests to 38 state departments of correction and the fifteen largest counties in the United States. We also scoured academic literature and news media, and read policy documents and rules of the road for various EM programs. Where possible, we interviewed parole agents, corrections officials, and EM company executives and employees.[7]

By weaving together the contents of personal stories and data from various sources, we established at least two facts. First, from the statistics we were able to gather, we concluded that electronic monitoring is becoming more widespread and more intrusive. Second, the stories from impacted people provided evidence to support our conclusion that electronic monitoring is not an alternative to incarceration but an alternative form of incarceration, one with a wide range of pernicious implications for the present and future of freedom and social justice in this country and beyond.

THE GROWTH OF ELECTRONIC MONITORING

A variety of sources provide strong evidence of the growth of EM. The key data comes from local jurisdictions and departments of corrections. Statistics from a number of important sites highlight the widening net of electronic monitoring. Perhaps the most illustrative example is in Marion County, Indiana, which we can label as the capital of EM usage in the United States. Marion, with the main hub of Indianapolis as the driver, operates the largest pretrial EM program in the country. Marion doubled EM usage from 2015 to 2020. In 2018 alone, more than fourteen thousand people in Marion County were on a monitor at some point.[8] Brian Baron, head of Track Group, the firm contracted to handle EM in Marion, linked the rise in monitoring to issues in the jail. He explained to a local reporter, "The fact that there is a major jail overcrowding problem here and technology is cheaper than it used to be [means] there is a lot of pressure to use monitors." Baron saw his year-on-year profits rise by 39 percent in 2016 alone.[9] Profits rose another 11 percent in 2019.[10] By May of 2020, the county's daily EM count had reached 4,300.[11]

Another hot spot of EM growth is Cook County, home of Chicago, where Sheriff Tom Dart runs the nation's second-largest program for pretrial electronic monitoring. In operation since the late 1980s, a 1995 report on this program boasted that it was "considered the best of its kind, serving as the prototype for programs all over the world." Local officials even claimed that visitors from Russia, China, and the Netherlands had come to see how Cook County was implementing electronic monitoring.[12] Rather than serving as a global prototype, Cook County's EM program has become a mad, often contentious scramble to keep up with demand for devices while enforcing some of the most oppressive electronic monitoring regulations in the country. Maintaining the scale and punitive character of the program has meant intense political battles with prison abolitionist and criminal justice reform organizations including the Chicago Community Bond Fund, the Coalition to End Money Bond, and the ACLU, which have maintained that EM budgets should be redirected into programs to keep people out of jail.[13] The growth of EM in Cook County has been steady and considerable, with annual EM enrollment doubling from 2010 to 2014 then spiking again during the pandemic. Daily population counts increased from 2,357 at the end of December 2019 to more than 3,600 by January of 2021.[14] Apart from the sheriff's program, the county's chief judge, Timothy Evans, heads a separate, smaller pretrial EM operation in Cook County. In 2020, during the pandemic, EM use rose so quickly that the county ran out of devices, prompting the sheriff to take the ultra-punitive stance of keeping people in jail during the spread of COVID while they waited for EM devices to become available.[15] In response, the county commissioners granted Sheriff Dart a request for $13 million in December 2020 to purchase 1,310 GPS monitors.

In Massachusetts, one of the few states that compiles statewide figures, EM usage tripled between 2012 and 2020. About 40 percent of people on parole in Massachusetts must wear GPS monitors.[16] Such increases have been replicated around the country in a number of smaller counties. San Francisco, for example, showed one of the most dramatic increases, growing from 178 devices to 725 from 2017 to 2018.[17] Kate Weisburd's research has also helped quantify usage in a number of states where EM abounds. According to her 2021 report, Florida had over 5,000 people on EM in 2019, and Colorado was not far behind with 4,814 in 2018.[18]

In the immigration sphere, usage of electronic monitors under ICE's authority ballooned from 9,300 in 2015 to nearly 54,000 by 2020.[19]

Apart from EM device counts, the activity of firms in the industry has also indicated a shift of resources into e-carceration. A 2003 survey of companies in the EM sector contained only twenty firms.[20] But by 2020, at least fifty firms were active in providing or producing electronic monitors in the United States.[21] The net increase in providers took place despite frequent mergers and acquisitions initiated by the larger producers and distributors of monitors, another indicator of the vibrancy of the sector. The GEO Group's buyout of BI in 2009, noted earlier, was the most important such transaction. The other major providers of EM devices and services were also active, indicating their belief in the future of EM. Sentinel Offender Services, a large-scale player in the private probation sector, added to its EM portfolio in 2012 by taking over G4S Justice Services, a global, integrated security company.[22] Securus, a long-standing supplier of phone service for prisons and jails, entered the electronic monitoring world by acquiring major EM operator Satellite Tracking of People (STOP) in 2013.[23] Israeli firm SuperCom, a global provider of digital IDs as well as electronic monitoring, bought out California-based LCA in 2015.[24] LCA held contracts for electronic monitoring in several California counties, including San Francisco and Alameda. Prison profiteers clearly saw future revenue streams in e-carceration.

BEHIND THE GROWTH IN EM

Three interlocking factors precipitated this growth in electronic monitoring. First, the arrival of GPS capacity in the late 1990s was key to the advance of e-carceration. Though the shift was slow, according to the Pew Survey, by 2015 the market share of GPS monitors had reached about 70 percent, rising to 88,172, up from 2,897 in 2005.[25] This technical advance coincided with cries for increased surveillance that emerged after 9/11. By the end of the second decade of the twenty-first century, virtually all new contracts and purchases were for devices with tracking capacity.

Then in the 2010s, critics of mass incarceration began to focus on eliminating cash bail. This drove additional carceral consumers to electronic monitoring. Sheriffs and judges responded to pressure for change by releasing more people awaiting trial and putting them on monitors. These stabs at reform were far from ideal for activist leaders like Pilar Weiss, the director of the Community Justice Exchange. Weiss heads a national coalition of over a hundred community-based funds that post bail for people who cannot afford to pay to get themselves out of jail. She called EM a "fallback the system uses when it claims to be making reform."[26] Judge Carla Baldwin of Youngstown, Ohio, described EM as part of a "pre-conviction" process. Baldwin, who has an unusual passion for bail reform for someone in the judiciary, observed that decision-makers often opt for a monitor simply because they've "always done this," rather than taking the time to study the issue. For her, monitors provide an "easy excuse for the system to not ask why."[27]

Third, the pandemic of 2020 became a catalyst for the expansion of EM. This resulted largely from public pressure to reduce the prison and jail population, since imprisoned people faced a greater risk of contracting and spreading COVID-19. The Prison Policy Initiative (PPI), a nonprofit policy think tank, pointed out the difficulty of maintaining social distance in such confined quarters and noted that incarcerated people were more likely than the general population to have chronic health conditions. PPI also emphasized the overrepresentation of Black and brown people in prisons and jails, highlighting demographic disparities among COVID-19 sufferers. More importantly, incarcerated people themselves staged dozens of actions behind the walls. In a year of enormous popular uprisings under the banner of Black Lives Matter, the spirit of rebellion also touched people in prison. Their actions aimed to draw attention to the fact that they, more than anyone, faced the most intense direct confrontation with the deadly virus. According to a report from the *Perilous Chronicle*, an independent digital research and media project, people in over a hundred prisons and immigration detention centers staged acts of resistance during the first ninety days of the pandemic alone.[28] These actions began in two facilities at opposite ends of the country: an immigration detention center in Essex, New Jersey, and a Monterey County jail in California. From there, hunger strikes and other protests spread to thirty-five states. The hot spots of resistance were immigration detention centers, where nearly 40 percent of these actions took place. People inside the Mesa Verde ICE detention center proclaimed that they began their "protest in memory of our comrades George Floyd, Breonna Taylor, Oscar Grant, and Tony McDade. Almost all of us have also suffered through our country's corrupt and racist criminal justice system before being pushed into the hands of ICE."[29] Prison authorities responded to these actions with intensive repression in the form of pepper spray, rubber bullets, sting balls, and billy clubs, with outside police often called in as backup.

Despite these protests and the uprisings in communities, decarceration in most jurisdictions proceeded somewhat slowly. However, companies such as SuperCom were quick to take advantage of the crisis. They accelerated their marketing efforts with tactics such as re-packaging their electronic monitors as "quarantine management" systems. SuperCom executive Ordan Trabelsi maintained the firm was uniquely positioned to offer a "solution" to COVID. "We'll just be tracking people that are not essentially offenders but unluckily were exposed to the virus," he said in a 2020 interview.[30]

Over the course of the last decade, all of the factors noted above contributed to electronic monitoring's widening net. At the same time, voices critical of the ankle shackle grew in volume and began to appear in debates and struggles over policy.

THE LIVED EXPERIENCE OF EM

Johnny Page, who spent ninety days on an electronic monitor after serving more than two decades in Illinois prisons, summed up his EM experience: "You get to pay your own bills. You don't have to wait in line for the shower, you don't have to wait for the telephone, but you're still in jail." When people asked Page how it felt to be out of prison during his time on the monitor, he had a simple reply: "I'm not out. It's just another form of incarceration." Alisha Coleman had a similar response after being released on EM as a result of California's

AB 109, a 2011 reform bill that targeted people with low-level, nonviolent offenses. "Why would you let me out of jail to put me in another jail inside my home?" she asked.[31]

Challenging E-Carceration interviews and discussions with dozens of people who have been impacted by EM across the country reveal sentiments very much akin to Page and Coleman's views. For example, after ninety days on the monitor after twenty-three years in prison, Challenging E-Carceration researcher Emmett Sanders concluded that "almost no aspect of a person's life is unaffected. You are wearing a jail anywhere you go, on your leg, in your phone." In Sanders's case, the omnipresence of the monitor was particularly obtrusive as he had to wear the ankle shackle to his own wedding. Sanders's extensive research for Challenging E-Carceration emphasizes the psychological impact of wearing an ankle shackle: "It is a daily reminder that there are people who view you as sub-human." He argues that most monitoring regimes are disempowering, "robbing people of their agency."[32]

In many instances, the regulations for determining whether a person should be on a monitor are extremely opaque. Ru-El Sailor spent fifteen years in prison on a murder conviction before he won his exoneration. However, Ohio rules dictated that a person who is released from a high security prison must go on a monitor. Since Sailor was in a maximum security facility, even though he was exonerated, he still had to spend four months on EM.[33]

Moreover, in neighborhoods of the criminalized, ankle shackles have become normalized. Kentavious Caldwell-Pope wore a shackle while he played basketball for the Los Angeles Lakers. Rappers such as Meek Mill and Rick Ross were "strapped," not with a Glock but an ankle monitor. Students in a Los Angeles high school reported the presence of special rooms for students to plug in their monitors.[34] For those without houses or without power in their houses, the local McDonald's has become a hangout not for the fries or Egg McMuffins but because it has wall plugs to connect an ankle monitor. EM even gained legitimacy in circles of respectability when errant celebrities like Lindsay Lohan, Charlie Sheen, and Martha Stewart landed on the e-shackle. In 2018, the superhero of the movie *Ant Man and the Wasp*, played by Paul Rudd, wore an ankle monitor and his movement restrictions were a key part of the plot. To top it off, members of the cast of characters of the Trump presidency, such as Paul Manafort and Michael Cohen, also wore the shackle as a way to keep them from having to mingle with the working-class, criminalized sector of the population in local jails. Yet the normalization of these devices has not done anything to relax the draconian rules that apply to EM regimes.

THE DRACONIAN RULES OF ELECTRONIC MONITORING

Research by Sanders and many others has revealed the harmful effects of exceedingly harsh EM rules and regulations.[35] The restrictions do not just limit physical movement; they block social interaction with family and community, the practice of religion, and the ability to tend to basic medical and health needs. The rules are a product of the punitive mindset of control that infects EM, a mindset often riddled with racism, gender bias, transphobia, and homophobia. Sanders says these restrictions amount to a "massive loss of freedom . . . you lose the right to take care of yourself." This is especially acute when it comes to Black and brown bodies, he emphasizes, noting even the simplest task can be forbidden. "When you take away the ability to go to the store to buy toilet paper," he observed, "you are completely disempowering people."

Rules and regulations for electronic monitoring constitute a carceral regime imposed on the individual and their household. Monica Cosby, who like Sanders spent two decades in Illinois prisons only to land on a monitor as a condition of parole, especially felt the way the monitor transformed living space. "When you're on electronic monitoring, any place of residence—whether it's in the home of your family or a halfway house—that place becomes like a satellite prison." She compared being on a monitor to "an abusive relationship where you never know when you go out if you're going to do something wrong and get in trouble when you come back home for breaking some rule."[36]

Ultimately, electronic monitoring with house arrest is designed for a cisgendered, *Leave It to Beaver*–style household of well-to-do white people.[37] The rich and famous icons of EM, such as Martha Stewart and Charlie Sheen, have spacious, well-furnished houses with full refrigerators, high-speed Wi-Fi, cable TV, functioning smartphones, and in-house washer-dryers. They may even have servants or personal assistants. Resources are readily available for the delivery of products and services to the home. In these scenarios, a person on house arrest can relax in their own personal space, binge-watch television, contact people via their phone, and avoid being a nuisance to other people in the house. Their class privilege allows them to avoid jail and to experience electronic monitoring as a glitch that temporarily limits their life of comforts.

But the reality for most people on electronic monitoring looks very different. They typically come from households with low incomes and precarious access to services. Power bills may not get paid regularly, making it difficult to charge their device. Phones may be cut off periodically, rendering their GPS signals inaccessible to the authorities. Because of overcrowding, various individuals may be sleeping on floors or couches at all times of the night and day. That house may be the least likely place for a person on a monitor to stay out of trouble. For these individuals draconian rules can also create a host of problems in simply carrying out the basic necessities of life. In Milwaukee, people on pretrial EM have to get authorization to go grocery shopping (maximum one hour per week), to use a laundromat (two-hour maximum once per week), and to attend church (four hours once per week).[38]

These problems may be especially acute for youth. Emmanuel Andre, a Chicago attorney who specializes in youth justice cases, says that "a lot of times you are forcing people to go back to a place where there is harm."[39] Father David Kelly, who has run youth programs in the predominantly Latinx and Black area of Back of the Yards in Southwest Chicago for many years, echoes Andre's depiction. He notes that the house where youth are assigned for EM may be "not helpful," or even "toxic."[40] In 2017, legal scholars and students at UC Berkeley completed a comprehensive study of juvenile EM policy and laws in all fifty-eight California counties. They exposed shocking rules impacting households where youth were on EM. Several counties required that the youth be taken into custody in the event of one of the frequent power outages in California. At least five counties required the presence of an adult any time a juvenile on EM was in their place of residence.[41]

EMPLOYMENT

Although most programs formally encourage granting movement for job purposes, in practice, accessing and maintaining employment is extremely difficult for people on EM. When they are able to find work, most people are relegated to precarious jobs or contracting through temp agencies. The monitor impedes the employment process at every level. Responding to calls for interviews on short notice is rarely feasible since the individual must contact their supervisor to be granted the movement. In most instances, this involves dialing a call center. Operators in these centers are notoriously slow to respond. "They can take hours to pick up the phone," Johnny Page recalled—a familiar mantra from people who have been on EM. Page reported waiting on hold for four hours on one occasion before anyone answered.

Supervisors often impose complicating rules about applying for jobs, such as requiring their clients to inform employers during the interview that they are on an electronic monitor and will have to follow a specific schedule. Alisha Coleman complained that the mere presence of "this big old thing on my ankle" scared away employers, especially in a job where she might have had direct contact with the public. One young man in Illinois reported that he landed a sales job in a sports shoe store without revealing his device. At one point, the cuff of his pants caught on the monitor and another employee noticed it. She went home and told her parents that she was working with a "criminal." The next day, her parents came to the shop and the man with the monitor was fired.[42]

Even though a GPS device is supposed to inform authorities of a person's location at all times, most EM regimes don't allow work that involves travel or frequently changing workplaces. This eliminates a whole range of jobs including driving, delivery, yard work, house cleaning, and catering. In addition, nighttime jobs are typically verboten. Upon his release on EM, Edmund Buck was refused permission to work a graveyard factory shift, though it was the only job he could secure after nineteen years in Illinois prisons.[43]

Some EM rules simply eliminate movement outside the house for work as an option altogether. Illinois's Cook County is especially strict on this. Timothy Williams was released on EM pretrial and wasn't allowed to work for six months. He finally landed a job driving a forklift for a temp agency. "Jarrett" (not real name) told the Chicago Community Bond Fund that his parents' house was designated as his residence upon pretrial release. For some reason, the court's Pretrial Services personnel began checking for him at his grandparents' house in the middle of the night. When they didn't find him, they took him into custody for violating the terms of his pretrial release. At his next court date, the judge placed him on twenty-four-hour home confinement and refused to give him permission to work. He lost both his jobs and was not allowed out of the house for four months.[44]

Even efforts to earn money through donating plasma can be blocked for people on a monitor. Ron Schroeder, on EM in Milwaukee, went to a local blood bank to give plasma. He was told they didn't accept plasma donations from people on EM.[45]

MEDICAL SERVICES

Although accessing work is the most frequent complaint regarding movement restrictions, difficulties in obtaining movement for medical purposes also rate high on people's lists of grievances. The most disturbing moments are medical emergencies, including emergencies involving loved ones. In an Illinois legislative hearing on EM in 2019, Colette Payne, who had been on EM herself years earlier, described her experience as the mother of a son who was on an electronic monitor. He was put on the device by Illinois parole authorities after an incident in which he suffered a gunshot wound in the testicle. After some time, Payne concluded that her son's wound was becoming infected. They attempted to arrange a visit to the doctor, but the parole officer didn't grant permission. She told the legislators that "as a mother, it was my duty to take him to the hospital," even at the risk of a rearrest. She took him to the hospital. He was later rearrested for an electronic monitoring violation.[46] Payne's difficulties in getting her son to the doctor are not unique. Some officers of the court in Cook County even require a faxed message from the practitioner before approving movement for a mental health consultation for youth traumatized by gun violence.[47]

Coco Davis had medical issues of a different sort. First, when she was on a monitor in 2013 after serving more than a decade in prison, she got word that her son had gotten into a fight and was taken to hospital. When she phoned the EM supervisor, no one answered. She took a chance and went to the hospital, and only managed to avoid being sent back to prison by getting a note from her son's school verifying he had been taken to the hospital. Her uncle was not so fortunate with the monitor. Not long after being freed on EM after serving twenty-four years in prison, doctors diagnosed him with Stage 4 cancer. Davis had constant battles with EM authorities to get her uncle movement to go to the doctor. After just a little more than two months of freedom, he passed away with the monitor still on his leg. The hospital authorities refused to remove the device, and the Department of Corrections didn't show up to cut it off. Parole officials told Davis that if she cut it off, she would have to pay the replacement charge and also could be sent back to prison. Eventually the company handling the burial arrangements moved the body out of the hospital, but they wouldn't bury her uncle until the Department of Corrections took off the ankle shackle. Her uncle's body stayed in the mortuary for nearly a month before the authorities arrived and removed the device. "This story about electronic monitoring can go on and on and on," she said in an interview. "It took a toll on me. . . . It's like modern day slavery. They keep tabs on you when you're in prison. Then they keep tabs on you in a halfway house. When you finish halfway house, then they gotta monitor you. So therefore you're not free. You'll never be free." In the case of her uncle, they monitored him even after he had passed.[48]

Even during the pandemic people on EM had problems accessing medical care. Ronald Molina, on a monitor in Lake County, Illinois, was denied movement to get a vaccine for COVID-19. According to the conditions of his supervised release, he was not allowed to be in a place where children congregate. He had an appointment to get a vaccine at a school that had been closed down in order to serve as a vaccination site. His parole agent refused to allow him to go to the school, even though there were no children present, thus denying him access to lifesaving treatment.[49]

In addition to blocking access to medical treatment, the device itself precipitates health problems for some people. Researchers from the Kathryn O. Greenberg Justice Clinic at Cardozo School of Law Freedom for Immigrants and the Immigrant Defense Project gathered data from a nationwide survey of 150 people who were on electronic monitors under ICE. They also drew on data provided on 1,400 cases from legal service providers who handle immigration cases. Their findings showed that one in five reported electric shocks from the device. Ninety percent said that they experienced harm to their physical health from the shackle. They noted aches, pains, cramps, and numbness. Mental health concerns also surfaced, with 73 percent of those polled mentioning difficulties with sleeping. Perhaps most surprising of all were the complaints from 12 percent of experiencing suicidal thoughts. One interviewee maintained that EM brought back memories of repression in their country of origin.

> When I was in prison in my country, I was attacked and beaten. The ankle shackle reminds me of this and makes me feel constantly stressed, afraid and despairing. It reminds me of my torture and I cannot stop thinking about it, as if I am still in prison. This ankle shackle is the worst thing for my health right now. I feel desperate.[50]

While fear of legal recriminations has kept most people on EM from making their health issues public, a few individuals have taken the legal route. Michael Robinson of Joliet, Illinois, who was placed on an alcohol monitor pending trial on a DUI charge, had repeated infections on his leg from the device. When he complained to the company, they switched the device to the other leg. The same infection recurred. Since Robinson got no relief from his complaints, he took the company to small claims court. The company lawyers contested his claims and eventually he lost the suit.[51] Robinson is not alone in his complaints about the device causing skin irritation. One individual in Indianapolis sued for damages when his ankle monitor caught fire, causing severe burns on his leg.[52]

At least as important as the issue of physical injuries is the trauma from wearing these devices. Tracie Bernardi of New Haven, Connecticut, who spent four months on a monitor after twenty-three years in prison, said the monitor tells everyone "I'm being monitored for something." She called it a form of "collateral damage that keeps you being judged and perpetuates the stereotype that you are still a criminal." It basically sends the message that "she's a criminal and we don't trust her."[53] Researcher Lauren Kilgour, who has investigated the impact of monitors, concluded, "Wearing an ankle monitor is a little bit like being required to wear a criminal record on your body. . . . It may jeopardize opportunities to form strong bonds within communities or maybe to obtain or maintain employment." She looked into the historical background of such stigmatization, concluding that "there's a long, broad and profoundly prejudiced history of taking people and marking them in ways that are meant to effectively act as a type of punishment." She also noted that these devices contribute to deputizing members of the public into becoming surveilling authorities as well.[54]

Chicago activist Mohawk Johnson, placed on a monitor while awaiting trial on charges stemming from his participation in 2020 Black Lives Matter protests, described wearing the shackle as a forced surrender of part of his body. "I wake up every fuckin' day and a part of my body don't . . . belong to me anymore, it belongs to the state. It's like I'm not a person anymore."[55]

CHILDBIRTH

Electronic monitoring can even add a punitive element to the experience of childbirth. Kristie Puckett-Williams became pregnant during her time on EM in North Carolina. As the pregnancy proceeded, her legs swelled up, putting additional pressure on her ankle. To find relief, she tried to insert a ruler in between the monitor and her skin. This triggered alarms from authorities, who threatened to return her to jail and charge her with tampering, a misdemeanor criminal offense in North Carolina. Fortunately for Puckett-Williams, she got the monitor off before the birth of her child.[56] Sarah Hanna of Pipe Creek, Texas, was not as lucky. Her monitor, for which she paid a monthly fee of $300, remained on her leg throughout the pregnancy, creating fears on her part that its alarm would ring during the delivery and police would come barging into the hospital. The baby arrived without an EM incident, but after the birth, one of the hospital staff made a note of the presence of the device and, assuming Hanna was thus a criminal, phoned Child Protective Services (CPS). Hanna had to remain in the hospital an extra day and a half until she was cleared by CPS.

The impact of electronic monitoring on childbirth also extends to fathers. Jerry Freeman of Chicago, on a monitor while awaiting trial, was denied permission to attend the birth of his child.[57] Authorities told him he had "no proof" the child was his.

ELECTRONIC MONITORING AND GENDER-BASED VIOLENCE

The dynamics of EM become especially complicated in households where gender-based abuse or illegal activity is taking place. In addition to dealing with pregnancy, Kristie Puckett-Williams was confined to a Charlotte household where she had been repeatedly physically abused. She ended up unable to show up for her court appearances because her abuser and her ongoing addiction kept her in the house. "I had a real problem keeping the device charged. I had to sit still for two hours straight. I was still addicted. The way things were in my house, it was hard to sit still for two hours. So they kept dinging me, telling me I had to charge the device or accusing me of tampering with the device. Eventually I ended up back in jail for violating curfew too many times." She concluded, "This is the situation with many people who are living in a violent household. They don't need a device on their leg, they need to stop getting beaten up. They aren't a flight risk. They aren't going anywhere."[58]

For Chicagoan Rashanti McShane, the threats didn't come from an abusive relationship but from the sheriff's office personnel sent to "check up" on her while on EM. McShane, a Black transgender woman, reported repeated abuse, including authorities deadnaming her.[59] They also threatened her with reincarceration in the men's jail where she had been originally placed because of the court's refusal to recognize her gender. They added to the punishment by denying her movement to pick up HIV medication that she was supposed to take daily. Even requests to go shopping for food were refused. At times she reported all she had to eat was crackers. One day she only had rice and corn. "I sprinkled a little sugar on it to make it taste better." In her words, "they made my house hell for me . . . treated me like the scum of the earth."[60] McShane's fears were not unfounded. In Illinois and other states, a number of lawsuits and criminal charges have emerged over the years against probation and parole officers who sexually assaulted their clients.[61]

EXCLUSION ZONES

As noted in chapter 2, a large number of those on electronic monitoring are not only limited in terms of leaving the house, they are also banned from entering certain parts of the city. These people, most of whom have been convicted of some sexually related offense or are alleged "gang members," have exclusion zones programmed into their devices. Exclusion zones demarcate forbidden areas—places the individual cannot go without triggering an alarm and possibly being re-incarcerated. For individuals with convictions for sexually related offenses, exclusion zones focus on places where children congregate in large numbers: schools, day care centers, and parks are the most common places excluded. These regulations operate on the assumption that everyone convicted of a sexually related offense needs to be kept away from children, regardless of the nature of their conviction.

Regulations for people with convictions for sexually related offenses usually specify a distance that a person must stay from schools and parks. These distances vary depending on the state or city, but typically range from 300 to 2,000 feet.

Exclusion zone regulations for electronic monitors work in concert with other laws and regulations aimed at punishing people convicted of sexually related offenses. These include registries or public housing statutes that ban people with certain kinds of convictions. These laws and regulations also create exclusion zones, without the aid of electronic monitors. In some cities, the exclusion zones take up nearly all urban space. For example, a 2006 Georgia law banned people with certain offenses from being within 1,000 feet of a school, day care, playground, or school bus stop. Advocates studied the Georgia map and found that this would have made 99 percent of Georgia into an exclusion zone, since the state had an estimated 350,000 school bus stops.[62] The law has since been slightly modified. In Miami, people with sex offense convictions accused authorities of setting up "postage stamp parks," a strategy in which a small piece of land in a neighborhood is designated a park solely for the purpose of keeping people on the registry from living nearby. In response to such a policy in 2009, several dozen people with convictions for sexually related offenses relocated to a spot about forty miles out of town and called it Miracle Village, creating their own community with no exclusion zones. The late Rev. Richard Witherow, who founded Miracle Village, argued that people with convictions for sexually related offenses were becoming "modern-day lepers."[63] Anti-registry activist Laurie Jo Reynolds of Chicago refers to housing restrictions for people on the registry as "banishment."[64]

Exclusion zones raise a number of concerns about the impact of excessive monitoring of specific communities on urban space and movement. Many cities already make use of ordinances such as bans on "camping," living outdoors, soliciting money, or feeding people in public to criminalize survival activities and exclude poor people from upmarket areas.[65] Electronic monitors that are programmed with exclusion zones can potentially create "geofences," virtual perimeters for real-world geographic areas, to enforce group punishment by requiring people to have permission to leave or enter certain areas. For those with alleged gang affiliations, the exclusions apply to zones designated as high-crime areas where gangs supposedly operate.

"TWENTY-FIRST-CENTURY SLAVERY, ELECTRONIC STYLE"

As with all aspects of mass incarceration, Black people are particularly harmed by electronic monitors. Though racial breakdowns of EM populations are difficult to find, the few statistics available show that Black people are disproportionately targeted for EM. A study in Michigan's Wayne County in 2018 and 2019 found that Black people were twice as likely as white people to land on a monitor.[66] Cook County data showed that in a county that is 25 percent Black, about 70 percent of those on pretrial monitors were Black.[67] In San Francisco, where Black people make up only 6 percent of the overall population, they comprised 44 percent of those on EM, according to a 2020 report from the sheriff's office.[68] Data for people on parole showed similar disparities. In Ohio in 2018, Black people were 42.1 percent of those on electronic monitoring post-prison in a state where they were just 12 percent of the general population. Figures for Kansas were similarly skewed, with Black people constituting 31.7 percent of those on parole EM in a state where just 6 percent of the population is Black.[69] In the immigration sphere, anti-Black racism also surfaced. Aggregate data from 955 clients of three legal service providers revealed that only 15 percent of those responding to a survey questionnaire were Black but 31 percent of those on EM were Black people.[70]

Even when placed on EM, Black people and other people of color are more likely to face obstacles. Law professor Kate Weisburd concluded from her extensive research and courtroom defense work that "African-American youth and youth from poorer neighborhoods are more likely to have a probation officer document noncompliance and are more likely to receive more severe consequences."[71]

For many Black people, the ankle shackle triggers historical memories of the oppression of their enslaved ancestors. Renowned author Michelle Alexander has labeled electronic monitoring and e-carceration the "Newest Jim Crow."[72]

Stories from impacted people further surface the anti-Black nature of electronic monitoring regimes. The late Ernest Shepard had spent forty-five years in prison before landing on a monitor for a parole violation. Looking at his ankle monitor, he said:

> I could imagine how slaves would be on a ship and they would be chained to the ship and their feet would be anchored to some steel. [That black plastic strap] always inspired me to want to get a sense of relief, to escape, or to break it off. My life was miserable. How could I be expected to sit day and night and accommodate myself to a voluntary misery, and I'm trying to do something to rehabilitate, to make a life . . . and I got this nagging misery? I feel like a chattel slave and I say, "If I don't rebel, what kinda dude am I?"[73]

J. Jhondi Harrell refused to be placed on a monitor while in a halfway house after serving eighteen years in federal prisons. Even though rejecting the monitor limited his opportunities to visit his family, he declined to be a part of what he called "virtual slavery." He added that it was "the new slavery . . . [where they] make your house into a cell."[74]

Arissa Hall, former director of National Bail Out, a project that puts up bail for Black mothers, says EM has a special impact on Black women:

> We know when a Black mother is in a cage, so is their whole family and community. Black mothers and caregivers are usually the primary caretakers within our communities. So when a Black mama is on a monitor and has her movements restricted and a possible curfew, it will restrict her ability to be physically present at school and child-related events. It will limit her opportunities to generate

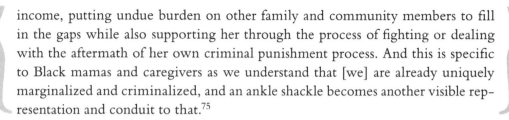

income, putting undue burden on other family and community members to fill in the gaps while also supporting her through the process of fighting or dealing with the aftermath of her own criminal punishment process. And this is specific to Black mamas and caregivers as we understand that [we] are already uniquely marginalized and criminalized, and an ankle shackle becomes another visible representation and conduit to that.[75]

THE HOUSE IS ON FIRE

In 2017, Kent Shultz was on an electronic monitor in Lansing, Michigan, making toast when the wiring in the toaster shorted out. The next thing he knew, his kitchen, then the entire apartment was on fire. Shultz ran out into the street and phoned the people in charge of his EM program as he watched the fire spread. Their response was "Where's the box?" referring to the control box of Shultz's device. When Shultz responded by telling him it was still inside the burning apartment, the call center operator ordered Shultz to go back into the apartment to retrieve it. Risking his life, Shultz went back into the burning apartment and retrieved the box. He then phoned the police to let them know he wouldn't be in his apartment that night due to the fire, so they should ignore any warrants that might come for him. The Red Cross put him in a hotel for the night, but when he went to report to the police station the next morning, they told him there was a warrant for his arrest since he had absconded from his house. They put him in a cell for several hours until his lawyer came to solve the issue, then Shultz went back to the cinders of his apartment to sort things out.[76] Shultz's harrowing night starkly demonstrates the dangers inherent in the vagaries of electronic monitoring regimes. While his particular escapade was perhaps exceptional, the punitive response of the authorities to Shultz's tragedy was all too typical of life under the shackle.

ELECTRONIC MONITORING: CONNECTING THE DOTS

Though the enforcement of electronic monitoring takes place at an individual level, the impact extends far beyond the person being monitored. Family members and friends can become virtual prison guards. In addition, as Emmett Sanders observes about those on the monitor, "when they are not on this thing, they are actively participating in this community, they are working, they are consuming, they are watching the neighbor's kids. You can't take the people out of a community and make it stronger." He portrays individuals on monitors as "dead spots," places where "the thread that holds the community together is pulled out." Sanders has special concerns about the impact that isolating people on home confinement has on children. "Kids model behavior; if you remove social interaction, you are telling these kids there is no place that is safe. . . . The kids know that prison is a place they don't want to go, but when it is in the home, there is no safe space."

But there are far more dots to connect in terms of broader notions of privacy, state surveillance, and corporate domination. In an era where data has supplanted oil as the essential element for economic growth, and where electronic monitors increasingly capture more data, no meaningful change can occur without an effective strategy to curtail e-carceration. Electronic monitors—whether ankle shackles, phone apps, or whatever new devices loom on the technological horizon—will remain repressive tools in the toolbox of the criminal legal and immigration systems. As their capacity expands, monitors of all kinds will become further intertwined with the surveillance state and become far more blatant and threatening. And as Sanders and Arnett stress, the impact will not fall equally on everyone. The criminalized sector of the working class, primarily Black and Latinx, will bear the brunt of these evolving forces of e-carceration and will thus need to be at the center of any movements of resistance.

PART TWO

CONNECTING THE DOTS: FROM ANKLE
SHACKLE TO SURVEILLANCE STATE

6

IMMIGRATION AND ELECTRONIC MONITORING: SMARTLINKS AND GEO-FENCES

Tech is transforming immigration enforcement. As advocates have known for some time, the immigration and criminal justice systems have powerful allies in Silicon Valley and Congress, with technology companies playing an increasingly central role in facilitating the expansion and acceleration of arrests, detentions, and deportations.

—Who's Behind ICE?, *report compiled by immigrant rights organizations, 2018[1]*

On August 7, 2019, over six hundred ICE agents conducted raids on a set of poultry processing plants in Mississippi, taking 680 workers into custody.[2] The operation targeted plants run by five companies: Peco Foods, Pearl River Foods, Koch Foods, A & B Inc., and P H Food Inc.[3] While this raid was larger than most, these types of actions by ICE agents have become normalized.[4] They take place not only in workplaces but in court rooms, during traffic stops, as part of alleged drug raids, and on campuses where migrant children attend schools. Immigrants in handcuffs marching with their heads down or their face covered are part of the daily news feed. Along with the handcuffs, many of them are also shackled with a GPS ankle monitor placed on them by ICE. Jacinta Gonzalez, senior campaign organizer of the

Latinx/Chicanx social justice organization Mijente, maintains that the Mississippi raid was among the first occasions in which U.S. authorities had used GPS tracking to secure court permission for such an action.[5] Policing operations like the Mississippi factory raids, along with the technologies involved, are redefining e-carceration.

The mainstream news's framing of the Mississippi raid failed to incorporate the new realities regarding borders and their enforcement. That reporting and subsequent stories have continued to give an impression of armed border police constantly in hot pursuit of migrants fleeing justice. The reality is that the management of the flow of bodies across U.S. borders—especially the Southern border—no longer focuses on high-speed chases and neighborhood shakedowns. Increasingly, this has become an exercise in how data management systems—with electronic monitors playing a key role—sync with law enforcement. The use of electronic monitors on immigrants has increased significantly, but the monitors do not operate in isolation. They are linked to a wide variety of databases developed by companies, such as Palantir, functioning as predictive policing specialists.

Today, borders are no longer static lines on a map or walls between states; rather, they are dynamic, increasingly re-formed, and re-shaped. University of Illinois researcher Daniel Gonzalez has pointed out how a border may be demarcated by a set of technologies that controls who can and cannot be present in a space, part of a process of e-carceration. "Border enforcement increasingly relies not on physical structures, but on surveillance and big data technologies," he asserts.[6] As Jacinta Gonzalez notes, in the twenty-first century a border is also a "site of technological experimentation."[7]

What happened in Mississippi reflects this new concept of a border, but it also has historical continuity. Since the first emergence of legislation to restrict immigration in the 1800s, the policy of controlling the cross-border flow of bodies has rested at the crossroads of three often contradictory agendas: the need for labor (especially of the cheap, unregulated variety), the desire to preserve the white supremacist, imperialist national identity of the United States, and the mandate to promote the narrative of this country as a peaceful melting pot that welcomes the tired and weary of the world "yearning to be free."

In the 1920s, patrols from the agency known as Customs and Border Protection rode on horseback along the Rio Grande looking for migrants wading in the water. In fact, for most of the twentieth century, enforcement of immigration policy involved screening at border crossings or hunting down those who were not permitted inside the United States, then arresting and deporting them. In addition to a militarized force of immigration police, enforcement demanded a vast bureaucracy of regulators and record keepers, steadfastly reviewing laws, policies, and hand-recorded statistics to preserve the order deemed necessary by decision-makers and public opinion.

Policies and enforcement varied, depending largely on both the needs of U.S. employers and the economic and political conditions in Mexico and other countries that were sources of that labor. Underpinning any importation of labor was a deep-seated racism. A Chamber of Commerce spokesperson summed up these arguments in testimony to Congress in 1926:

> We, gentlemen, are just as anxious as you are not to build the civilization of California or any other western district upon a Mexican foundation. We take him because there is nothing else available. We have gone east, west, north, and south and he is the only man-power available to us.[8]

During the days of the Great Depression, exclusion became the dominant dynamic, largely to prevent immigrants from draining the budget of Roosevelt's New Deal programs. According to historian Francisco Balderrama, during the 1930s, the United States deported over one million Mexican nationals, 60 percent of whom were also U.S. citizens of Mexican descent.[9]

During World War II, the government changed direction, taking action to guarantee a steady flow of Mexican workers to replace members of the U.S. labor force who had joined the military. Despite the mobilization of over three million women to work on farms under the auspices of the Women's Land Army of America, there was still a labor shortage, especially in California and the Southwest, which accounted for the majority of the nation's agricultural produce.[10] In response, from 1942 to 1964, federal authorities ran the Emergency Farm Labor Supply Program, popularly (and later officially) known as the Bracero Program. This program featured an agreement with Mexico that allowed hundreds of thousands of

Mexican agricultural workers at any given time to gain temporary work permits to plant and harvest crops during the war years. All told, nearly five million Mexican workers enrolled in the Bracero Program over the course of a little over two decades. According to stories from some of these workers, the line to join the ranks of the braceros stretched for half a mile from the U.S.-Mexico border.[11]

While immigration authorities did monitor the legal status of immigrant labor forces, in many instances, enforcement, steeped in the racism of the day, meant ignoring violations of minimum-wage and other labor regulations. Harsh treatment abounded. Even before these workers picked their first strawberry or planted their first lettuce, they were often stripped and sprayed with DDT in order to kill any lice they supposedly might be bringing with them.[12]

At times, certain alleged attempts at enforcement were meaningless rituals. For instance, stories from the workers reveal that the predecessor of the present-day ICE, Immigration and Naturalization Services (often referred to as "La Migra"), would round up all the workers without permits, drive them to the border, get them to sign a contract, and drive them back to the fields.[13]

Still, the flow of Mexican workers across the U.S. border was never a seamless process. At times, Mexican authorities wanted to stem the northward migration due to their own need for a labor force to expand industry. At other moments, poor treatment of Mexican workers led to conflict and even caused the Mexican government to suspend the program from 1948 to 1951. But even during the suspension, workers streamed across the border, doing whatever it took to access wages that were twenty times what they earned back home.[14]

During these decades, enforcement of immigration laws was strictly an analog affair. People had paper records that were checked by employers. Immigrants could only be tracked by being sighted or through landline phone and mail contacts. Sharing IDs and the use of other people's names and Social Security numbers were common practices. La Migra conducted raids on undocumented people by grabbing them if they overstayed a visa, visiting them at their home or workplace, or tracking them if they got picked up for a minor offense like shoplifting.

In some periods, the pro-deportation forces on both sides of the border held the upper hand. For instance, in 1954, under a program bearing the racist name of Operation Wetback, the U.S. government initiated the forced migration of thousands of immigrants. Authorities shoved these people into buses, boats, and planes and, with the cooperation of Mexican authorities, sent them to central and southern parts of Mexico, supposedly to invigorate their home areas. Three times a week, a plane filled with immigrants would fly from Chicago to Mexico. U.S. authorities claimed more than a million people were deported under Operation Wetback, though some historians peg the figure at less than half that number.[15]

Like contemporary immigration raids, Operation Wetback obscured the real purpose of mass deportations: the regulation of the flow of labor into the United States. The mass deportations of the 1950s largely aimed to coerce employers into legalizing the employment of Mexican workers who were not registered under the Bracero Program. While Operation Wetback contributed to an enormous increase in the legalization of workers, the price for enabling that change wasn't extracted from employers who violated the law but from the enormous abuses visited upon workers.[16] Deportation was often cruel and violent, with authorities herding workers into public parks that the Border Patrol had converted into concentration camps, or loading them onto cargo ships that, in a later congressional investigation, would be likened to "eighteenth-century slave ships."[17]

THE RISE OF E-CARCERATION IN IMMIGRATION

Today's border control, despite the vast rhetoric and expenditure devoted to building walls, relies more on gathering data than patrolling a physical barrier or boundary. Immigration enforcement incorporates a range of technologies that supply the personal details of people and then connects them to create profiles at the family, household, community, national, and even international levels. This requires far more than a bird's-eye view of the terrain that immigrants cross.

Modern technologies of surveillance entered the immigration sphere in the 1970s, with the expansion of the use of aircraft, cameras, and infrared technology to monitor border activities and facilitate immigration management. But it was only in the early 1990s that technology became fully integrated into the immigration regimes, albeit initially with a minimal presence.

In 1994, the Border Protection broke precedent by procuring what was seen at the time as significant amounts of equipment, both analog and digital: six nightscopes to help agents spot illegal traffic crossing the border in darkness; forty seismic sensors to detect traffic around the clock; four-wheel-drive vehicles for patrolling the border; and eighty portable radios to enable agents in the field to communicate and coordinate operations.[18] A new electronic fingerprinting system, IDENT, was also initiated to assist agents in identifying who had been previously apprehended by immigration authorities or had criminal records.[19]

Ironically, these procurements by the Border Patrol took place amid the backdrop of the implementation of the 1994 North American Free Trade Agreement (NAFTA). This pact opened the U.S.-Mexican border to free trade in goods and commerce but tightened the clamps on labor flows. Hence, while championing NAFTA in 1994, the Clinton administration implemented Operation Gatekeeper. Based on the rationale of "control through deterrence," Gatekeeper involved constructing fences and militarizing the Southern border where it was most easily crossed. This was not a technology-based approach but rather a strategy of military maneuver. Instead of deterring or tracking undocumented immigrants, the new obstacles at the border shifted the immigrants' entry options and funneled them to treacherous terrain of deserts and mountains. Deaths due to dehydration, sunstroke, and freezing in the winter increased exponentially. In 1994, fewer than 30 migrants died along the border; by 1998, the number had risen to 147; in 2001, the official death count rose to 387; and by 2012 it reached nearly 500. All told, from 2007 to 2013, over 2,000 known migrant deaths occurred along the Mexico-Arizona border. Many more took place off the official records.[20]

A HYBRID SYSTEM: E-CARCERATION AND IMMIGRATION PRISONS

The major turning point for technological change in U.S. immigration policy came as a result of a 1996 federal law, the Illegal Immigration Reform and Immigrant Responsibility Act. This legislation added increased penalties for immigrants who committed crimes or

Criminalizing Immigration

For the first century after the founding of the United States, the federal government did not restrict immigration. However, racism and nationalism kicked into gear in the late 1800s with the Chinese Exclusion Act of 1882. This law made it a crime for anyone from China to enter the United States. This came after tens of thousands of Chinese workers had come to the United States to work on building the national network of railroads in the mid-1800s. The 1882 Immigration Act, passed two months after the Chinese Exclusion Act, offered a prime example of nineteenth-century ableism by banning "any convict, lunatic, idiot, or any person unable to take care of himself or herself without becoming a public charge."[21] The act also established immigration quotas in ways that radically reduced the numbers of permitted Southern and Eastern European migrants, who were deemed less "white" than other Europeans.

But in any given period, immigration policy toward different groups could vary. While U.S. authorities sought Mexican migrant laborers in the 1940s, they were hunting down and incarcerating people of ethnic Japanese ancestry in the West Coast of the United States, regardless of their citizenship status.[22]

remained in the United States without a visa or permit. This laid the foundation for the draconian USA PATRIOT Act, the response to the 2001 World Trade Center attacks. In 2002, the federal government formed the Department of Homeland Security (DHS), reconstituting what was previously the Immigration and Naturalization Service. The newly founded DHS incorporated Immigration and Customs Enforcement (ICE) and Customs and Border Protection (CBP), along with U.S. Citizenship and Immigration Services, under its umbrella.

In 2002, ICE established a set of programs known as Alternatives to Detention (ATD) to be operated by a nonprofit organization without any electronic supervision. The ATD programs were supposed to offer more support to immigrants, especially by providing assistance in navigating the court system. The next year, the parameters changed and a call for proposals went out to private companies for a five-year supervision program for immigrants.

The Colorado-based BI won the contract to operate the Intensive Supervision Appearance Program (ISAP). Under ISAP, BI's approach moved away from support to intensified surveillance via telephone calls, unannounced visits, and electronic monitoring. E-carceration was rising to the fore in the world of immigration, with the nation's largest EM provider in charge.[23]

Post-9/11 financing for border enforcement technologies was plentiful. Border control and surveillance became focal points of the law-and-order paradigm. The CBP budget grew from $6 billion in 2004 to $11.4 billion in 2010. The extra funding helped support an acceleration of border wall construction. By 2009, the border wall had grown from a length of 75 miles to over 600 miles.[24] In 2005, the implementation of Operation Streamline added a statutory dimension to the enhanced enforcement by reclassifying border crossing, changing it from an administrative matter punishable by deportation to a fully fledged criminal offense. Authorities retooled the system for rapid processing of deportation cases, often via mass hearings of up to eighty people at the same time.[25] The result was a spike in the incarceration of immigrants. By 2011, noncitizens were occupying 35 percent of the cell space in a rapidly growing federal prison system, a dramatic increase from 1980, when they occupied just 4 percent.[26]

What was emerging was a hybrid system of punishment and control, combining traditional policing and tracking, incarceration in steel and concrete cages, and technologies of e-carceration. ISAP evolved to extend its technology beyond electronic monitoring. The Bush administration tried to add another set of tools with the ill-fated Secure Border Initiative (SBINet) of 2005. SBINet aimed to create a "virtual fence" along the border, as well as produce a common operating picture (COP)—a uniform presentation of activities within specific areas along the border. Sensors, radar, and cameras were supposed to combine to gather information and transmit it to COP terminals located in command centers and agents' vehicles. However, the program stumbled owing to management problems and claims that it was an inappropriate one-size-fits-all approach to extremely varied terrain. President Obama scrapped it in 2011. Homeland Security spokesperson Michael Fisher explained that DHS now opted for a more high-tech plan that would "utilize existing, proven technology tailored

Palmer Luckey's Virtual Wall

In 2017, the crowded marketplace of border surveillance added Anduril Industries, which was under the stewardship of then twenty-five-year-old ultra-conservative entrepreneur Palmer Luckey. Anduril Industries claimed to use technology to "solve complex national security challenges for America and its allies" by creating a "digital wall that is not a barrier so much as a web of all-seeing eyes, with intelligence to know what it sees." The key components of Luckey's "wall" were thirty-two-foot towers marketed as "Lattice." These towers combined radar, communications antennae, and laser-enhanced cameras to identify motion within a two-mile radius. This was yet another dimension of e-carceration as applied to border guarding, a techno-wall involving no sheets of steel, no razor wire—just sound and video devices that were getting smaller by the day.

to the distinct terrain and population density of each border region." The new plan included more advanced surveillance systems, unmanned aircraft, thermal imaging, and tower-based video.[27]

ICE's move toward deeper levels of e-carceration continued with a second five-year immigrant supervision contract with BI in 2009 for $372 million. This included supervision of 27,000 people with GPS-enabled electronic monitors. In the immigration world, radio frequency was a thing of the past. This second ISAP contract was also a motivator for the 2009 purchase of BI by the GEO Group.

Noticing the lucrative potential of e-carceration demonstrated by the second ISAP contract, the private prison operator GEO Group secured the buyout of BI that year, a clear sign e-carceration would have an important place in the future market of immigration law enforcement.[28]

THE ADVENT OF BIG DATA

The 2009 BI agreement coincided with the emergence of Big Data. This brought four crucial new developments to immigration enforcement.

First, ICE introduced the widespread use of the Risk Classification Assessment (RCA) in

2013. The RCA, drawing from risk assessment methods in pretrial courts, provided a supposedly scientific system for categorizing immigrants and determining how they should be handled. Within five days of detention, all immigrants were supposed to undergo a risk assessment that would determine if they were to be detained or released. If they were to be detained, the RCA would determine their custody classification and their immigration bond amount. If they were to be released, the RCA would assign them a community supervision level that could include GPS monitoring. Of course, the criteria used by risk assessment tools baked in racial biases by incorporating criminal history, immigration violation history, and carceral disciplinary infractions in the calculation.[29]

These biases blatantly surfaced in a 2018 suit filed by the New York Civil Liberties Union, which alleged that the federal government had altered its RCA algorithm to make it virtually impossible for someone in immigrant detention to be released on bond.[30] The filing contended that the algorithm was altered to reflect the Trump administration's immigration policy, labeled by journalist David R. Jones as embodying the president's "hateful, racist vision of a white ethno-state," which "overwhelmingly impacts immigrants of color from South America, the Caribbean, Africa and parts of Asia."[31]

The second development began as early as 2012, when ICE entered into a series of contracts with Palantir Technologies, a firm with a long history of engagement in military and predictive policing software. In 2020 Palantir CEO Alex Karp made it clear that the company he runs develops tools that are used "to kill people."[32]

Likely the company's most important contract with ICE was the 2015 agreement to apply the company's Analytical Framework for Intelligence (AFI) to immigration. AFI could draw from federal, state, and local databases to compile profiles of individuals.[33]

AFI contains detailed personally identifiable information of millions of individuals including full name, address, age, gender, race, physical characteristics, marital status, residency status, country of citizenship, city and country of birth, date of birth, Social Security number, vehicle information, travel information, document information, passport information, law enforcement records, and familial and other contact information. CBP uses AFI to provide "analysts with different tools that assist in detecting trends, patterns, and emerging threats, and in identifying non-obvious relationships."[34] Former president Donald Trump referred to the type of searches done by AFI as "extreme vetting."

AFI combines with Palantir's Investigative Case Management (ICM) software, which, according to the Department of Homeland Security, "contains extensive information related to individuals including targets of investigations, associates of targets, victims, informants, and other third parties," as well as "identifying data [and] information about individuals' locations and activities."[35] In the ICE context, this meant gathering data on those under ICE supervision and maintaining that data in a digital file, much like a client file in a social service agency. Through ICM that file might include data from intelligence platforms maintained by the Drug Enforcement Administration, the Bureau of Alcohol, Tobacco, Firearms and Explosives, the Federal Bureau of Investigation, and an array of other federal and private law enforcement entities. It can provide ICE agents access to information on a subject's schooling, family relationships, employment information, phone records, immigration history, foreign exchange program status, personal connections, biometric traits, criminal records, and home and work addresses.[36] In connecting these databases to electronic monitoring, University of Illinois researcher Daniel Gonzalez describes the process as using the location data of a person on a GPS monitor to put dots on a map, then bringing in ICM to connect those dots and describe patterns and relationships.[37] In terms of EM, this is a crucial convergence of GPS monitors and the broader surveillance state.

The third technological innovation that affected immigration enforcement was the switch to cloud computing. The cloud enabled servers, networks, storage, development tools, and applications to operate through the internet rather than on individual machines or local networks. The cloud created the possibility of permanently sharing data across a number of DHS databases. This meant a person's database record could contain their criminal record, immigration history, past and current use of public benefits, interaction with public health authorities, driving record, and credit score. In 2010, the Federal Office of Management and Budget released the Cloud First Policy, mandating government departments to investigate cloud options before making any new investments in data management.[38] From that point, the cloud began to dominate the digital world. The Trump administration built on the foundation established by Obama in terms of immigration data. By early 2019, more than half of ICE's two-thousand-plus databases had moved to the cloud under the aegis of Amazon's AWS cloud services and relocated to Amazon centers on the West Coast.[39] All told, ICE, CBP, and U.S. Citizenship and Immigration Services counted for 42.6 percent of DHS's spending on IT.[40]

The fourth technological advance for ICE was the advent of BI SmartLINK in 2018. SmartLINK is an app that replaces the function of the ankle shackle. It can operate on a dedicated BI phone device or on a personal mobile phone. SmartLINK has facilitated the conversion of ankle monitors from location trackers to full-blown surveillance devices. With BI SmartLINK, ICE potentially has access to sets of data via video conferences, face and voice recognition, self-reporting, and interactive calendars and media. If downloaded to a personal phone, the company could likely gain access to all data on that phone as well. SmartLINK and similar applications allow authorities to link what is recorded on a person's phone to the vast databases of ICE.

Federal budgets reflected the shift to technologies of e-carceration. From 2017 to 2020, Customs and Border Protection received $743 million from Congress for tech and surveillance.[41] This included drones manufactured by Anduril, Lockheed Martin, FeelLIR Systems, AeroVironment, and General Dynamics that were used to patrol the border. In addition, CBP contracted with commercial data broker Venntel and software firms Grayshift and Cellebrite to enable the hacking of people's phones without warrants.[42] The first budget of the Biden presidency continued the trend of expanding the use of technologies of e-carceration as part of border surveillance.[43]

These advances in technology provide concrete evidence that data capture has outpaced location tracking in importance and value. The captured data blends into the Integrated Case Management/Cloud Computing system then connects to a personal data trail from other sources. These data trails are a lucrative source of revenue for data brokering firms like Thomson Reuters and LexisNexis. Both of these companies have contracts with ICE and with Equifax, which houses mega-sets of utility data. In fact, a person's data pipeline often begins with utility bill information. This data can be cross referenced with jail bookings and information from license plate readers to develop profiles of individuals. Researcher Archana Ahlawat reports that in some cases companies can build a detailed data profile of an individual from a starting point of knowing only their first name, the first name of a family member, and the street where they live.[44]

All of these data potentially can be tied into a punitive package—forcing an immigrant, for example, to pay outstanding bills or run the risk of deportation. Moreover, this data itself has become a commodity in the digital marketplace, fetching returns for product promoters, bill collectors, and various arms of the agencies that govern researcher and social justice advocate Virginia Eubanks's "digital poorhouse," a collection of data-driven tools "that profile, police, and punish poor and working people."[45]

Although the comfortable classes may legitimately fret over the invasion of their privacy by Big Data, the concerns of immigrants and the other sectors of the criminalized population are much more fundamental. The gathering of their data is part of a process of weaponization. Their data holds connections to freedom, border crossing, family reunification, and access to employment and services. All of these are in jeopardy when the rubber of the weaponized databases meets the road of risk assessment and ICE enforcers.

THE MISSISSIPPI FACTORIES: THE REST OF THE STORY

When ICE officers showed up at those factories in August of 2019, they knew exactly who they were looking for. According to the affidavit filed in court to legally sanction the raid, ICE had proof through its GPS tracking that a number of undocumented people who were under ICE supervision were working at Koch Foods, one of the raid targets.[46] This information was complemented by inputs from HSI Tipline and Falcon-TL, both products of Palantir. HSI Tipline records tips about suspicious, potentially criminal behavior, then an operative feeds the contents of the tip into Falcon-TL, which creates a report and triggers searches of other databases, generating more geospatial data, including information from news reports and content from public records such as litigation, criminal history, and state incorporation records. All of this facilitates ICE's ability to "visualize the data to help identify

IDENT

Beginning in the early 1990s, ICE used IDENT to build personal profiles. By 2019, IDENT held the biometric and personal data of 230 million unique identities, 36.5 million face records, and 2.8 million irises belonging to people who have either entered, attempted to enter, or exited the United States, or done any combination of those things. The DHS developed the Office of Biometric Identification Management (OBIM) to oversee this work. Though fingerprints were used as identity markers in criminal investigations since as early as 1892 in Argentina,[47] OBIM management involves a new method—combining theses fingerprints with facial recognition data points. Designed and implemented by the Thales Group, a French aerospace company, the digitization of this data is a step toward developing a virtual passport available via smartphone. In 2018, DHS announced that it was upgrading IDENT to a system called Homeland Advanced Recognition Technology (HART), which would have capacity to hold more biometric data including iris scans and voice recognition. According to Mijente's Jacinta Gonzalez, voice recognition holds the key to expanding authorities' understanding of networks.[48] Via tracking calls and other conversations, voice recognition allows rapid differentiation between conversations worth the attention of authorities and mere social interaction of no surveillance value.

relationships."[49] ICE did not arrive at those particular factories by accident. The workers in those plants had scored organizing victories, having won lawsuits in 2018 against their employers for $3.75 million in response to claims of racial and sexual harassment as well as harassment based on national origin. In addition, two of the plants had formal union contracts with the United Food and Commercial Workers International Union.[50]

This was the actionable data at that time, in that place, garnered from DHS databases and company information. Though DHS systems are secretive, the workers targeted in those Mississippi factories are connected now in many more databases that focus on labor. Today, ICE records are not simply about making sure that those who enter the United States have a work permit and a visa. This is a macro data management project to optimize immigration outcomes for employers and the state. Identifying productive workers who are not on the troublemaker list is one priority. But the case management software designed by Palantir can also potentially reveal whether these workers are a drain on government budgets. Hence, one's risk is not only about their "behavior" in school or the criminal legal system, but also fits into a cost-benefit analysis. The Trump administration put this into action by issuing a final rule in August of 2019 that applied a risk assessment to determine if an immigrant was inadmissible due to it being "likely" that he or she would "become a public charge."[51] Becoming a public charge meant accessing public benefits for an aggregate of twelve months over the preceding thirty-six months. That rule was reversed in March of 2021.

RESISTANCE

While the use of e-carceration on immigrants has been growing, various sectors have resisted both the technology and the companies that design it. Within the industry, a number of groups have staged protests and filed petitions against their employers—which include major tech companies like Microsoft and Google—for their involvement in supplying software and data for ICE. In 2017, employees at Google

A Message to Amazon Workers

Paige Panter of the Tech Workers Coalition wrote this message to Amazon workers in 2019:

If you're an Amazon engineer and you're reading . . . about a deep learning–based image-recognition product you're working on, and you know very well what law enforcement could do with a database of millions of faces, or you work at Microsoft and you were able to kind of tune out the ramifications of its contract with ICE until we saw the images of violence and violations of the human social contract on the border—the workers who are speaking out right now, for them . . . growing unease kind of instantaneously became a collective aghastness at the way their daily work was connected to it.[52]

headquarters in Mountain View, California, staged a demonstration against then president Trump's ban on immigration from certain countries. They carried signs reading "Silicon Valley: Built by Immigrants." In 2018, two former employees of Facebook started a fundraiser on the platform to raise $1,500 for migrants who needed legal assistance. Within three days, they had raised more than $5 million and eventually surpassed $20 million.[53] In a 2019 letter to CEO Satya Nadella, a group of workers at Microsoft urged the company to "cancel its contracts with ICE and with other clients who directly enable ICE." They added that "those creating powerful technology have to ensure what they build is used for good, and not for harm."[54]

Much of this organizing was driven by the Tech Workers Coalition, a broad-based formation of people in the industry that includes software designers and other computer experts along with cleaners, cafeteria workers, and security guards. Their activities focused not only on the ethics of their companies' investments and contracts but also on the struggle of contract and non-tech staff to improve working conditions and to unionize.

IMMIGRANT RIGHTS ORGANIZING

In 2019, a coalition of social justice groups including National Immigration Project, Mijente, and the Immigration Defense Project produced a report on the role of tech companies in ICE titled *Who's Behind ICE?* This document, written in conjunction with workers at all levels of Big Tech, exposed the complicity of these companies in deportations and other dehumanizing policies of ICE and the federal government. The report outlined the state of play for immigration and Big Tech, stressing how immigration enforcement and detention had become big business for Silicon Valley. The spending is astronomical, with data management taking about 10 percent of the entire DHS budget. The authors point out how huge corporations like Amazon and Palantir have built a "revolving door to develop and entrench Silicon Valley's role in fueling the incarceration and deportation regime." In their view:

> Unchecked, these tech companies will continue to do the government's bidding in developing the systems that target and punish en masse those it deems

"undesirable"—immigrants, people of color, the incarcerated and formerly incar-cerated, activists, and others.

Moreover, the report emphasizes the irony that these companies insist their products and services are "free from bias, racism, profiling, and abuse, while being highly profitable."[55]

Although much of the resistance to Big Tech's immigration operations has come from largely Latinx-led groups, Black immigrants have also been deeply involved in pushing back against ICE. Organizations such as the Undocublack Network, the Black Immigration Engagement Initiative, the Black LGBTQ+ Migrant Project, and the Black Alliance for Just Immigration (BAJI) have fought for community-driven programs and services as alternatives to electronic monitors for their constituencies.[56] They highlight the fact that Black immigrants are disproportionately targeted for deportation. While composing only 7 percent of the immigrant population, Black people make up 21 percent of those facing deportation as a result of engagement with the criminal legal system.

In recent years there have been incidents in which police have shot Black immigrants dead—including, in 2015, David Felix in New York, and, in 2016, Alfred Olango in El Cajon, California. Likely more killings have gone unrecorded.

According to Opal Tometi, executive director of BAJI and a co-founder of Black Lives Matter, the harsh immigration laws passed by the Clinton administration in 1996 that expanded the criteria for detaining and deporting immigrants have also disproportionately criminalized Black people. Writing in *Time* magazine with BAJI attorney Carl Lipscombe, Tometi stressed that immigrants' rights and racial justice advocates should address the "intersectional impact of mass criminalization."[57]

In addition, a number of campaigns have pushed through legislation and local government policies to protect immigrants from the surveillance state and ultimately from capture by ICE. The implementation of Secure Communities in 2008 required that if an immigrant landed in police custody their fingerprints and other details should be shared with DHS and ultimately ICE. As a result, the number of submissions of immigrants' data to DHS rose from just over 800,000 in 2009 to nearly 3.5 million in 2010.[58] Removals increased as well, growing from 14,333 in 2009 to 83,578 in 2012.[59] Consequently, a number of cities and several states including Illinois, New York, and Massachusetts declined to cooperate with Secure Communities by refusing to forward data on undocumented people in their custody, contributing to a decrease in deportations of over 30 percent.[60]

Ultimately, this refusal was about the federal government's invasion of people's data privacy and helped pressure President Obama to halt the program in 2014, though President Trump resumed it in 2017.

Apart from organized efforts on the issue of immigration data, resistance also involves the heightened awareness of users and social justice campaigners. Researcher Daniel Gonzalez argues that people need to recognize that the new forms of e-carceration don't just track individuals but households and entire communities. Award-winning historian Simone Browne argues that users need to develop a "critical biometric consciousness" about technology and surveillance that enables people to recognize they are the rightful owners of any data that emerges from their bodies and should have control over what is done with this data.[61] Moreover, efforts to regulate or control that data may be overruled by the speed with which Big Tech can modify their apps to avoid regulatory efforts. Daniel Gonzalez makes note of the implications of this rapid technological change, linking EM to the broader surveillance state, where

> systems like Individual Case Management . . . incorporate EM's geographic information while also folding in data from a person's entire social network, which includes data on both noncitizens and citizens. So, everyone associated with a person in the ICM system is now potentially put under DHS's watch. These technologies should be seen as part of a larger political economic project that is trying to strip away democracy and human and civil rights."[62]

Immigration occupies a cutting edge of research, debates, and activism on these technologies of e-carceration. The data captured by electronic monitors, especially those such as the BI SmartLINK, which have grabbing capacity well beyond location tracking, are a jumping-off point for painting more elaborate portraits of targeted groups, the criminalized layer of the population. Mijente's Jacinta Gonzalez points out how this technology is expanding "without us having a framework to fight back against it . . . we need to understand that when technology is outpacing the understanding of its use, then these technologies can do real-time harms"—deportations, family separations, even criminal charges.[63]

This is a challenge immigrants' rights activists have been addressing for several years. In 2020, the pandemic and the murder of George Floyd broadened the spectrum of resistance to the advance of e-carceration technologies. Activists began to tackle both the privacy challenges of collecting public health data and the issues of transforming policing. We turn to these issues in the next two chapters.

7

THE PANDEMIC AND
THE GROWTH OF E-CARCERATION

The first priorities of what we're trying to do . . . are focused on telehealth, remote learning, and broadband. . . . We need to look for solutions that can be presented now, and accelerated, and use technology to make things better.

—*former Google CEO Eric Schmidt reimagining New York post-COVID*[1]

We demand the use of COVID-19 data for the abolition of the structures, systems, policies and narratives that have made Black people defenseless and vulnerable to COVID-19. We reject any use of COVID-19 data to police, surveil, control and target Black communities and any use of COVID-19 data to reinforce the narratives about Black people that have made race a risk factor, while blatantly ignoring the central role of racism.

—*Data for Black Lives*[2]

For more than two decades, the ankle shackle has remained the standard electronic monitoring device. As cellphones, tablets, smartwatches, and laptop computers evolved, the black plastic band remained—bulging out under socks and scraping the skin of criminalized legs. This is because entrepreneurs in the criminal legal system had little motivation to evolve this technology. With the core model of mass incarceration continuing to imprison more than two million people, the technological alternatives of e-carceration held out minimal prospects for profits of the scale that prisons and jails could bring. Furthermore, as British EM expert Mike Nellis noted, even with GPS capacity in the U.S. context the electronic monitor was not sufficiently punitive to warrant massive investment and innovation.[3] Hence, many ankle monitors in 2020 still required a landline phone to function. They retained ancestral ties to the analog age.

The advent of COVID-19 in 2020 brought change to this monitoring landscape, bringing about an increased use of location monitoring but also, more importantly, the melding of these devices with the more complex technology of the surveillance state. As journalist Sam Biddle of *The Intercept* argued, the pandemic had created "a climate of perpetual bio-anxiety" where fear of contracting the virus "paved the way for broader acceptance of carceral technologies."[4] As local authorities looked for ways to defund policing, new technologies became one of the carceral "solutions" they employed to dilute the demands for transformation. Rather than addressing the structural inequities, these technologies expanded the reach of e-carceration in the name of reform, creating major changes. The players in this industry looked for new markets opened up by the crisis and enhanced the power of monitoring devices to both increase revenue and broaden the scope of surveillance.

THE INITIAL SPARK

Initially, the spark for change came from the rampant presence of COVID-19 in U.S. jails and prisons. Michelle Jones, who spent twenty years in Indiana prisons, referred to prison cells as "killboxes." Jones was among many anti–mass incarceration advocates and loved ones of people in prison who pressured authorities to implement social distancing and isolation measures behind the walls.[5] This prompted decision-makers to seek a way to release people while promising "public safety." In many jurisdictions such as Indianapolis and Cleveland, the electronic monitor became the policy tool of choice. In Pittsburgh, Chicago, and

Milwaukee, decarceration with EM grew so quickly that authorities ran out of monitoring devices.[6] Decision-makers in Pittsburgh reacted by placing people on home detention without an electronic tether. Their Chicago counterparts took the draconian course, making people wait in Cook County Jail (where seven incarcerated people had already died from COVID-19) until monitor inventories could be replenished.

Advocates argued that release on EM presented serious dangers under COVID-19.[7] The typical requirement of EM regimes, that of needing official permission to leave the house under any circumstances, posed a huge dilemma for a person who suddenly showed symptoms of COVID-19. Delaying a visit to the doctor while waiting for permission could have dire health consequences. On the other hand, an unauthorized visit to the doctor could result in reincarceration. Moreover, daily fees that could reach as high as $35 added enormous burdens to many households already stretched to the limit due to increased unemployment resulting from the pandemic. In the face of massive layoffs and reductions in working hours, the challenges of earning enough to pay rent and put food on the table became overwhelming for many people. An additional fee for an electronic monitor, coupled with a threat of incarceration for non-payment, added even more trauma to the COVID reality.

FROM SHACKLE TO CELLPHONE

In addition to expansion in the use of EM, COVID-19 prompted changes in the actual technology. Smartphone-based apps began to replace the ankle shackle. A primary advantage was they could be installed without violating social distance dicta, since a program staff person was not required to physically strap a device on a person's leg. BI, the nation's largest electronic monitoring company, was the market leader in this arena. Its SmartLINK app, already the go-to device for ICE, became the front-runner for the indefinite future. As of May 8, 2021, BI had over thirty-two thousand people under ICE supervision on SmartLINK, nearly triple the figure for June 2019.[8] Although BI remained guarded about the functionalities of SmartLINK, reports revealed that users could be required to enter the contact details of five friends or family members in the United States when they logged on, setting them up for ICE surveillance.[9]

BI also aggressively marketed SmartLINK as an add-on to other supervision regimes. For example, at the start of the shelter-in-place COVID restrictions in April of 2020, Illinois parole agents ordered clients not already under EM to download the SmartLINK app to their personal phones.[10] This allowed agents to practice safe distancing through video check-ins rather than in-person meetings since users could log onto the app through facial and voice recognition. SmartLINK also claimed to offer services such as court date reminders and lists of local resources. Probation authorities in Akron, Ohio, adopted a similar course, ordering a thousand of their four thousand people on probation to download a rival app, Outreach Smartphone Monitoring.[11]

Another major player in this cellphone-based sphere was the Guardian app, made by prison phone profiteer GTL. Guardian was promoted as an "ultra-modern" smartphone app with the slogan "Don't give them an ankle bracelet, give them a hand."[12] Once downloaded, Guardian had the capacity to pick up sound from the location where the monitored person was located, adding another dimension of techno-invasion. An article in *Gizmodo* estimated that by mid-2020, users had downloaded the Guardian up to fifty thousand times, but also noted that the app had such a history of technical failures, such as inaccurate location reporting, that the authors categorized it as "faulty to the point of being unusable."[13]

Unlike producing ankle monitors, developing an app does not require a factory and a workforce. Hence, start-ups began to flow into this space. Cellphone-based apps such as Pokket, designed by the platform Acivilate, and Promise embodied the spirit of new market players fully in line with the notion of carceral humanism. While SmartLINK and Guardian each struggled to distance itself from its parent company's past profiteering from EM and prison phones, Pokket and Promise didn't carry that baggage. They emerged in the Obama years when providing "alternatives" to incarceration began to be mainstream. Acivilate's Pokket cloud service focused on "safely sharing information" by providing the parole officer with the "full context of the client's progress and challenges" in order to "break the cycle of recidivism."[14] CEO Louise Wasilewski framed the purpose of Acivilate squarely in line with carceral humanism, stressing that her company's app was "very much about people getting access to their own information" while avoiding requirements for users to pay fees.[15]

Acivilate secured contracts in Maryland and Utah. Promise, launched via a capital injection from seven investors including rapper and entrepreneur Jay-Z's entertainment company, Roc Nation, boasted that its device was state-of-the-art tech, proclaiming that it was not a "clunky tool" like an ankle shackle but a "smart dashboard"—a "caring" app for "clients who need attention each day" for "ongoing and timely support" including court date reminders and lists of service providers.[16]

Libre by Nexus, an immigration bail bond company, took this carceral humanism to a new level. For years, Libre had been in the business of lending immigrants bail money, then charging them $14 a day to be on EM, plus a debt service fee on the loan. When one of the company's clients died of COVID-19 with the shackle still on their ankle, company president Mike Donovan had an EM epiphany, declaring, "I can't accept that our family member, someone we advocated for, died without their family and with a piece of plastic strapped to them." Donovan decided to reject the technology of electronic monitoring, arguing that "placing a tracking device on someone simply isn't effective in actually solving problems associated with immigrants in detention or pretrial criminal defendants in U.S. jails." Labeling ankle monitors "unreliable" and "unhelpful," Donovan asserted that "ending the use of body affixed GPS technology was a goal all governments should be committed to achieving."[17] He capped his critique by announcing that the seven thousand individuals on Libre by Nexus ankle monitors would move to cellphone apps, which would not only track location but offer access to telemedicine opportunities and appointment reminders.[18]

Despite cellphone-based apps' claims of providing services, many researchers and policy makers remained skeptical. Researcher Daniel Gonzalez noted that while some smartphone-based technology might be useful for short-term public health purposes during the COVID-19 crisis, in the long run, it poses two distinct dangers. First, developers can create new apps and mandate the downloading of updates with such speed that keeping up with the changes or enacting regulation in response become virtually impossible. Second, as we have seen in immigration, these cellphone-based electronic monitors can set up an enormous data matrix by combining audio/video connections and location tracking with databases that contain information on individuals living in the same house or nearby.[19]

ELECTRONIC MONITORS, EXCLUSION ZONES, AND QUARANTINE MANAGEMENT

In the midst of the pandemic, cellphone apps represented a blending of carceral electronic monitoring and coronavirus quarantine management. This meant both reframing tracking technology in the discourse of public health and a deeper infusion of carceral logic into the public health sphere. The prototype of this hybrid approach was Israel-based SuperCom, an established EM provider in the United States. According to the head of SuperCom's Americas division, Ordan Trabelsi, "Many customers and potential customers around the world asked us if we could use that same platform to do COVID-19 home quarantine tracking and compliance. And we thought, of course we can because it's exactly what we do in the offender tracking space."[20] SuperCom began marketing their trackers as quarantine management software in a number of countries including China, Sweden, Bulgaria, and Latvia.

A second set of coronavirus-dedicated technologies involved contact tracing via the use of Bluetooth. These necessitated a critical mass of people downloading a Bluetooth-based application to their phones that alerted the user when they came into contact with another user who had tested positive. A surprise partnership between competitors Google and Apple led the field in creating these applications; national governments in Singapore, Taiwan, Australia, and several other countries initiated similar platforms.[21] In the United States, Utah along with North and South Dakota became early adopters in this market, followed by Rhode Island with its Crush COVID RI application.[22]

Data collection in China and India took a different approach. With the advent of COVID the Chinese government, in partnership with local mega-corporations Alipay and Alibaba, the Chinese equivalents of PayPal and Amazon, compelled virtually the country's entire online population to download an app that would apply a risk assessment tool to the person's health data. This process yielded an Alipay health code, which converted to a QR code housed in the person's phone. This code determined the individual's freedom of movement, creating a customized geo-fence that defined where a person could go. Public banners in the city of Hangzhou highlighted the rules: "Green code, travel freely. Red or yellow, report immediately." Those with red or yellow could be quarantined at home or taken to a medical isolation unit for up to fourteen days. A *New York Times* report alleged that such personal data were added to the individual's police record, ultimately framing a person's COVID history as part of a background of criminality.[23]

While Chinese assessments were individualized, India deployed the government-established Aarogya Setu ("bridge to health") app to color code entire neighborhoods. Through the process of grabbing health data from the more than 120 million people who downloaded the app, the government was able to geo-fence entire sections of cities. People who lived in a green zone had pretty much unrestricted movement, while those residing in a red zone were compelled to spend the bulk of their days sheltering in place. Apart from the colored zones, households with residents who tested positive could be placed in a containment zone, a category used to restrict movement by a smaller number of people than the red zone.[24]

Other countries used technology to construct simpler forms of geo-fences to digitally limit people's movement. The best example is the notion of "COVID passes" or "immunity passports," documents which provide proof that the bearer has tested negative for COVID-19. The World Health Organization rejected immunity passports, citing a lack of evidence proving their efficacy.[25] Nonetheless, Estonia implemented such passports and a number of countries, including Italy, the UK, Germany, and Chile, gave it serious consideration.[26] South Korea took a different path to movement control by requiring international visitors to download an app and remain in quarantine for fourteen days upon arrival.[27]

THE UNIVERSITY AS EXPERIMENTAL LAB

While government authorities dealt with overall policy in the first few months of the pandemic, universities in the United States, which typically start their academic year in August or September, began to look at systems of surveillance and control as a way for their campuses to minimize the spread of COVID-19. Although a number of universities simply chose to switch to online learning, institutions with extensive engineering and computer science capacity viewed the pandemic as a challenge, both for setting up a safe system for their students and for developing tracking and tracing technology with application beyond campuses. The University of Illinois at Urbana–Champaign (UIUC), for instance, created a system requiring all students and staff to complete a saliva-based test twice a week. The test was accompanied by an app, Safer Illinois, designed by university faculty, which provided users with their testing results.

According to UIUC authorities, the app also offered a "self-assessment symptoms list, personalized tips for health and wellness . . . and contact information for virtual care teams from local health care providers," meaning it was being presented as a helpful and practical option for its users.[28] Similar to the Chinese national app, Safer Illinois contained an icon to inform campus building security officers if the bearer had been "granted" or "denied" access to various buildings. University of Illinois professor William Sullivan, who headed the team that developed Safer Illinois, suggested that the app would provide an opportunity to "use ourselves as a laboratory for how community can solve this problem."[29] Like the Chinese and Korean apps, Safer Illinois could detect if the user had been in proximity to anyone who had tested positive. This would, according to Sullivan, "give everyone confidence that the people in the building around them have recently tested negative." University authorities also claimed that the app ensured privacy by not capturing location or personal data from any individual phone. Scientists at the campus worked on providing users with the capacity to track the progress of their COVID-19 test processing in real time. Dr. Melvin Fenner called it the "Grubhub experience. You know when your order's been placed. You know when it's on the way. You know when it's been delivered."[30]

PERSONAL TRACING DEVICES: THE BIOBUTTON

Another variation on this theme of using universities as a "sandbox" for technological experimentation arose with the "BioButton" device implemented by Michigan's Oakland University. The BioButton, a small handheld device manufactured by biotech firm BioIntellisense, records the user's heartbeat, blood pressure, and respiration rate. Just before the opening of term, university officials declared BioButtons mandatory for all students.[31] More than two thousand students quickly signed a petition against such an approach, which led the university administration to make the BioButton voluntary. The version of the application contemplated for use at Oakland University only tapped into a few of the device's metrics. Apart from the three metrics used at Oakland, the device has the capacity to remotely measure skin temperature, heart rate, respiratory rate, gait analytics, coughing and sneezing frequency, sleep quality, body position, steps, and activity level. It can also detect if a person has vomited or fallen.

At the high school level, another set of data grabbers emerged. Rekor Systems launched OnGuard, a program that claimed to "advance student safety" by using license plate readers, facial recognition, full-range cameras, and 24/7 social media marketing to compile a "threat assessment."[32] These can be forwarded to school administrators or law enforcement to target individuals who may be contemplating undesirable activities.

These innovations raise concerns about privacy, especially given the extent people rely on their phones for personal data storage. UIUC authorities asserted that they had adequately ensured the privacy of their students. However, similar apps and other devices used in university settings raise other concerns. According to the Surveillance Technology Oversight Project (STOP), a nonprofit organization that researches mass surveillance, such contact tracing apps almost inevitably gather some personal data. According to STOP's research of fifty contact-tracing applications available for Google devices, thirty access call history, text messages, photos, videos, the camera, the microphone, network connectivity settings, or other personal data. Disturbingly, only sixteen of these apps promised to take the minimal step of anonymizing, encrypting, and anonymously aggregating users' data.[33] Moreover, the existing privacy laws may allow relatively easy access to data for law enforcement and immigration officials, putting serious limits on the privacy of university contact tracing records. That could be avoided by deleting records after a fixed period. However, such restrictions might have undermined the grander plans that UIUC had for that data.

SMART CITIES

Professor Sullivan's suggestion about using the university as a laboratory was not simple product hype. The Illinois COVID-19 system is connected to another university initiative, the Rokwire platform, which is billed as a "living lab" that aims to build "the operating system for the cities of tomorrow." Rokwire brings together an interdisciplinary team dedicated to building "the ecosystem for Smart Cities," with the university functioning as a pilot. Smart Cities are set up to gather data through devices and sensors and then use that data, with interventions from artificial intelligence, to improve management of the city.

University of Illinois: Smart City Model for the Rich

UIUC promotes itself as the teaching and learning lab for building Smart Cities of the future. But how representative is the university population of the state as a whole? According to a 2017 survey, the average family income for a University of Illinois student was $109,000, significantly higher than the state average of $65,030. Furthermore, the demographics of UIUC are decidedly white. Its student body in 2020 reported Black enrollment at just 5.1 percent, which represents only a little more than a third of the 14.6 percent Black presence in the state. Similarly, the university had a 9.25 percent Hispanic or Latino enrollment, slightly more than half the corresponding figure for Illinois (17.5 percent).[34] Those in the criminalized sector of the population, who largely fall within the 12.1 percent of those below the poverty rate, may find that staying off the radar may offer a more promising option than trying to plug into a high-tech urban reality.[35] Their data will most likely contribute to more sophisticated mechanisms of exclusion and punishment rather than providing a pathway to the promises of the Smart City innovators.

Ultimately, technology of virtually all varieties offers different possibilities and impacts for individuals and communities, depending on variables such as race, class, national origin, gender identity, and ability. The impact of using technology to track location and gather data relates directly to who controls the technology, who owns the data, and how much control the individual who "owns" the data has over how it is used. Although professional critics and litigants constantly bemoan loss of privacy, far more crucial is the loss of power and the capacity to survive outside a carceral space that most surveillance technology, the technology of e-carceration, embodies.

Rokwire's promotional videos repeatedly remind viewers that a college is an ideal site for experimentation with such data-gathering systems. "If it works at college, it can work in cities too" is the mantra of these promotions. University president Robert Jones called the Rokwire initiative a "contemporary high-tech tool to sustain us for the next 150 years," an innovation that will "build something that will become the envy of everyone in the world."[36]

MOMENT OF CRISIS, MOMENT OF CHANGE

While the onset of the pandemic and the resulting technological changes seem sudden, this is a moment for which people like former Google CEO Eric Schmidt, Bill Gates, and Jeff Bezos have been preparing. In a talk to the National Security Commission on Artificial Intelligence in 2019, Schmidt outlined his vision of a techno-future.[37] He envisaged a world in which Big Tech increasingly took over the functions of government—not unlike the Smart City. In this model, more and more profits go to a small circle of firms that control the technology infrastructure. Those on the other side of the digital divide, who are not connected to the mainframes of 5G and beyond, fall into the wilderness. For Schmidt, the lethal coronavirus came along just in time to become the great enabler for his vision, moving online mega-players such as Amazon and Zoom onto the economic center stage. As millions of workers waited for a few hundred dollars in unemployment and stimulus checks, and the national GDP fell by 9.5 percent, the major tech players gobbled up mega-profits. According to figures for the second quarter of 2020, Facebook's profits grew by 98 percent, Amazon revenue rose by 40 percent and its profits doubled, and Apple hit $2 trillion in market capitalization for the first time.[38] By April of 2021 Amazon was reporting another 44 percent rise in sales over the previous year. Profits grew even more astronomically, expanding by 220 percent to $8.1 billion for the first quarter of 2021.[39]

These major corporate players in the tech world are closely related to the kingpins of e-carceration. As surveillance was expanding during the pandemic, Big Tech was widening its data-gathering net even further. For Amazon, every increase in online purchases is also the addition of more data to their cloud computing services. This data is the raw material for more profit-making opportunities. This Big Tech expansion has serious implications for equity. Organizations such as the ACLU pinpoint the civil rights and privacy issues of this expanding technology. A 2019 ACLU report on COVID-19, *Temperature Screening and Civil Liberties During an Epidemic*, urged people to "skeptically scrutinize new products and proposals, especially where they have implications for our privacy or other civil liberties."[40] Global social justice watchdog Human Rights Watch expressed similar concerns about the use of mobile location data in the COVID-19 response, noting that such data "usually contains sensitive and revealing insights about people's identity, location, behavior, associations and activities."[41]

One outcome of these critiques could be the creation of legislation akin to the European Union's General Data Protection Regulation (GDPR).[42] This regulation, passed by the EU in 2016 and activated in 2018, aimed to provide some legal guarantee of privacy for the personal data of individuals living in EU countries. To this end, it compels data controllers to disclose any data collection, state for how long the data will be kept, and disclose any third parties with whom the data will be shared. This also applies to data controllers based outside of Europe if they are selling goods and services to European countries. For 2020, European Union authorities recorded an average of 331 data breaches daily.[43] By that year's end, cumulative GDPR fines had reached a total of 245 million euros (about $332 million). Google was the biggest corporate target. In December of 2020, it incurred penalties of $100 million for having placed advertising cookies in personal computers via its search engine. Amazon was billed $35 million for a similar illicit practice.[44]

Although the GDPR might inspire some legislation in the United States, any oversight of data gathering in this country should assess the racial impact of new technologies. Think tanks such as historian Ibram X. Kendi's Center for Antiracist Research, along with independent journalists such as Zoë Carpenter, systematically gathered data on racial inequalities and disparities in COVID-19 cases and deaths, incontrovertibly connecting these to structural racism. Kendi argued that these data allow us "to provide policymakers with the ability to make evidence-based policy decisions to curtail health disparities during the pandemic."[45] Such critiques are crucial in determining which aspects of data gathering pertain to public health and which are widening the net of e-carceration by disproportionately targeting people of color.

The array of geo-fences that has emerged during the pandemic demonstrates how the technologies of e-carceration could morph into a far more systematic mode of segregation, on the basis of not only a person's criminal background but a range of data that might go into their digital profile, including the health data collected for COVID-19 detection. Indian urban authorities were able to color code neighborhoods and grant differentiated freedoms to residents of different parts of the city on the basis of health criteria. A U.S. version could easily replicate past systems of oppression using data from sources tainted by long-entrenched structural racism and inequality to create QR codes and geo-fences as the digital foundation for twenty-first-century segregation.[46]

8

CAMDEN, NJ, AND
THE "SILICON VALLEY WAY OF DOING POLICING"

When you match courage with compassion, with care and understanding of the community—like we've seen here in Camden—some really outstanding things can begin to happen. . . . I want to focus on the fact that other cities across America can make similar progress.

—*President Barack Obama, speaking to Camden, New Jersey, police, May 2015*[1]

Camden is what happens when liberals hijack "defund the police."

—*Brendan McQuade, author of* Pacifying the Homeland:
Intelligence Fusion and Mass Supervision[2]

In 2013, Camden, New Jersey (population: 79,000), hit the big time in the criminal justice world with bold moves to dismantle its entire police department. At the time, this experiment was widely touted as a model for reform. Not only did this restructuring of law enforcement make major changes to policing; it also, by design, facilitated the flow of new streams of resources to Camden's well-heeled.

This piece of Camden's history returned to the national limelight in the wake of the 2020 murder of George Floyd in Minneapolis and the ensuing rise of a movement to abolish and defund the police. A romanticized version of Camden's tale drew headlines as an example of a city that had disbanded its police force and prospered.[3] Camden County Police chief Scott Thomson became an instant celebrity, called upon for more than three hundred interviews, including from outlets as distant as New Zealand. Despite the rash of people singing praises for the Camden model, what actually emerged from this New Jersey experiment was what researcher Brendan McQuade called a "Silicon Valley way of policing."[4] Essentially, the authorities in Camden had found yet another way to squeeze a criminalized, predominantly Black urban population more tightly. Instead of a model for transformation, Camden, viewed through the lens of e-carceration, offers a fine-grained cautionary tale for activists who seek to redress systemic injustices but also want to ensure high-tech policing doesn't sneak in the back door.

CITY INVINCIBLE

The background to the restructuring of Camden's police force is a complex process of race and class struggle that unfolded as a by-product of the decline of U.S. industrial capacity. Though located slightly outside the boundaries of what is usually called the Midwest Rust Belt, Camden's history feels very much like that of Youngstown, Ohio, or Flint, Michigan. Despite having a population that is 83 percent Black and Latinx and a reputation as "the poorest city in the nation and the most dangerous city in the nation all in the same place," Camden didn't always symbolize urban decay.[5] During its industrial zenith, Camden confidently adopted the motto etched above the entrance to City Hall: "City Invincible." The phrase comes from a poem by Camden native Walt Whitman, in which he depicted his hometown as a city "that led the rest."[6] "Invincible" Camden was once home to 365 different industries. In 1950, with a population of 124,000, Camden provided 43,000 manufacturing jobs. The city's destiny was associated with a number of corporate giants of the mid-twentieth century. Campbell's invented condensed soup in Camden and went on to produce it there for decades. In the pre-digital days, electronics company RCA employed twelve thousand workers in Camden, mostly in production of radios and components. But the crown jewel in Camden manufacturing was the New York Shipbuilding Corporation plant, which produced a major portion of the U.S. Navy's fleet during both world wars, as well as the *Savannah*, the only nuclear passenger ship ever built.[7]

By the mid-1950s, time began to rush past these companies' products and management models. The decline in demand for wartime ships led to the shipyard's closing in 1967. Campbell Soup held on until 1991, when both its plants shut down as production relocated to Ohio, Texas, and North Carolina. RCA failed to keep up with a rapidly changing electronics and broadcast industry. It sold off the bulk of its branding to General Electric and other firms. In the late 1980s, wrecking balls demolished most of RCA's production sites in Camden. The demise of major industry sparked familiar processes—white flight and severe poverty—both of which increased in parallel with a flourishing drug trade. As Brendan McQuade, who spent years researching the policing in the context of urban development in this city, described it: "Camden's decline is an extreme example of larger processes: the deindustrialization of the United States, the rollback of the welfare state, and the increasing use of the criminal legal system to contain complex social problems."[8]

As economic opportunities declined in Camden, rates of incarceration increased. The jail population in Camden County more than doubled from 1970 to 1990, a ripple effect from the post-1970 economic crisis that struck all rustbelt cities and triggered the exodus of U.S. industries to overseas locations.[9] During the same period, the portion of Black people in the city's population rose from 39 percent to 56 percent, while the portion of white people fell from 60 percent to 19 percent.[10] Staggering levels of corruption exacerbated the situation. From the 1970s to the early 2000s, three of the city's mayors ended up in prison after engaging in various forms of plundering the public till. Blight had become a feature of the landscape. By 2000, more than three thousand houses stood vacant and 44 percent of the population was living in poverty.[11] In 2004, Camden had the highest crime rate of any city in the United States.[12] An injection of $175 million from the state's Municipal Rehabilitation and Economic Recovery Act had little impact. Joshua Ottenberg, then the county prosecutor, lamented that "the drug economy is the economy. That's been the truth for a long, long time." Some drug kingpins claimed to be making up to $7,500 a day.[13] The police complained about being helpless. Police Chief Edwin Figueroa said, "I feel like I'm in Fallujah [Iraq]. I don't have enough soldiers. The enemy is out there. And we're fighting the same battle over and over and over again."[14]

Enter the restructuring of policing initiative, featuring a heightened role for the technologies of e-carceration. This restructuring aimed to not only decrease local government spending and reduce crime and violence, but also help secure a grand plan of economic revitalization led by George Norcross, Camden's homegrown magnate and veteran union-buster. Norcross offered a vision of a gentrified Camden that included a vibrant, tightly policed, and technologically surveilled downtown area.[15] E-carceration was on his agenda.

The first step was for Police Chief Scott Thomson and Norcross ally Mayor Dana Redd to slash the police force in 2010 from 368 to 200 officers. These reductions prompted "sick-in" responses from the remaining police force. On some days there were as few as twelve on duty to cover the entire city.[16] Predictably, by 2012 another wave of violent crime hit the city. Policing was not making headway. Instead, excessive force complaints kept arising, with little done in response. In 2010, five officers were charged with planting evidence, fabrication, and perjury, leading courts to overturn the convictions of eighty-eight people arrested by those officers.[17]

The rising constellation of power brokers, led by Norcross, found a new solution, something no other city had ever tried: completely disbanding the remaining police force. Their plan was the reassignment of the city's unionized municipal police force to the jurisdiction of the county as non-union employees. Planners' estimates projected that getting rid of the union would enable authorities to trim officers' benefits, producing a reduction in police expenditure of about 25 percent, a total savings of $14–16 million per year. With the backing of then governor Chris Christie, Norcross, and Mayor Redd, plus support from Thomson and six out of seven city council members, the measure to disband the Camden City Police went through. The union was broken—clearing the way to restructure the police under the authority of Camden County. The new force would feature low-wage officers under a different model of policing involving beat cops working with local informants known as "neighborhood sentinels." This triggered widespread arrests for petty offenses and, most crucially, the introduction of surveillance technologies and e-carceration.

On May 1, 2013, Camden laid off its entire police force and contracted policing to the county for $62 million in operational costs. The county leased the city's administration building for one dollar.[18] State attorney general Anne Milgram appointed Thomson the new top cop in the Camden County Police Department. A salary increase of $66,800 brought Thomson's pay to $230,000.[19] Thomson then hired dozens of new, inexperienced officers at much lower salaries than the city scale.

VIRTUAL PATROLS: POLICING THE "SILICON VALLEY WAY"

The restructured Camden police force bore down on the criminalized in two ways. First, police began to gather data on the population by walking the streets, talking to residents and taking notes, encouraging the growth of networks of informants. This street-level intelligence magnified in importance as Camden grew regional and national connections to the world of digital surveillance. Second, county deputies moved toward so-called broken windows policing. Broken windows holds that any slight sign of petty crime, such as a broken window, needs to be addressed by law enforcement before it spirals into a crime wave. In Camden, police began to turn every violation of the law into a citation. Petty offense dockets went up from 28,000 in 2013 to 125,000 in 2014. That meant a big increase in arrests and summonses for minor crimes such as loose license plate holders or riding a bicycle without a bell.[20] More importantly, these arrests provided opportunities to collect more data on the local population, which could be fed into the array of local and national databases Camden was joining.

Neighborhood information was upgraded to database input through a new system called the Interactive Community Alert Network, or "iCan." The increase in foot patrol–derived citations was part of a management model officials called "community intelligence–led po-licing."[21] Much of the information came from the "neighborhood sentinels."[22] This network allowed residents to report crime or suspicious activity in real time as they saw it in their neighborhood. Becoming part of iCan required registration, a series of background checks, and training, the last of which could take up to a year. iCan members became an elite force of neighborhood spies on the ground, linked through the $4.5 million in technologies of e-carceration spread across the city.

Camden became a live testing ground for every e-carceral toy and piece of equipment. A total of 121 cameras watched virtually every inch of sidewalk; thirty-five ShotSpotter micro-phones, which record the location of gunshots, were put in place; police cars were fitted with scanners that read the license plate number of every passing vehicle; and Skypatrol, a mobile forty-foot-high information-gathering tower, became normalized as part of the community landscape.[23] iCan and police on the beat were complemented by "virtual patrols," a scan of the vast network of cameras and other surveillance devices to target police operations where crime was supposedly happening. E-carceration was also personalized, with residents being asked to download the STOPit app, which enabled people to report crimes and gunshots anonymously.[24]

These localized efforts were linked to a vast set of regional and national intelligence net-works. The most important of these was the National Network of Fusion Centers. These centers were intelligence-gathering hubs established across the country in the wake of 9/11. Though initially focused on tracing "terrorist" plots, they soon morphed into information centers for surveilling a wide variety of activities, including the types of drug operations ac-tive in Camden. By 2018, seventy-nine fusion centers were operating nationally.[25] Camden's affiliate to the National Network was the Real Time Regional Operations Intelligence Cen-ter and fusion center (RT-ROIC), a police hub of cloud computing that enabled investigators to connect all the data.[26] In 2013, yet another hub arose, the Real Time Tactical Operational Intelligence Center (RT-TOIC), working under the authority of the county police. This center didn't just process data from other sources, but carried out its own surveillance. In a visit to the RT-TOIC, journalist Rachel Everett observed civilians working on contract through a third party as "crime analysts" and "virtual patrollers." Each person was in charge of monitoring six computer screens that displayed video feeds from surveillance cameras, maps, real-time police call data, and "the intelligence they've collected to make sense of it all."[27] This was the back end of a system of e-carceration. The Invincible City was learning to use the weapons of the surveillance camera, the database, and the algorithm to buttress the power of Glocks and tasers.

Camden's fusion center attracted attention from the Department of Justice (DoJ), which invited the city to share its experience of digital policing. Commenting on the DoJ move to gather representatives from six cities selected to develop a national Violence Reduction Network (VRN), New Jersey's U.S. attorney, Paul Fishman, said: "It is gratifying that Camden has been selected as a partner in the VRN, so we will be able to build on what we've started and ensure federal resources are being used as effectively as possible to create safer communities."[28]

The fusion center was not Camden's sole link to the world of digital policing. Camden County law enforcement was also part of the Delaware Valley Intelligence Center (DVIC). Based in Philadelphia, the DVIC served as a regional fusion center, connecting intelligence operations across Pennsylvania and much of New Jersey. The DVIC's goal was to "open up important lines of communication between the fusion center, law enforcement and the business community on matters of crime and terrorism."[29]

In 2015, President Obama visited Camden during a White House–led two-day "design sprint" for the Police Data Initiative, which aimed "to help envision what a truly effective technology system could look like." Camden was one of twenty-one cities chosen for inclusion. The two-day deployment was targeted at enabling police departments like Camden's to find the solutions that most fit their needs. Camden was moving to the cutting edge of the Silicon Valley way of policing.[30]

Connecting the Camden County Police to other intelligence and policing operations across the country was more than an exercise in attending planning seminars and workshops.

Camden authorities took part in coordinated national actions in intelligence-led policing that aimed at reducing crime and the presence of drugs. Spearheaded by federal authorities, these exercises included up to four major components: warrant sweeps of "wanted" individuals, compliance checks for people on parole and probation, periodic check-ups on "chronic" offenders and saturation patrols sent to locations identified as real or potential crime hot spots via surveillance, and data sharing.[31]

The coordinated action with the highest profile was Operation Padlock, which largely targeted drug traffic. A classic example of intelligence-led policing deploying the technologies of e-carceration, Operation Padlock was nine months in the planning. It encompassed ninety-three operations during a seven-week period spanning August and September in 2012. The total haul in Camden was 535 arrests, the impounding of nearly seventy vehicles, and the seizure of over $35,000 in cash and $44,300 in drugs. A key element in Operation Padlock was the compiling of "gator guides," pocket-sized booklets compiled by the fusion center. The guides contained key details, including pictures, of local targets for "chronic-offender" hunts. The fusion center drew from its network of field operators, neighborhood informants, and national links. Playing a central role at this level were records from probation and parole, which often contained far more individual details than a routine background check or police file would.

In 2015, under the leadership of the U.S. Marshals, Camden police took part in a six-week national sweep of fugitives and suspects of violent crimes across seven cities, yielding more than 7,100 arrests (84 of these arrests came from Camden). To carry out this operation, the Marshals had created a counter gang unit in each of the cities that provided "real time, ground level intelligence."[32] A similar national raid a year later led to the arrest of seventy-four people in Camden.[33]

Such operations had direct support from the regional forces of intelligence-led policing. The New Jersey State Police, the lead agency at the fusion center, also sent an "intelligence collection cell," a group of troopers to embed with Camden police. As a senior trooper explained to Brendan McQuade, "We're actually going to ride along with you and, when you lock up somebody in Camden, we're going to debrief them and interview them. We're going to gather intelligence and send it back here for analysis."[34]

Camden's new role as a practitioner of weaponizing data drew praise from people in high places. New Jersey U.S. attorney Paul Fishman led the chorus of commendation: "We have seen extraordinary things from what we call C-4, the unprecedented fusion center in Camden that brings together federal, state and local partners in a truly collaborative approach to fighting violent crime." He highlighted the multi-party efforts to make Camden "the safe city its residents deserve."[35]

REBRANDING THE POLICE

An onslaught of rebranding accompanied these technological upgrades. One-time warrior cop Scott Thomson was mastering the vocabulary of reform. He told a reporter in 2014,

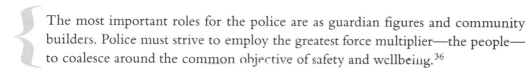

The most important roles for the police are as guardian figures and community builders. Police must strive to employ the greatest force multiplier—the people—to coalesce around the common objective of safety and wellbeing.[36]

The cultural shift to "embrace a guardian—rather than a warrior—mindset" was accompanied by a policy framework that included gestures toward accountability. Pressure for these changes came primarily from local citizens, especially in light of a 2014 incident in which a police encounter left twenty-year-old Black resident Xavier Ingram with a broken neck and unable to move his limbs. Under pressure from a Black population already outraged by the police murders of Michael Brown and Eric Garner, the county police created "clear and comprehensive policies" for use of force, mass demonstrations, and consent for searches. Police also incorporated de-escalation strategies in their Guardian Culture Program.[37] Other training topics included community policing methodologies and racial bias. Two of the trainers boasted that some of the curriculum was "adapted from the Marines' effective 'winning hearts and minds' efforts overseas."[38] Even Chris Christie joined the mantra, proclaiming, "You had to change the underlying principles of the way police officers were being trained and taught, and the culture in the department." For Christie, "the most effective way to do that was to start over."[39]

The new approach included cordiality as well. "We bring in ice cream trucks and put them on the corner," Chief Thomson told an NPR reporter. "And we tell our community cops that when they're out there walking the beat, to tell everybody, 'Hey, come and get some free ice cream.'"[40] "It's about treating people with respect and dignity and making the lives of the people of the city better," Thomson suggested in a 2017 Bureau of Justice documentary on Camden. He said the events in Ferguson surrounding the murder of Michael Brown and the brutal 1965 attack by police on civil rights marchers on Edmund Pettus Bridge in Selma, Alabama, inspired his change of philosophy.[41] Camden and its once warrior police chief, Scott Thomson, were becoming icons of carceral humanism, repackaging their policing as a caring service. Ralph Thornton, a Black officer also interviewed in the Bureau of Justice film, claimed, "We started giving people their neighborhoods back." He reported residents giving officers a round of applause after they began walking the beat.[42] But while the public face of policing was projecting a caring image, the back end of law enforcement was the rapidly expanding technologies of e-carceration. As Brendan McQuade observed,

> Police don't need M-16s and Mine Resistant Ambush Protected armored personnel carriers to be "militarized." The massive intelligence system hidden from public view suffices.[43]

CAMDEN RISING AND THE BROTHERS NORCROSS

The carceral humanist rhetoric and the renewed pressure on the criminalized in Camden were predictably accompanied by the rich getting richer. While police were undergoing de-escalation training, learning the ins and outs of databases, walking the neighborhoods, and squeezing out soft-serve ice cream, a new round of capital investment under the banner of "Camden Rising" was taking place. Norcross's advocacy, buoyed by a collaboration with his brother Donald, a member of the state legislature, drove this process toward a more successful outcome than previous efforts. Two key policy measures provided the catalyst for Norcross's bid to bolster investment in Camden: a $1.6 billion break in state property taxes and a local tax abatement that would reduce taxes by about 70 percent for twenty years. A third Norcross brother, lawyer Philip, used his legal skills to help draft language for this legislation. These tax incentives, coupled with the county declaring Camden City a special low-tax "Opportunity Zone," sparked a capital flow of more than $2.3 billion into this former icon of urban blight.[44] Subaru announced plans to bring its U.S. headquarters to town, promising 550 new jobs.[45] Energy equipment supplier Holtec International promised a $260 million complex in the city. American Water joined the trend by making Camden its global headquarters.[46] With these industries came the expansion of Rutgers University and Cooper University Hospital, in line with a shift toward "eds and meds" (education and medical facilities).[47] Even pro sports teams got involved, with the Philadelphia 76ers setting up an $82 million training complex in Camden.[48] These impressive new investments, concentrated outside the reach of the criminalized, served to further cement inequalities in the Invincible City.

THE CAMDEN MODEL: "NO LONGER A SLAVE PLANTATION"

By 2020, county police officials claimed that violent crime in Camden had decreased by 46 percent since 2013.[49] Police also reported a decline in the use of violence in their ranks. From July 2015 to October 2016, Camden police responded to over 2,400 calls for armed persons, but made only 370 arrests and had only one "officer-involved shooting." According to the department, complaints of excessive use of force had dropped from the range of thirty-five to sixty-five a year in the first years of the county force to fewer than five by 2020.[50] Scott Thomson gave full recognition to the role played by the technologies of e-carceration in this process. Speaking at a Department of Justice conference in Camden in 2019, he noted, "Technology can be a force multiplier in the work we do and have an outsized impact on our success ensuring the public's safety and maintaining a peaceful community."[51]

Although national policing authorities and Department of Justice bureaucrats have applauded Camden as a model for the nation, leaders and activists in the local Black population conveyed little such enthusiasm. The late NAACP activist Dr. Doris Carpenter expressed shock at the praise for her city. "When I heard that we were a model city, I almost fell off my chair," she said, adding that Camden Rising had failed to incorporate the perspectives of the city's most marginalized residents. "Until people rise, Camden won't rise, and so often [city officials are] making decisions for us. We need to be present at the table—this is no longer a slave plantation."[52]

Darnell Hardwick, also of the local NAACP chapter, had an even harsher response: "They want to tell CNN and all these big places that the city is rising, the police force is perfect and it's a bunch of bullshit," he said. "We don't have a relationship with the police here."[53]

Black community leaders like Keith Benson, president of the Camden Education Association, a local teacher's union, questioned the validity of the crime figures. He argued that the crime rate fell largely because gentrification was pushing out residents who were living on the margins. "The people are not there anymore," he said. "That type of thing really has nothing to do at all with the police."[54] He also claimed that policing remained unevenly distributed. "In the visible areas, like the central part along the business district, are they there?" he asked. "Yeah. Are cars patrolling? Absolutely. But in places where people live, are they walking up and down the street? Hell, no."[55]

The alleged drop in the crime rate also didn't trigger a move toward eradicating poverty. The core underlying factors that had precipitated the crisis of crime and policing didn't change significantly. The poverty rate in Camden reported in 2013, at 39.8 percent, had only fallen to 36.8 percent by 2018. Although unemployment had declined to 6.8 percent by May 2019, as compared to 9.9 percent in 2012, the city still maintained the highest unemployment rate in the state. Even some law enforcement data indicated there were still problems. In the twelve-year period from 2008 to 2020, when prison incarceration in the state of New Jersey fell by 30 percent, the Camden County jail population decreased by just 11 percent.[56]

Camden now has a waterfront with a big aquarium, a state-of-the-art sports facility, a number of major corporate offices, and neighborhoods of renovated houses to accommodate the professional classes, who are disproportionately white. The city has promoted a business improvement district where companies use their tax savings to contract services such as sidewalk cleaning, snow shoveling, and graffiti removal through private deals with providers, typically employing non-union, low-wage workers.

Rather than being a model for defunding or dismantling the police, Camden instead demonstrates how the technologies of e-carceration can be packaged with policing and neoliberal restructuring to control surplus populations. The reality of Camden Rising was only possible because the technologies of e-carceration, coordinated through the presence of fusion centers, were present to enforce the boundaries of privilege. Data flowing through operational centers became the foundation for exclusion and inclusion. The police handed out soft-serve ice cream cones, momentarily masking a restructuring that only deepened Camden's underlying inequalities. Barack Obama may herald the progress of Camden as a great lesson for all cities to follow, but Camden's real lessons from the years 2010–19 are not about progress for the criminalized and marginalized. Instead, a Silicon Valley model of policing with neighborhood sentinels wired into e-carceral control centers has produced a tightly policed, secured corporate gentrification that has offered little more than the extended surrender of data and continuing disenfranchisement to the Black and brown populations of Camden. In this model, the technologies of e-carceration help keep investments and profits flowing, unhindered by street crime or, more importantly, the kinds of Black-led uprisings that spread across the United States in the summer of 2020.

9

E-CARCERATION, SETTLER COLONIALISM, AND THE OPEN-AIR PRISON

Here we have no borders and no life. Where are we supposed to go? We ask for our rights. I have the right to have a country. I have a right to have a home.

—Palestinian woman resident of the open-air prison of Gaza; her son was shot dead by Israeli soldiers in 2020[1]

The combination of growing opposition to mass incarceration, the evolution of the technologies of e-carceration, and the intransigence of those who remain loyal to the prison-industrial complex is driving us toward a hybrid system of punishment. This hybrid will contain two parts: The first is the existing prisons, jails, immigration detention centers, and other carceral institutions that continue to physically confine people under the authority of the criminal legal and homeland security systems. We can label the second component "open-air prisons," or a collection of institutions, programs, and practices that exist outside the walls of traditional prisons. Some of these, such as parole and probation, are directly linked to the criminal legal system, while others, such as substance abuse programs and group homes, are part of the widening net of social services that follow a punitive rather than a restorative, transformative, or even a rehabilitative approach.

Although reform has definitely been in the air since 2010, the edifices of mass incarceration that sprung up in the 1980s and 1990s are not going to turn into a carceral rustbelt any time soon. Statistics show a lot of life remains in the built environment of punishment.[2] Allowing for accelerated prison depopulation during the pandemic months up until April 30, 2021, the total prison population in the United States has fallen by about a fifth since the peak year of 2009.[3] In 2018, analyst Nazgol Ghandnoosh of the criminal justice reform think tank The Sentencing Project noted that it would take seventy-five years to cut the prison population in half at the then existing rate of decarceration.[4] Releases and policy changes during the pandemic have somewhat accelerated that timetable, but the speed of change remains extremely gradual and uneven. As of December 2020, nineteen state prison systems remained at 90 percent capacity or higher.[5]

Although the turn to e-carceration and open-air prisons implies an expansion of probation and parole, the annual statistical reports of the Bureau of Justice Statistics don't bear this out. In fact, the number of people on parole and probation has remained fairly stable over the last two decades. Even the pandemic did not change this reality. According to the Prison Policy Initiative, most parole boards actually granted fewer paroles in 2020 than in 2019.[6] Rather, as we have chronicled throughout this book, the criminal legal face of e-carceration primarily involves adding *new* dimensions of technologies of control to probation, parole, and pretrial release. In addition, the drivers of the open-air prison will involve the application of e-carceral technologies such as risk assessment and facial recognition in the realms of social services, education, and health care and on city streets where they didn't previously exist.

OPEN-AIR PRISONS

The late anti-police activist Jazz Hayden was among the first people to apply the term "open-air prison," in the U.S. context. When commenting on the intensification of policing and surveillance in poor neighborhoods of color, Hayden stated that he had seen New York police "turn our community into an open-air prison." He added, "I've been to prison so I know what I'm talking about."[7] This terminology is useful for reminding us that deprivation of liberty is a daily reality for the criminalized sector of the working class wherever they may be living, walking, driving, or just hanging out. But what does this really mean and what are the defining characteristics of open-air prisons?

To begin with, like many forms of e-carceration, open-air prisons break the boundaries of space and time. Facial recognition or drone surveillance can capture data and monitor location at any given time and place. The boundaries of a geo-fence created to limit a person's movement can be extended or reduced to any degree and at any time. The tracking of an individual's location or monitoring of certain biometrics may last for a day, a week, or a lifetime.

Second, changes in technologies of e-carceration are not usually subject to due process. While prison sentences and most electronic monitoring regimes (though not all) are determined in a legal proceeding, altering the details of how technologies of e-carceration operate usually does not take place in a transparent open hearing. These changes can be done by a parole or probation agent, a program coordinator, or even a technician by simply altering the settings on a digital dashboard. In treatment programs, counselors or case managers may make those decisions. In the future, such determinations will increasingly become data-driven, meaning the terms of liberty deprivation will be delineated by an algorithmic calculation rather than a human decision. Already in many cases, confinement in lockup mental health facilities and other institutions dedicated to individuals with various types of disabilities does not involve legal proceedings or courtroom decisions. The signature of a medical authority is the equivalent of a sentence by a judge.

Technologies of e-carceration in an open-air prison can be individualized or used as collective punishment. Although today some court cases, especially in immigration, have multiple defendants, legal proceedings are tailored to the individual level. By contrast, e-carceration can punish entire communities through the use of cameras, fusion centers, drones, or targeted algorithms. While the existing criminal legal system remains dominated by structural racism, blanket punishment is not typically delivered collectively and explicitly to people *because* they are classified as a particular race or live in a certain neighborhood. Rather, the system punishes individuals from targeted groups one by one. E-carceration has the capacity to target collectively and instantaneously through the use of data and mathematical formulas rather than human judgment. Hence, technology can instantaneously enact a set of punitive policies for those who fit a certain data-derived profile—whether just one individual or millions of people, whether they live in one community or are scattered across the globe.

Lastly, the imposition of many technologies of e-carceration in open-air prisons may not be known to the targeted individual or community. As Chicago's Johnny Page replied when asked if he was on a GPS or radio-frequency monitor during his parole, "I don't know what that thing did."[8] But Page was at least aware a device was tracking him. In other instances, such as being subject to facial recognition or the target of social media tracking, a person may have no idea that surveillance is even taking place. Even when an individual or a community is subjected to e-carceration in an open-air prison, they may have no idea exactly what the conditions or rules of governance and surveillance are or how the management structures of the prison enable the supervising authority to capture data or control access to and monitor communication beyond the geo-walls.

Although these are the main features of open-air prisons, it is important to recognize the full spectrum of practices we might categorize under this heading. Using the security categories of the prison system, as problematic as they might be, is helpful in differentiating levels of control and punishment in open-air prisons. For example, a community with extensive police cameras capturing what happens on the street might be termed a minimum-security open-air prison. In such a situation a carceral presence is everywhere via this technology of e-carceration. Yet the sense of intrusiveness and threat is far less pronounced than in far more carceral open-air settings, such as what we will explore below in the open-air prison in the Palestinian territory of Gaza.

In the world of open-air prisons, Gaza could be considered a super-maximum-security facility. A further exploration of both the daily life inside the open-air prison of Gaza and the historical circumstances that gave rise to its existence will help provide some parameters for examining open-air prisons in the United States.

THE OPEN-AIR PRISON OF GAZA

Gaza is a densely populated area in the Middle East that is home to roughly two million Palestinians. It covers about 139 square miles, approximately the size of Detroit.[9]

The historical roots of the open-air prison in Gaza are deeply connected to the establishment of the nation of Israel and the perpetuation of Zionism.[10] Originating in Europe in the late 1800s, Zionism is a nationalist political ideology that historically had called for the creation of a Jewish state.[11] From the outset, Zionists longed to establish a Jewish homeland in a place distant from the anti-Semitism of Western Europe. As early as the 1880s, Zionist Jews began to migrate to Palestine with this in mind.[12] However, the full-fledged open-air prison of Gaza we know today only emerged after two major Israeli military offensives dispossessed the Palestinian people from a land where they had lived for centuries. The first occurred in 1948 in what Palestinians often refer to as "the Nakba," roughly translated as "catastrophe." The Nakba led to the creation of the state of Israel on Palestinian territory. During this incursion, the Zionist goal was a Jewish state that Israel's first president, Chaim Weizmann, suggested would become "as Jewish as England is English."[13] According to an *Al Jazeera* report, the Zionists' armed invasion and occupation of Palestine in 1948 resulted in the expulsion of an estimated 750,000 Palestinians and the destruction of 530 villages. Fifteen thousand Palestinians died in this attack.[14] This amounted to an ethnic cleansing of the Palestinian people and the establishment of systems for future control of the surviving population.[15]

From that time forward, all of Palestine, including Gaza, was under the rule of the Zionist occupiers. For the next fifty years, with the support of the United States and European powers, Israel became a major military power and colonial oppressor of the Palestinian people. The oppression of Palestinians intensified as a result of repeated acts of military aggression by the Israeli government. The most important was the Six-Day War with Egypt in 1967, through which Israel expanded the territory under its control. In 2008–9 the Zionists launched an offensive in Gaza against Hamas, a militant Palestinian opposition political party that had been elected into office.[16] Since 2009 two more major Israeli offensives have taken place.[17] According to a UN report a 2014 attack by Israel resulted in 2,251 Palestinian deaths including 1,462 civilians. Six Israelis also died.[18] In 2021 further military interventions by Israeli forces killed 250 Palestinians, 66 of them children. Thirteen Israelis also perished.[19] Apart from the deaths, in 2021 70,000 people in Gaza had to seek refuge in schools run by the UN due to the destruction of their homes. The ongoing threat of military attacks is magnified by the scale and sophistication of the Israeli defense industry, which from 2016 to 2020 was the eighth leading global exporter of arms.[20]

The events of 2008–9 converted Gaza into an area of multidimensional, open-air incarceration, enforced by military might and the technologies of e-carceral surveillance.[21] By 2010, John Holmes, spokesperson for the UN undersecretary-general for Humanitarian Affairs and Emergency Relief, stated that people in Gaza were "living in a large open-air prison."[22]

GAZA'S OPEN-AIR PRISON REALITIES

Since 2008, Gaza has been a totally closed territory. Israel, with a little help from Egypt, controls all entrances to Gaza, by sea, air, and road.[23] Technology, in combination with military checkpoints and physical barriers, keeps Palestinians confined to Gaza, where standards of living have seriously deteriorated in the last two decades. Yousef Munayyer, executive director of the U.S. Campaign for Palestinian Rights, contended in 2018 that "Gaza is a place that has been testing the limits of what the minimum level of sustainability is before a total humanitarian catastrophe. We inch closer every day to finding where that threshold is."[24]

About 50 percent of the workforce of Gaza is unemployed,[25] and 80 percent of the population requires international aid to survive.[26] Ninety-five percent of the groundwater is undrinkable, which forces the population to buy expensive commercial water.[27] Electricity is intermittent, usually available for only about four to five hours a day.[28] About 70 percent of the population of Gaza relies on the services of the UNRWA, with more than three-quarters of those dependent on the UN agency for food. A UN report in 2012 declared that Gaza would be unlivable by 2020.[29] Yet people still live there. For most, there is no escape.

In addition to fears of military attacks, people in the open-air prison of Gaza live under one of the most sophisticated e-carceral surveillance systems in the world—Israel's. Israeli firms are major players in global security markets. In 2014, Israeli firms exported over $6 billion worth of products and services in the cyber sector. A 2016 Privacy International report on the global surveillance industry identified twenty-seven Israeli surveillance companies.[30] The Mer Group, a key firm in the sector, includes numerous alumni from Unit 8200, the intelligence branch of the Israeli Defense Forces.[31] Israel's arsenal of e-carceration technologies is enhanced by its position as one of the world's leading exporters of attack drones.[32] In addition, two of the global corporate powers in the world of electronic monitoring, Attenti and SuperCom, are based in Israel.

According to Israeli scholar Neve Gordon, one of the reasons behind Israel's outsized presence in the surveillance sector is that its decades-long occupation of Gaza and other territories, along with periodic wars, "provides a laboratory for testing and fine-tuning different commodities that are created, or different technologies."[33]

DAILY LIFE IN GAZA

Amnesty International has stated that "for half a century, Israel's occupation of the Gaza Strip has resulted in systematic human rights violations against Palestinians living there."[34] This occupation has a major impact on daily life for Palestinians in Gaza.

To begin with, in Gaza all Palestinians must carry digital IDs,[35] which are linked to a facial recognition database to block against the use of fake documents.[36] The boundaries with Israel are surveilled by Integrated Fixed Towers. These are mobile devices about eighty feet high and capable of seeing detail on objects up to eight miles away.[37] Elbit Systems, Israel's largest surveillance equipment manufacturer, produces these towers.[38] Company supervisor Oren Matzliach described the use of one of Elbit's app products like this: "[a battalion commander] inputs enemy target data to his smartphone or tablet, and will receive fire quickly, just like ordering a book on Amazon or a pizza in a pizzeria."[39] While no evidence exists that these towers use this app, the chilling equating of ordering a hit with ordering a pizza has serious implications for how the company's surveillance technology may be used in the future.

At present, police at checkpoints inside Gaza force Palestinians to produce ID, endure searches and interrogation, and face possible arrest or beatings. *Haaretz*, a major newspaper and information service in Israel, in 2019 claimed surveillance of Palestinians is "among the largest of its kind in the world. It includes monitoring the media, social media and the population as a whole."[40] Since Israel controls the import and export of goods to and from

Gaza, officials have gone so far as to create a list of foods that are banned for import.[41] The list includes items as innocuous as instant coffee and coriander.[42] At times, authorities have banned the import of fuel, creating a crisis in terms of delivering power and providing basic services including health care and the processing of sewage.[43] Apart from blocking trade, Israel exercises control over telecommunications in Gaza, limiting access to the internet, blocking social media, or tracking online posts to identify political opponents. Observers such as Helga Tawil-Souri have referred to Israeli control over telecommunications for Palestinians as "digital occupation."[44] As she observes, "the Israeli regime continuously produces, reproduces, shifts, and fine-tunes digital borders to dynamically enclose Gaza." Even international phone calls in Gaza must be routed through Israeli providers.[45] Activist Abdallah Abu Sharekh wrote on his Facebook page on June 23, 2017, "The reduction of internet hours in Gaza is a terrible violation of human rights and even a crime against humanity!"[46]

The situation of Palestinians living under Israeli occupation is so extreme that many analysts, including a 2017 team from the United Nations and Human Rights Watch, have argued that Israel's actions in the Occupied Territories of Palestine, which include Gaza, meet the criteria for apartheid[47] since Palestinians are restricted by an external power and, on the basis of nationality and ethnicity, do not have full and equal rights. International reports have also characterized Israel's actions in Gaza as "collective punishment" in violation of Article 33 of the Fourth Geneva Convention.[48] According to Professor Michael Lynk, a UN special rapporteur on the Occupied Palestinian Territory, "Collective punishment is an inflamed scar that runs across the entire fifty-three-year-old Israeli occupation of Palestine."[49]

OPEN-AIR PRISONS IN THE UNITED STATES

What lessons can we take from the open-air prison of Gaza?

At the moment, in the absence of a full-scale civil war, an exact replication of the open-air prison of Gaza seems unlikely in the United States. Yet the close relations and historical parallels between Israel and the United States open up a range of possibilities. Both Israel and the United States rely heavily on the military to enforce their political profile. In Gaza, the military intervenes directly, while in the United States, a militarized police force plays that on-the-ground role, with only an occasional presence of the military during times of uprisings. Another parallel is that both Israel and the United States are unrepentant settler-colonial regimes. As award-winning Native American historian Roxanne Dunbar-Ortiz reminds us in her epic book *Indigenous Peoples' History of the United States*, "In a settler society that has not come to terms with its past, whatever historical trauma was entailed in settling the land affects the assumptions and behaviors of living generations at any given time, including immigrants and the children of recent immigrants."[50] Thus, an open-air prison system in the United States will reflect, among other things, the historical trauma of the enslavement of African people, the conquests of territories that were once part of Mexico, and the genocidal warfare against Native Americans. In the late twentieth and early twenty-first centuries, the legacies of settler colonialism found expression in the xenophobic attacks on immigrants and the mass incarceration and mass criminalization of people of color. This is the foundation on which a regime of open-air prisons in the United States will be built. For the moment, the level of military aggression carried out in the Occupied Palestinian Territories does not appear a likely pathway for U.S. open-air prisons. Here authorities will rely on e-carceration along with more traditional forms of policing and imprisonment.

OPEN-AIR PRISON INFRASTRUCTURE IN UNITED STATES

A key piece of the infrastructure of open-air prisons in the United States is security cameras. The number of security cameras in the United States hit roughly 72 million in 2019, which translates to about one camera for every 4.6 persons.[51] Unlike in China, the bulk of these cameras are privately owned. Typically installed for security reasons, they are increasingly weaponized by property owners to monitor and keep away those who may not be seen as "suitable" for the neighborhood. An important example of this is Amazon's Ring app, which links a camera at a person's front door to a doorbell. When someone comes near the front door or rings the bell, the owner can see that person remotely, either via a camera in the house or from a device such as a phone from another location. Ring can integrate with another Amazon app, Neighbors, through which users can post videos of "suspicious activity" and crimes outside their house to people within a five-mile radius. *Vox* reporter Rani Molla referred to Neighbors as part of a collection of "fear-based social media apps whose focus on crime gives people the mistaken perception that crime is rising" when it is at an extremely low level.[52] "Working together we can all help to make our neighborhood safer," came the call from a video ad for Ring.

In 2019, a journalist's investigations revealed that not only were these devices connected to phones, but they were networked to police databases in over 1,300 law enforcement agencies. Police also had a tool to request access to the footage recorded on household Ring cameras. While advertisements for these devices targeted "porch pirates," activists worried about the potential of these technologies to racially profile those doing everything from looking for yard work to campaigning for political candidates to participating in nearby demonstrations. Myaisha Hayes, campaign strategies director for MediaJustice, one of the organizations leading the campaign against Ring, argued that the platform provided police with "unprecedented access to data recorded by its video doorbell devices, effectively bringing police surveillance to our front doors."[53] She claimed this was "digitizing racial profiling while perpetuating the routine criminalization and over-policing that communities of color already face." In Hayes's view, Amazon was "fueling its surveillance empire" by stoking a false panic about rising crime."[54] As policy analyst Matthew Guariglia of the Electronic Frontier Foundation, a privacy watchdog, notes, "Once you have a centralized network of cameras that police can easily have access to without a warrant, you essentially have a police CCTV network by another name."[55] Some analysts refer to this as "digital stop and frisk."[56] Policing expert and researcher Brendan McQuade elaborates further on Guariglia's observations, emphasizing that facial recognition is the key component of this process, because if a person's face is identified in a certain place, everything about them can be connected to any data referring to that place and everyone who is present.[57] This is one of the central ways in which the network of technologies that feed into e-carceration can function to intensify open-air imprisonment.

PRISONS BY ANOTHER NAME

As the technologies of e-carceration spread and the notion of open-air prisons in U.S. cities has become more widely accepted, a number of analysts have attempted to label and describe what is taking place. An important strand of writing emphasizes the expansion of mass supervision. In their inspiring book, *Prison by Any Other Name*, writer-activists Victoria Law and Maya Schenwar point out the ways in which reformist programs and social service agencies have become sites of carceral practices, embodying the punishment paradigm rather than any notions of healing, personal development, or even rehabilitation. They describe how "locked buildings are being replaced with slightly less-menacing locked buildings, [and] brutal surveillance with surveillance that may appear less brutal."[58] Law and Schenwar also point out how proponents of such programs frame their ventures in the carceral humanist language of "helping" or providing "support." As an example, Law and Schenwar highlight the way that many drug treatment programs, mental health centers, and anger management courses are geared far more toward control and profitability than removing people from the revolving door of poverty and the prison-industrial complex. "In the context of probation and electronic monitoring," they write, "community" supervision means being confined outside prison walls."[59]

Researcher Brendan McQuade also frames this issue in terms of mass supervision. McQuade argues that mass supervision is not only about "managing surplus populations"; it is also part of restructuring the state, shifting power away from social welfare into high-tech administration, a structure that he calls "authoritarian statism." At the heart of this authoritarian state sits the supervision and surveillance apparatus, largely the technologies of e-carceration. Optimistically, he suggests this is a "passing development," a "morbid stage" that will wither away.[60]

While the term "mass supervision" does indicate the scope of these technologies, it doesn't quite capture the punitive nature of this process. The activists of the volunteer-run group Stop LAPD Spying Coalition offer an alternative terminology. They position open-air prisons as part of the formation of a "surveillance bureaucracy" acting on behalf of a "stalker state." They argue that the development of such a bureaucratic stratum cannot be part of a reform process, that "entrusting the state to regulate surveillance" legitimizes its right to sur-veil and opens the doors to further extending the use of data for profit-making.[61] Radical im-migration rights activists like Mijente and Just Futures Law prefer to describe the expansion of mass surveillance under ICE as "digital prisons."[62] As the technologies of e-carceration expand, the search for terms that fully capture the punitive nature of this technology, its per-vasive quality without neutralizing it will continue.

DISABILITY RIGHTS AND CARCERAL ENCLOSURES

In considering decarceration and open-air prisons, disability rights activist and theorist Liat Ben-Moshe draws our attention to the history of efforts to deinstitutionalize mental health and developmentally disabled people in the late twentieth century. In her view, these ef-forts were successful in terms of closing lockup mental health hospitals and releasing people who were confined in them. However, plans and rhetoric of deinstitutionalization featured community-based mental health facilities that didn't materialize. Instead, two destructive options arose to serve the needs of those who were no longer confined in mental health institutions: psychotropic drugs and prisons. By the early 2000s, jails and prisons had be-come the dumping ground for people with mental health challenges. Moreover, according to Ben-Moshe, with the growing push for decarceration and the closing of prisons and jails, many programs that focus on people with mental health challenges or disabilities have moved people from behind bars to what she calls "carceral enclosures." These include the many group homes and nursing facilities that require all who are admitted to take psychotropic medications.

Some group homes intensely surveil sexuality and compel women residents to take birth control pills.[63] For Ben-Moshe, carceral enclosures refer "not only to physical spaces of con-tainment but to particular logics and discourses" that lead to deprivation of liberty in ways other than restriction of movement. Her perspective and that of other disability rights ana-lysts adds a new dimension to the understanding of confinement, a mental and psychological incarceration created by medical and chemical interventions.[64]

FUTURE COMMODIFICATION OF BODIES

In this chapter we have seen how e-carceration involves a network of punitive technologies that can be weaponized in numerous ways to punish targeted individuals and communities. But these technologies also suggest a new form of the commodification of human bodies. In the prison system of mass incarceration, some bodies (though not the majority) were used as cheap labor for corporations. Other bodies helped keep the prison system going through their labor by performing basic maintenance, cooking, and menial office work inside the institution. They made mass incarceration affordable for the state and helped, at least in many states, to subsidize the bloated wages of prison staff who earned far more than the market would have otherwise dictated. But as we move deeper into e-carceration, the commodification of bodies takes a different turn. Instead of being commodified as labor, bodies are becoming commodified as data. And as billionaire tech investor and TV personality Mark Cuban reminds us, "data is the new oil, the new gold." Not surprisingly, as is the case with oil rig workers and miners, the wealth from this commodity does not go to those who deliver the raw material to the marketplace but to those who own the process and have the power to scrape people's data: the Amazons, Palantirs, and Googles of the world. In the next chapter we will examine their future strategies for commodifying that data and turning it into the grist for the speculative investment mill.

10

DATA PROFITEERING FROM
THE BODIES OF THE CRIMINALIZED

I believe that the power of making money is a gift from God. . . . I believe it is my duty to go on making money and still more money, and to use the money I make for the good of my fellow man according to the dictates of my conscience.

—*John D. Rockefeller, oil magnate, interviewed in 1905*[1]

The first 50 years of Silicon Valley, the industry made products—hardware, software—sold them to customers, [it was a] nice, simple business. For the last 10 years, the biggest companies in Silicon Valley have been in the business of selling their users.

—*Roger McNamee, author of* Zucked: Waking Up to the Facebook Catastrophe[2]

On September 6, 1781, the British ship *Zong* set sail for Jamaica from the West African city of Accra with 470 enslaved Africans on board. Aiming to maximize profits, Captain Luke Collingwood overloaded the vessel with Black bodies. After more than two months at sea, supplies of food and water began to dwindle. When the ship hit "the Doldrums," an area in the Atlantic so named for the periodic absence of winds encountered there, people started to die of sickness and starvation. When it was determined that seventeen crew members and fifty enslaved people were dead, the captain made a momentous decision: he ordered 122 of the African captives thrown overboard. Ten other Black people threw themselves into the water rather than face the rest of the journey. The captain apparently called jumping overboard "an act of defiance."

When the ship arrived in Jamaica, the owner filed an insurance claim for the loss of "cargo" en route. This was the beginning of a long series of legal battles where experts debated, among other things, whether the managers of the *Zong* enterprise had packed enough food and water to equip the journey. In the first legal round, a Jamaican court found in favor of the owners, but a subsequent appeal by the insurers swung the pendulum in their favor.

Subsequently, the renowned British abolitionist Granville Sharp attempted to force criminal charges against the captain, crew, and owners. This effort brought a sharp rebuke from the bewildered solicitor general, Justice John Lee, who asked, "What is this claim that human people have been thrown overboard? This is a case of chattels or goods. Blacks are goods and property; it is madness to accuse these well-serving honourable men of murder. . . . The case is the same as if wood had been thrown overboard."[3]

The *Zong* massacre, as historians have labeled it, represented a turning point in the struggle against slavery in Britain. While the incident highlights the dehumanization of African people and the greed of slave traders, it also provides a key to understanding how financial markets intersect with systems of oppression. Enslaved Black bodies were not only used for insurance claims; they were collateral for credit. When slave traders bought Black bodies, they often used British manufactured goods as the medium of exchange. Merchants were willing to extend credit to the slave traders for those goods because they knew that the bodies to be captured in the future would fetch a return in the marketplace. Some historians estimate that traders paid for 70 percent of the goods they bought with credit based on the future capture of Black bodies.[4] This form of a futures market, financially similar to how farmers might secure loans against the future slaughter of livestock, became central to the economy of global capitalism. The financial flows from the slave trade played a vital role in the growth of the British banking industry. They heralded a shift from an economy based almost completely on trading goods and services to one that relied heavily on profits from the financial sector. Historians Zenia Kish and Justin Leroy conclude that the slave trade's greatest contribution to the English economy was "the evolution of financial institutions whose innovation and persistence was due to the fact that their use was not restricted to the slave trade; they could be applied to any kind of industry in a credit economy."[5]

The financial instruments catalyzed by the event lasted long beyond enslavement. Apart from creating new financial instruments that used Black bodies as collateral, the massacre heralded a series of reforms of the conditions of slavery that reduced the harm and propelled the movement toward abolition. The *Zong* massacre spurred Granville Sharp to help organize a flurry of petitions to Parliament that were critical of the slave trade. Partially as a result of his advocacy, Parliament passed the Slave Trade Act of 1788, described by historian Jane Webster as "the first attempt in over 200 years of British slave trading to regulate the business by law."[6] In terms that echo measures of mild contemporary prison reforms, the Slave Trade Act addressed overcrowding by limiting the number of enslaved people allowed on a ship to 1.67 enslaved people per ton, up to a maximum of 207-ton burden.[7] (As a point of comparison, according to Webster, there were 4.0 people per ton on the *Zong*.)[8] The act also curtailed insurance language that allowed owners to receive payment for death to an enslaved person due to "all other Perils, Losses and Misfortunes."[9] "All other Perils" included throwing enslaved people overboard. At the heart of this matter was the extent to which the corporations of the day should be held accountable for any harm done, including mass Black death, through their commercial activities.

MASS INCARCERATION AND THE *ZONG*

Fast-forward to the era of mass incarceration. Angela Davis and Ruth Wilson Gilmore have shed light on the political economy of mass incarceration, depicting in great detail what they call the prison-industrial complex (PIC), a system that connects a range of elected leaders, government bureaucrats, financial institutions, and corporations who have accumulated power and profits through the caging of bodies. These bodies are disproportionately Black, but prisons, jails, and detention centers welcome all bodies. As we move deeper into the digital age, we find that the bodies of the criminalized, like the enslaved people on the *Zong*, can become sources of profit through the creation and restructuring of financial markets. Investors are working to develop vehicles to exploit the bodies of incarcerated populations and other sectors of the criminalized sector of the working class—not for their labor, or even their presence in a prison cell, but for their data. The harvesting of data by brokers such as Thomson Reuters and LexisNexis has been well documented. Even state governments are profiting by selling the data of their customers.[10] In 2020 the state of Pennsylvania made $90 million through the sale of information about the state's licensed drivers. A similar transaction by the Pennsylvania Department of Motor Vehicles in 2013 included 36 million photographs.[11]

Yet simple sales of data may not be enough to satisfy profiteers. Investors may be moving beyond straightforward selling of data. We are in the early days of the creation of speculative investment vehicles based on our data. However, we already have an experimental vehicle, the social impact bond (SIB)—also known as a life bond or a Pay for Success, or PfS, scheme—which is a worthy successor to the enslavement insurance schemes of the *Zong* era. Not surprisingly, the first such bond was launched in a prison.

SOCIAL IMPACT BONDS AND PAY FOR SUCCESS

Social impact bonds are financial vehicles that aim to attract investments from wealthy people or companies in programs directed at social change. Starting with a stated goal of addressing poverty and inequality, investors use SIBs to inject capital into welfare projects in the hope of gaining a profit as well as securing bragging rights for doing good deeds. SIBs are a form of speculation where the investors aim to profit by accurately "speculating" on the outcome of chosen social service programs. These bonds emerged in the wake of the economic crisis of 2008 and the ensuing populist Occupy Wall Street movement. The central message of

Occupy was that the United States had become a society in which a layer of the super-rich, whom Occupy labeled the "1 percent," were ruthlessly dominating the other 99 percent of the population. But Occupy was not confined to the United States. The framing of Occupy found a foothold across Europe, as well as in Australia and South Africa. Occupy had an important impact on public consciousness. Although causation in shifts of public opinion is difficult to isolate, Pew Research showed that the percentage of people in the United States who perceived "strong" or "very strong" conflicts between the rich and poor rose from 47 percent in 2009 to 66 percent in 2011.[12]

Although venture capitalist Thomas Perkins subsequently claimed the "progressive war on the American one percent" might lead to a Nazi-style "pogrom" of billionaires, Warren Buffett and Bill Gates saw the moment differently.[13] They looked for a course of action that might improve their public image. Buffett and Gates came up with "The Giving Pledge," a measure that aimed to "help shift the norms of philanthropy to give more and . . . give in smarter ways." In that founding document, Gates and Buffett joined with thirty-eight others from the ranks of the super-rich and committed to "giving the majority of their wealth to philanthropy."[14] To qualify as a signatory, a person had to have at least $1 billion in personal wealth. Although the pledge was merely a moral commitment and not legally binding, by 2020, it had drawn 211 signatories from twenty-four countries. Nothing in the document even specified whether the donations were to be made immediately or willed after death. Signatories to the pledge included Richard Branson, founder of Virgin Atlantic, and his wife Joan; investment and media mogul Michael Bloomberg; the late David Rockefeller, head of Chase Manhattan Bank; and Facebook founder Mark Zuckerberg and his wife, pediatrician Priscilla Chan. At the time, the media lavished praise on the initiative, with *Fortune* magazine concluding that "society cannot help but be a beneficiary here."[15] Trevor Neilson, president of the Global Philanthropy Group, a consultancy that advises philanthropists, offered the optimistic "Ten Reasons Why the Giving Pledge Will Reshape Philanthropy."[16]

As with the debates and attempts at market regulation that took place within the British investment circles after the *Zong* massacre, these moves by Buffett and Gates were part of a dual process of continuity and change. The continuity was committing to keep doing business as usual. The change was framing it in a new way. This new frame would allow the development of investment vehicles that could mean new profit-making opportunities that could simultaneously be cast as reform. This is where social impact bonds entered the fray as tools to refresh capitalism—by finding new ways of profiting from the populations that global capitalism had already impoverished. In the wake of the global economic crisis of 2008, leaders across the board began to explore social impact bonds. Like the Slave Trade Act of 1788, this would reduce relatively minor harms caused by the system but keep it intact.

In October of 2011, President Barack Obama called a meeting of over sixty corporate leaders and philanthropists at the White House to discuss "impact investing." Obama allocated $100 million for SIBs in his 2012 budget, then leveraged $65 million more from the private and nonprofit sectors. The Rockefeller, Bloomberg, and Laura and John Arnold foundations were key players in the Obama plan.[17]

The dialogue continued into May of 2012, when thirty-five of the Giving Pledge signatories gathered in Santa Barbara, California, to discuss "impact investing," or how to invest money to make profits and do good at the same time—"doing good while doing well" in the parlance of investors. Some of the key programs targeted for such investment were education, medical research, and—of course—poverty.[18] These were primarily areas where the corporate sector argued that public-sector provision was failing to deliver. But while the 1 percenters in the United States were still talking about impact investing, their counterparts in the UK had moved into action.

THE FIRST SOCIAL IMPACT BOND

Just three months before the Giving Pledge became public, the first social impact bond launched in the UK at Peterborough prison, located in the city of the same name about eighty-five miles north of London.

The goal was to raise private finance for a program that would provide support for the rehabilitation of people returning from prison. The central partners in the venture were the

British Ministry of Justice and the UK-based charity St Giles Trust, which was charged with project oversight. Their project, One Service, provided case workers to help people newly released from prison to develop a life plan. One Service also provided continuing support for these life plans over the course of the first year after release. The organizers raised five million pounds (approximately $8 million) from seventeen trusts and foundations for the effort, including the U.S.-based Rockefeller Foundation.[19] A report on the project by the RAND Corporation noted the motivation of investors: "There was an appetite for mission-aligned investing among the charitable organizations."[20] These funds backed the setup and operating costs for the project. Investor return was linked to reducing the number of participants from the program who returned to prison, commonly called the "recidivism rate." The target of the plan was to reduce the recidivism rate of two thousand people with short sentences by 7.5 percent. If the rate fell by 7.5 percent or more, investors would get their investment money back plus an additional return as profit. The profit was generated from the money saved by the Ministry of Justice by not having to pay for the incarceration of these individuals. After five years, the recidivism rate had fallen by 9 percent, and the investors received a 3 percent annual rate of interest for the duration of the bond. The first social impact bond was declared a success.[21]

SOCIAL IMPACT COMES TO RIKERS ISLAND JAIL

The first attempt at a Peterborough type project in the United States took place at Rikers Island jail in New York in 2012. The Rikers SIB raised $9.6 million from Goldman Sachs for the Adolescent Behavioral Learning Experience (ABLE)—a cognitive therapy program for three thousand sixteen- to eighteen-year-olds incarcerated in the men's jail. Following an ethically questionable social science protocol, ABLE divided the cohort of three thousand into two groups. One group was provided a set of services, while the other group served as a control and did not receive services. The terms of the bond meant that if the recidivism rate of the fifteen hundred of those men receiving services fell by more than 10 percent over the course of three years as compared to the control group, the investors would receive a profit. A local nonprofit, Manpower Demonstration Research Corporation (MDRC), which had extensive experience in program evaluation, selected the service provider and monitored the program and its outcomes. The charity wing of former New York mayor Michael Bloomberg's corporate empire, Bloomberg Philanthropies, gave $7.2 million to help guarantee the bulk of the investment. The Vera Institute of Justice was the evaluator. At the close of the trial period in 2015, Vera evaluated the data and concluded that the program was not successful. Those who took part in the ABLE program fared no better in terms of recidivism than the control group. Hence, the investors got no return.[22]

Another important cautionary scheme, this time using the "Pay for Success" title, took place in Utah. In this case, a Goldman Sachs–funded program aimed to reduce the number of kindergartners "at risk" of landing in special education. This scheme's goal was to save the school district money for often costly special education programs. In its project report, Goldman Sachs claimed that the PfS scheme had helped 99 percent of the kindergartners avoid the special education stream. Investors received a payment for each of those children. Yet, when an investigative team from the *New York Times* examined the issue more carefully, they found that other such interventions typically only reduced special education enrollment by 10 to 20 percent, with the best-resourced programs achieving a maximum of a 50 percent reduction. Moreover, they found the method of identifying students who were "at risk" to be questionable. Essentially, a group of researchers concluded that the students in the Pay for Success scheme, rather than being "at risk," were unlikely to have ended up in special education even without the intervention. In this program, the bar for success was set at a 50 percent reduction, at which point Goldman Sachs would have received a 5 percent return on its investment. According to the *New York Times* report, that is a higher rate than school authorities would have paid if they had borrowed money through traditional channels rather than using Pay for Success.[23] Selectively choosing measures of success is key to Pay for Success schemes, a process that is ultimately the result of a negotiation between investors and the issuers of the bonds. For investors, the lower the bar, the more likely a return on their investment. If the bar for success is set very low, the bond may be evaluated in a positive light even though the program doesn't provide any meaningful change for its participants.

Despite the failure at Rikers and the dubious outcomes in Utah, social impact bonds, increasingly adopting the name of Pay for Success schemes, have mushroomed across the United States and internationally in recent years. Though still representing only a tiny sliver of global investment, by January 2019, there were 134 such projects globally, totaling $370 million of investment.[24] Initially, much as in the days of the *Zong* massacre, the most dehumanized bodies of our era, the incarcerated population, were the experimental subjects. But Pay for Success schemes were not confined to the criminal legal system. As in the Utah case, they spread across areas where the private sector claimed that the public sector was failing to deliver adequate services or lacked resources to operate effectively. According to "Learning from Experience," a report produced by MDRC, a key player in the Rikers Island bond, PfS should be used to support:

(1) an innovative new approach not previously tried,

(2) a program with mixed-to-good evidence about its effectiveness on a limited scale but no reliable evidence about effects at a large scale,

(3) a program with strong information establishing effectiveness at scale.[25]

Pay for Success schemes continue to develop, typically couching their efforts in the triumphalist language of "win-win-win." They promise that investors will "do well while doing good" by bringing resources to underfunded government programs and not-for-profits and improving the lives of participants. Housing, workforce development, health care, and early childhood development have become key areas for social impact investment.

However, the scale of these operations to date cast them more as experiments in novel investment mechanisms rather than serious vehicles for catalyzing social change. Much like the junk bonds of the 1980s or the internet start-ups of the 1990s, these are creative innovations looking for a way to pad the portfolios of Goldman Sachs, Morgan Stanley, and other players in the world of private equity and hedge funds. With the arrival of more sophisticated algorithms and risk assessment vehicles in the 2010s, the possibilities for creating speculative vehicles for investment from the data of the criminalized population will inevitably grow.

SIBs: WHO REALLY BENEFITS?

Focusing on metrics and rates of return on investment overlook the reality that these schemes are a learning lab for commodification of the bodies of the criminalized. The process of increasing profit and sharpening the ability to gather "evidence" to assess success will involve deepening the role of the technologies of e-carceration and the surveillance state. Data about individuals directly involved, such as the incarcerated populations at Peterborough and Rikers, as well as data of nonprofit providers, is surrendered to comply with the dictates of profitability. For most investors, the welfare and the privacy of participants are not important.

To date, the evaluation of PfS schemes has focused largely on project design with an emphasis on framing and selection of outcomes that can be readily linked to profit calculation.[26] For example, by choosing to measure recidivism, decision-makers were plunging into a decades-long debate over both defining and measuring this variable.[27] Determining how long a period a recidivism calculation should measure, plus whether it should include only convictions for new criminal offenses or should also cover violations of conditions of parole, has vexed criminologists for years.[28]

Another topic that surfaced in an evaluation done by Urban Institute analyst John K. Roman was the problem of "wrong pockets." This term refers to the strategy of choosing a measure of success that may save money for a department that is not part of the scheme.[29] For instance, if a youth education program aims to keep young people from going to jail, a successful project will accrue savings to the local authority that runs the jail, not necessarily the school or service provider where the program takes place.

IMPACT BONDS AND THE PUBLIC SECTOR

Despite the slow proliferation of SIBs, the model still has detractors. For instance, Stanford University political scientist Rob Reich classified the Giving Pledge as "not much more than a website, a letter and a promise."[30] But the Giving Pledge was not simply about remaking the image of the 1 percent. Like social impact bonds, the pledge had another agenda: inserting corporate power in spaces previously reserved for the state and its reservoirs of taxpayer dollars. Investment banker Josef Stadler, head of the Ultra High Net Worth division at global finance giant UBS, predicted that the increasing concentration of wealth in the hands of the rich would mean that they would substitute for public institutions when it came to "the big questions of our lifetime. [Only] they have the money." Data compiled by economist William Megginson concurs with Stadler's assertions. According to Megginson's findings, at the time social impact bonds emerged, the world was in the midst of a massive transfer of wealth that would see an estimated $2 trillion of once publicly owned assets shifted to private hands during the 2000–16 period.[31] Key drivers of this transfer were the 1 percenters who were not only seeking more profits but also believed they had a historic mission to save the world from state-run economies.

Megginson and research partner Jeffry Netter concluded that this amounted to the "transfer of responsibility for public goods and services from democratic institutions to the wealthy, to be administered by an executive class."[32] Sectors once controlled by the public sector such as energy, education, water, housing, health care, and transportation landed in the hands of for-profit companies. These transfers happened via outright privatization policies, corporate buyouts, public-private partnerships, corporatization of government departments, and other methods that enabled consolidation of mergers and acquisitions. These initiatives also reached into the provision of social welfare through vehicles such as social impact bonds.

Supporters of the Pay for Success model, such as the think tank Urban Institute, define it as "an innovating financing mechanism that shifts financial risk from a traditional funder, usually government, to a new investor . . . to improve outcomes for a vulnerable population."[33] In this simplistic rendering, PfS is a mechanism that either succeeds by earning a

profit or fails by not earning a profit. A key element missing from this value-neutral defi-
nition is the extent to which such initiatives undermine the role of the public sector, often
the primary source of service provision for the criminalized population who are typically
the "subjects" in social impact bonds. In a review of SIBs, Michael Roy, Neil McHugh, and
Stephen Sinclair, a multidisciplinary research team from Glasgow University, expressed great
concern over "the unintentional (or otherwise) effect of introducing the SIB model into the
realm of service delivery previously infused with a public-sector ethos." They contend that
introducing a profit incentive fundamentally changes the relationship between the service
provider and user, amounting to "an ideological shift in welfare service provision." They
characterize SIBs as both an archetypal "solution looking for a problem" and an illustration
of the cultural supremacy of market principles and their insertion into all aspects of everyday
life, including politics and policy.[34]

As organization studies experts Carl Rhodes and Peter Bloom contend, SIBs and other
market-based interventions by the super-rich, which they refer to as "philanthrocapitalism,"
ultimately create a "social justification of extreme wealth inequality, rather than any kind
of antidote to it." In their view, "despite the apparent proliferation of giving promised by
philanthrocapitalism, the so-called golden age of philanthropy is also an age of expanding
inequality."[35] In the world of social development, philanthrocapitalism acts much in the same
way as what we have labeled "carceral humanism" when describing certain kinds of reforms
in the criminal legal sphere. Promises of help and support in the end simply result in program
changes along with new labels and terminology, but ultimately restructure the system in ways
that do not impact the fundamental dynamics of power.

THE "INVISIBLE SPIDER WEB" OF DATA SNATCHING

The early SIB and PfS projects examined here were launched before the consolidation of
algorithmic computer power. Mass surveillance has laid the groundwork for a rich database
of criminalized human subjects poised to live under an extensive set of program data man-
dates, such as those contained in PfS schemes. A working class for whom, as author Virginia

Eubanks stresses, these databases are already linked and weaponized into the formation of a digital poorhouse:

> Think of the digital poorhouse as an invisible spider web woven of fiber optic strands. Each strand functions as a microphone, a camera, a fingerprint scanner, a GPS tracker, an alarm trip wire, and a crystal ball. They are interconnected, creating a network that moves petabytes of data.[36]

Eubanks sums up the function of these technologies as "targeting, tracking and punishing" poor people in ways that "divert attention from the need for social change and erode democracy for everyone." Social impact bonds add yet another function of these technologies: gathering data to develop profit-generating investment vehicles.

Vienna-based activist-researcher Wolfie Christl reached similar conclusions in his research on global corporate surveillance. He contended that these databases may "limit the chances and choices of individuals and lead to the discrimination and social exclusion of whole population groups." He goes on to note that "algorithmic decisions based on digital profiles may reinforce existing biases and social inequalities and even become self-fulfilling prophecies."[37]

With the power of Big Data, PfS designers can construct algorithms that predict what specific data correlate with a profit-making project, and cherry-pick participants by either sorting the population according to specific criteria or linking investment to project designs in line with the demands of the algorithm. For example, if the professed outcome in a PfS scheme is securing housing for people on parole, the applicant's risk level score might be increased by a history of eviction, presence on a sex offender registry, or a drug conviction. A risk assessment tool might also target association with certain individuals as problematic, such as alleged gang members, undocumented workers, or people with histories of mental illness. Hence, for the party investing in such a scheme, the exclusion of people with high-risk assessment scores owing to such factors would likely be seen as increasing the investment's chances of success. This could lead to a selection process that would leave the individuals with the most difficult housing challenges unsupported. A data set and an algorithm make these decisions, typically offering no avenues of appeal. As we have noted repeatedly, race, gender, and class bias are baked into the formulas of the risk assessment tools and other forms of high-powered e-carceration. These offer new frontiers for the weaponization and monetization of data, a form perhaps appropriate for insertion into a global capitalism that geographer David Harvey argues embodies the "financialization of everything."[38]

CHALLENGES OF BEING A DATA TARGET

The rise of Big Tech and Big Data subject the criminalized sector of the population to new vulnerabilities. As social impact or other investment vehicles continue to evolve, an ever-increasing demand for data will be part of the formula for success and for profitability. But for the individuals in SIB programs, data collection presents several issues.

First, there are privacy questions. The data collected for the program is fed to the cloud, but the next steps remain opaque. In most cases, the individual has no control over whether that data is shared or sold, or who may access it. Privacy vulnerabilities become more severe for those in the criminalized population who are subject to parole or other forms of carceral control. For these people, Fourth Amendment rights to protection from illegal search and seizure have already essentially been suspended. In the 2016 case of *Samson v. California* the U.S. Supreme Court concluded that people on parole "agree in writing to be subject to a search or seizure by a parole officer or other peace officer at any time of the day or night, with or without a search warrant, and with or without cause."[39] The "no knock" open-door policy applies not only to their person but to their residence, workplace, and other surroundings. For people who are under some form of carceral control or surveillance, social impact bonds may ultimately expand state and corporate access to data related to new aspects of their daily lives, without the requirement of even a digital search warrant.

Not surprisingly, these questions of privacy are also racialized. The demographics of the 4.5 million people under some kind of legally mandated supervision in the United States are extremely skewed. Although African American people make up just 13 percent of the U.S. adult population, they account for 30 percent of those on probation and 37 percent of those on some form of post-prison supervision.[40] A report by the Brennan Center for Justice also found that African American and "Hispanic"[41] individuals remain on probation and parole longer than similarly situated white people.[42]

Second, the investment angle inevitably links the person in the program to the goals of the investor. As Leroy and Kish note, "The metrics of success for such social finance instruments reveal that intimate aspects of the everyday lives of bonded subjects are accounted for, and made accountable to, investor expectations."[43] The assumption is that this is a win–win situation where, for example, non-recidivism is a victory for both the investor and the person in the program. But if the demands of the program force a person to keep a job in a chemical factory that endangers their health or work hours that may have negative consequences for their children, the interests of the investor and the person in the program may collide. Exactly what intimate aspects of daily life might an investor assess as indicators of success? Might they come to include sexual practices, manner of dress, gender identity, or family members with a history of incarceration? Who has the power to determine the data required for the risk assessment? Moreover, if a person remains out of jail but is unhoused, unemployed, has no access to health care, and endures constant hunger and illness, does that sole metric of statistical success have meaning for them?

Third, the use of the classic social science tool of a control group presents enormous ethical questions in these schemes. In certain situations control groups may be useful. However, in the social impact bond schemes, one group is being provided a service and the other group is being denied that service simply for the sake of calculating the profit for the investor. The ethical question emerges when considering who is being denied access to a service that the experimenters believe is likely to be helpful to them in their future life. A fundamental premise of any research project is to first "do no harm," but denying services to a group of people for the sake of creating a control group violates this principle.[44]

Lastly, those in charge of the program on behalf of the state or a supervisory nonprofit will have a strong incentive to ensure that people do not fail, and if the funding stream from the SIB is linked to money for their salary or the operations of their department, they may understandably be motivated to influence the outcome. For instance, they might put extra pressure on participants to generate the required data, or might be less prone to punish people who are in the investor-backed program than those who are not in the program. Alternatively, there may be incentives to systematically exclude some data sets if they don't produce the desired results. This situation could become even more complicated if those managing or overseeing the program targeted by the social impact bond have also invested in the project.

THE FUTURE OF SOCIAL IMPACT BONDS

As the capacity of the technologies of e-carceration and the surveillance state grows, the dimensions of SIBs and other investment schemes will also expand. Each new app or platform offers additional opportunities for profit-making from the data of the criminalized sectors of the working class. At least three major emerging technological developments will likely seriously impact the world of e-carceration, surveillance, and digital investment vehicles. All of them are already working at some level.

The first is blockchain, a digitized form of record keeping that compiles a permanent, encrypted, and internet-based record of every online transaction. Unlike many other files or data that are saved to the cloud, blockchain is publicly visible, but the identity of the person involved cannot be detected. Moreover, a blockchain entry cannot be altered once it is posted. Blockchain first came into the public eye as the core of Bitcoin, the digital currency. In accounting terms, blockchain was the ledger or record of all Bitcoin transactions. The details of blockchain are complicated, but through the use of algorithms and lots of computer power, each transaction completed is stored in a block of information that is immediately shared with many other users. The entire record of all blockchain transactions anywhere is stored online in code. While blockchain records are anonymous, they are potentially the source of huge amounts of data that can be run through algorithms to make predictions and other calculations. Many high-profile corporations are using blockchain. Walmart applies blockchain to track global food supplies while FedEx tracks high-value cargo with this technology. The Russian branch of Burger King has developed its own cryptocurrency, the WhopperCoin, to manage its rewards program. Not surprisingly, Giving Pledge founder Bill

Gates is in on the ground floor of blockchain, deploying this technology in Microsoft's cloud computing service, Azure.

Blockchain-based cryptocurrencies like Bitcoin, along with many online cash apps, are precipitating a steady reduction in the use of cash. This means everything we buy, sell, or trade will eventually leave a digital record, a data trail that can become a source of revenue for investors. The move away from cash has important global advocates. The "Better than Cash Alliance," based at the United Nations, aims to push for the "transition from cash to digital payments" as a way toward the inclusion of the 1.7 billion people worldwide who are outside the formal financial system.[45] The alliance brings together seventy-five partners including the European Bank for Reconstruction and Development, as well as major tech figures such as the Bill and Melinda Gates Foundation and corporate players such as Mastercard, the Gap, and Coca-Cola. The alliance's goal of inclusion is not a neutral one—such inclusion would mean the availability of 1.7 billion people's data to investors.[46]

The second development is the introduction of digital IDs. In the United States, several million people lack an official, state-issued form of identification.[47] This population is disproportionately people of color and includes much of the criminalized sector. Essentially, this leaves them out of the banking system, makes them ineligible for many public benefits, and in some states blocks them from voting. A digital ID might offer them access to some of those benefits but would also collect considerable data about their personal lives and their activities. As a result, the Real ID Act, which passed in the United States in 2005, has drawn resistance, delaying its implementation until 2023. Resistance in the United States has come from both progressive privacy rights groups like the American Civil Liberties Union and libertarian organizations like the Cato Institute, as well as former president Barack Obama.[48] A national ID would bring people into the digital loop but leave a large segment of the population—particularly undocumented or transgender people—vulnerable. In the European Union in 2011, eighty civil liberties organizations called for an investigation on the legality of national IDs that included biometrics.[49]

From an e-carceration standpoint, a national digital ID would provide government with even more power to monitor people's activities and charge them for services, and it could establish a more direct link between payment of benefits and performance of tasks or labor. Centralized digital IDs also lay the groundwork for systems of mass surveillance and punishment, as they could lead to the enforcement of penalties via wage garnishment for illegal actions, failure to pay debts, or even missing appointments with authorities such as parole or probation officers.

The third development is the spread of the internet of things (IoT), which we discussed briefly in chapter 1. For the most part, at the turn of the century, only devices such as smartphones, tablets, and computers could communicate with the internet. But two decades later, almost anything can be connected via an attached or embedded sensor. These connections mean a person using their phone can, among other things, remotely adjust the temperature in the house, turn on the oven, put a vacuum cleaner or lawn mower into action, close the curtains, or set the living room light's brightness and color. These sensors not only receive commands but feed their data into systems that analyze that data, send reports, and, if necessary, alarms. Currently, the marketing of IoT primarily focuses on consumer convenience and household security. However, the advent of COVID has given us hints about how these networked sensors could be used to monitor and control behavior. These sensors could, for example, track mask usage or social distancing and enforce penalties for violations.

With regard to social impact bonds, IoT could offer more data for the investor and more sets of criteria to impose on programs where they want to invest. Investors could establish the criteria, and agencies seeking the funding would have to comply. This creates a number of possible outcomes. As more and more data accrue to social investment bond projects, investors and bond writers will develop more sophisticated risk assessment tools. Such tools could be similar to the social credit scores in China that grade almost every daily activity and link performance to certain privileges such as air travel and entering restaurants.[50] Moreover, since social impact bonds now fall under the heading of speculative investment, the possibility of creating some kind of credit default swap also arises. In this case, instead of investing money in the bond itself, a fund manager could create an investment vehicle that allows investors to bet against the successful outcome of the program. This means there would be some investors betting on the initiative to succeed and some betting on it to fail. This is similar to sports betting where gamblers may bet on either team to win; however, with Pay for Success, the outcome is not the score of a game but the fate of an individual or a community. This development in the social impact sphere resonates with what took place in the subprime housing market in the 2008 economic crisis. Not only had investors been buying bundles of mortgages, they were creating derivative investment vehicles in which they invested in the likelihood of homeowners defaulting on their individual bonds. In other words, the home-owner's loss was the investor's gain. In SIBs dealing with probation, this would mean some investors would win if the person failed their probation and went back to jail. Perhaps the real crunch emerges if more investors are putting their money on failure than success, or if individuals working for the probation department were investing in these bonds.

Mainstream commentators and product marketers view the blockchain, digital IDs, and IoT through the lens of the comfortable classes, arguing that these technologies increase ef-ficiency, enhance safety, and add new dimensions of convenience. However, these develop-ments take on a different hue when applied to the criminalized sector of the population. For this sector, the log of the past provided by blockchain, especially if embedded into an ID, creates a permanent, readily accessible digital record of virtually every moment of their lives during which something negative happened—a conflict with authority, a failure in school, or enrollment in drug treatment. The past cannot be expunged or altered. By contrast, for many in the comfortable classes, such a background scan likely offers a far more positive portrait, perhaps with a significant job history, educational accomplishments, and few if any encoun-ters with the criminal legal system.

ZONG, MASS INCARCERATION, AND ABOLITION

We began this chapter with the story of the *Zong* and the commodification of Black bodies in the financial markets of the nineteenth century. Then we traced the rise of Big Tech, Big Data, and the advance of algorithms during the past decade, and the ways it expanded the reach of the surveillance state and the net of e-carceration. In a way, this was a repeat of his-tory, demonstrating how the drive for profits continually creates new ways to commodify everything, what renowned Marxist geographer David Harvey classified as the "wholesale commodification of nature in all its forms," including data generated by of the human body.[51]

Ten years after the signing of the Giving Pledge, a few signatories had fulfilled their promises. Chuck Feeney, the co-founder of the Duty Free Shoppers Group, had given away over $8 billion in the previous two decades, much of it in line with the pledge. By 2020, he was no longer a billionaire, lived in a "modest apartment" in San Francisco, and had ordered his personal foundation, the Atlantic Philanthropies, to spend all its money on working charities. The foundation followed his orders, making its last grant in 2016 and closing its doors in September of 2020. Feeney was the model of the Giving Pledge, as were Marc and Lynne Benioff of Salesforce fame, who gave away $200 billion between 2017 and 2019. But these were the exceptions. For most, the Giving Pledge was a tiny downward bump on a profit curve sloping steadily upward. Ironically, while giving was moving slowly, the sixty-two U.S. pledgers who signed in 2010 saw their combined assets grow from $376 billion in 2010 to $734 billion in 2020.[52] A detailed study of the signatories by the economic analysts of the progressive Institute for Policy Studies (IPS) argued that the Giving Pledge was at least as much about tax breaks as philanthropy, suggesting that little of the funding would reach grassroots efforts. The report suggested that the billionaires' assets were "growing too fast to give away." IPS concluded that most "donations are going either to private foundations controlled by family members" or to donor-advised funds, which maximize tax benefits. According to IPS, the efforts of Buffett and Gates to create a public image of a caring 1 percent had been sidetracked as the fortunes of their signatories expanded rather than diminished. Although the signatories of the Giving Pledge have not become universal backers of social impact bonds or Pay for Success schemes, they are on the hunt for ways to profit from the data of the criminalized sector of the working class. This will be a fitting legacy of the *Zong*: the weaponization of philanthropy against the poor via the platitudes of the 1 percent investing in "social change."

Although regulatory measures and electoral victories may slow down the forces of data-based investment vehicles, as with the restructuring of the financial system post-*Zong*, the commodification of the bodies of the criminalized continues to move ahead with the speed of an algorithmic calculation. The Slave Trade Act of 1788 might have limited how many Black bodies could be legally squeezed onto a ship, but ultimately, halting chattel slavery required a new paradigm, not regulations about overcrowding. In this era of mass incarceration, e-carceration offers a range of opportunities for the 1 percent and their allies to recast their project in the language of caring. Fighting these capitalist mutations requires a new paradigm, informed by liberation and abolition tailored to the digital age. This paradigm will include not only freeing incarcerated people but decriminalizing the vast sectors of the working class currently under the shackles of a rising risk assessment and algorithmic dictatorship. In the final chapter, we will consider some ways to imagine that new paradigm and how to build an alternative world as we walk into it.

PART THREE

ABOLITION AND E-CARCERATION

11

ABOLITION AND CHALLENGING E-CARCERATION

In 1858, a year before the Harpers Ferry raid, Lincoln opined that slavery would last for at least 100 more years—or at least until 1958 or the 1960s. It is important to note that Lincoln's prognostication was meant to appease the slavocracy. It was not an assessment of the counterrevolutionary dynamic that would detonate after the war. What this means, of course, is that abolitionists were truly remarkable people who saw beyond the present into a time not yet born.

—Mumia Abu-Jamal, U.S. political prisoner[1]

We believe that data must be reclaimed and reimagined. For those of us living on the margins, who have found a way to thrive in a country that has Black life dispensable and Black survival optional, data is protest, data is accountability and data is collective action.

—Yeshimabeit Milner, executive director, Data for Black Lives[2]

The idea for this book began when Mary from the Illinois Department of Corrections showed up at my house two days after my release from prison and stuck that ankle monitor on my leg.

That was the moment when I began to rethink what freedom meant. Just three nights earlier, the guards had come at midnight and told me to pack "my shit" and come out of my cell. I asked them where I was going and they said "to the lieutenant's office." I grabbed my bags of clothing and my legal papers and the handwritten manuscripts of my novels and headed to the lieutenant's office. They put me in the "box," a small portable jail cell about the size of a broom closet—not even wide enough to stretch my legs. I had spent six and a half years in prison, but now, for the first time, I felt claustrophobic, even had an urge to scream. It was midnight and they usually released people after breakfast. I kept my eyes closed, took deep breaths, and tried to ignore the possibility of being in that box for the next eight hours just so they could have one last round of punishment.

Before I got to the screaming stage, the two guards took me out of the cage and we walked out into the warm night air, under the desert sky, to the front gate of the prison—a place I had not seen since I arrived at High Desert State Prison three years earlier. Another guard standing behind a counter gave me a box with my "dress out clothes." I stripped off the pants and shirt with "prisoner" written all over them and dressed myself up like the human being that I knew my mother, my partner, my sons, and my other loved ones wanted me to be once again. A blue dress shirt, black socks, some casual brown shoes, and an off-white jacket. The cop gave me my gate money—the standard $200 in twenties, plus the $3.17 that I had in my prison account. Then I went out into the night again and walked, without chains or cuffs or any restraints, to a black SUV. Some white guy who looked like everyone who worked at the prison told me to get in and we started to drive down the road, into the darkness of the high desert. Not a car or human being was in sight. The only lights came from the prison and they were fading into the background. I asked what the plan was, and he said, "We've got one but I can't tell you what it is." I kept scouring the brush on each side of the road, looking for truckloads of Ku Klux Klan members or any other white supremacist group I knew wouldn't mind seeing my carcass in a ditch. I fantasized the headline, "Former Fugitive Shot Trying to Escape." I took a deep breath, and in fifteen minutes we were in downtown Susanville at the parole office. A couple other white guys who looked like everyone who worked at the prison greeted me and had me fill out a bunch of forms.

Twenty minutes later, my wife walked down the hall, and we hugged and kissed in front of the gawking guys who looked like everyone who worked at the prison. They had probably never seen a white man kiss a Black woman before. When we walked out of the office, my partner started shouting for joy. I kept quiet. I thought for sure they would arrest us in this rural prison town where I imagined that everyone looked like somebody who worked at the prison. But I did feel free. I held that feeling on the three-hour drive to Reno, through my first night's sleep under soft sheets with a loving person next to me, then through the mountains to San Francisco, and through the airport on the flight to Illinois, where my family lived and where I would be serving my parole. I held that feeling as I visited my new home for the first time and hugged my mother and my two sons. I held that feeling until they put that device on my leg two days later, and then I realized that I would never quite feel free again, that there would always be some device, some trick, some twist of fate that would bind me to them. Probably race and class privilege had prevented me from realizing that before.

But the monitor got me thinking about all that, and I have been thinking about it ever since, about what it would be like to *not* have that feeling. It took me a couple years, though, to realize these thoughts were pushing me down a new ideological path, a view of the world that would help me to understand a lot about the dynamics of my six and half years in prison, about the reason they put this shackle on my ankle, why a punitive, money-sucking, racist system like the California Department of Corrections and Rehabilitation had even been able to exist. Those ideas were called abolition.

The uprisings of 2020 sparked a huge interest in abolition. As with many ideas that gain rapid popularity, abolition has taken on many different meanings for many people. For some people, abolition resounds as a personal philosophy, a method of dealing with the complexity and oppression of the twenty-first century, a tool to deliver inner peace and wellness. Looking at the challenges of daily life through the lens of abolition can definitely help people avoid resorting to violence or revenge in solving problems. But more importantly, abolition can inspire building community, constructing a political project. As activist and Critical Resistance co-founder Rachel Herzing notes, "A person may say: I want to do abolition in my house . . . that means I am going to make pickles. We're going to have a fermenting closet. . . . [This is] not the same as advancing an abolitionist politics. We want to transform society." Herzing stresses that if "we don't have our eyes on structural aspects," then we are not addressing the fundamental problems of people who are "vulnerable to state-sanctioned violence." Our aim is "abolition of the entire nexus of the prison-industrial complex."[3]

Central to any notion of abolition is the eradication of white supremacy. As Angela Davis stresses, "Attempting to undo the harm of policing and prisons without attending to these immense embodiments of systemic racism is doomed to failure." Ultimately, abolition calls for a total transformation of how we view the world and how we engage daily life. Having experienced six and a half years in prison, imagining abolition as a world without prisons made immediate sense to me. But Ruth Wilson Gilmore and Angela Davis have added another dimension by reminding us that abolition is about absence and presence. The absence goes beyond prisons and even police to include the absence of technologies of unfreedom—e-carceration, surveillance, and the weapons of war. Perhaps most importantly, abolition must be about the absence of the urge to continue to use these punitive, impoverishing, destructive tools. Researchers Fred Moten and Stefano Harney stress that abolition is "not so much the abolition of prisons but the abolition of a society that could have prisons, that could have slavery, that could have the wage, and therefore not abolition as the elimination of anything but abolition as the founding of a new society."[4] And such a new society would not imagine putting electronic shackles on people to track every move and record every biometric. Data gathering and observation would be dedicated to building healthy communities, advancing equity in distribution of goods and services, and preserving the planet; in short, developing the freedom to thrive. If we collected biometrics at all, it would not be tracking heart rates and voice cadence to predict criminal acts but to provide support for wellness.

As with nuclear weapons, many of these technologies cannot be re-tooled into vehicles for positive change. No matter how far artificial intelligence and machine learning may advance, the system will not reset itself. This change requires a mass movement, led primarily by people who have been most oppressed by racial capitalism and e-carceration; people with imagination, determination, organization, and a global vision acknowledging that the future of the planet and all humanity are at stake. No one can do abolition alone.

Instead of imagining a world without technology, we must recognize that technology is not inherently good or bad. Rather, it is how we design and use that technology that poses the challenge. In the context of abolition, we need to imagine a world where technology sustains the planet and the human spirit; operates in the service of eliminating racism, gender-based oppression, ableism, militarism, and imperialism; technology that builds relationships, cooperation, and collectivity. To do this we need to escape the prison of our existing imagination, which all too often channels us into tweaking the status quo rather than building anew. I suggest five key targets for action that will help to more concretely imagine what the abolition of the technologies of e-carceration means. You may think of others.

1. ABOLITION MEANS DISMANTLING THE POWER OF BIG TECH

The starting point for abolition in regard to e-carceration is the elimination of Big Tech as the owners and stewards of information technology. Google, Amazon, Microsoft, Facebook, and their Big Tech allies form the largest conglomerate of corporate power and wealth in human history. They control our technology and, all too often, our ability to imagine. Their CEOs can appear unassuming, even antithetical to capitalism; they may sometimes wear designer T-shirts instead of suits and come up with cool gadgets, but, in fact, they are no different from the robber barons of previous eras. The fundamental truth of capitalist accumulation holds: wealth comes through the suffering of workers and marginalized populations via expropriation of their labor power, resources, and humanity. Bill Gates, Jeff Bezos, and Mark Zuckerberg are the global robber barons of our era, building their empires on data and technology instead of oil and steel. They may devise clever schemes and marketing strategies, but they will ultimately use every weapon in their arsenal to defend their "right" to wealth and power. In their brief period of existence, they have already shown themselves to be reliant on and comfortable with the super-exploitation of workers both in the United States and abroad, to at best pay minimal attention to resisting white supremacy, to profiteer from gender stereotyping in employment practices and product marketing, and to mobilize their corporate resources in the interest of deepening the power of the U.S. global military machine.[5]

They will follow the dictum used by many revolutionaries—by any means necessary. They will bring armies of consultants, technology experts, and lawyers, and, if need be, armies of the most advanced military forces the world has ever seen to defend their privilege. They will engage in debate about change, but discussion will never persuade them to transform. Research papers and Twitter storms alone will not bring them down, but they may respond to the power of mass movements that wield a counter political power. We have seen snapshots of the power of such movements in recent times with Black Lives Matter, #MeToo, and the 2020 uprising. In the past, movements such as organized labor, women's liberation, and Black Power have shown the capacity to confront the state and advance an alternative narrative.

Although the robber barons of the 1800s employed private police forces such as the notorious Pinkerton National Detective Agency, known simply as "the Pinkertons," to defend their property, Big Tech doesn't need to outsource policing, or at least not the technology of policing and surveillance. They are its owners and authors. As long as they control the technology and the ideology that shapes technology, abolition or even significant reform will remain a fanciful dream rather than a light at the end of a very long tunnel. Even when Big Tech cleverly packages their exploitation and destruction as an online Amazon shopping experience of "everything to everybody," in a Gates Foundation call for proposals to meet Grand Challenges in Global Health, or in the SIB's motto of "doing good while doing well," they still rely on the technologies of e-carceration—the weaponization of data. This means that an abolitionist agenda must include strategies to challenge both the technologies of e-carceration and the political actions of these companies. While addressing the race, gender, and anti-worker biases of these companies represents an almost insurmountable task, equally daunting is confronting their role in facilitating and promoting the type of disinformation that proliferated during moments like the 2016 U.S. presidential election. Measures such as Twitter's application of fact-checking labels to the tweets of then president Trump or Google's pledge to invest a paltry $30 million to fight online misinformation are far from transformative responses.

Dismantling Big Data includes more than campaigning against companies. The institutions of the state that drive the power of surveillance, incarceration, policing, and the military are the heart and soul of e-carceration. Dismantling Big Tech also means dismantling the state institutions that perpetuate the power of Big Tech, from Homeland Security to the CIA to the Department of Defense. As activist Sarah T. Hamid reminds us, "We organize against carceral institutions, actors and systems, not surveillance."[6]

2. ABOLITION MEANS CONFRONTING REFORM

Many technologies of e-carceration, including electronic monitoring, first emerged as reforms, as efforts to fix the system rather than abolish it. Abolition means developing a specific approach to dealing with these reforms. We need to fight for change in the present, but it has to be change tied to a vision of the future. As the great Trinidadian Marxist C.L.R. James argued, we look for the future in the present and build on that.[7] The prison-industrial complex will not disappear overnight, but certain changes along the way can both reduce the harm done by the system and educate people further about the need for systemic change.

An essential strategic decision, then, is determining which reforms to support. Many abolitionists use a term created by European philosopher and activist André Gorz and popularized by Ruth Wilson Gilmore in the world of abolition: "non-reformist reform." This type of reform undermines the logic and power of the system without adding new forms of punishment and harm. Such reforms often embody what I refer to as "carceral humanism," the old wine of punishment with a new bottle labeled "caring and service."

Activists such as Mariame Kaba, Marbre Stahly-Butts, and Dean Spade, as well as the pathbreaking abolitionist organization Critical Resistance, have all suggested key questions to ask about specific reforms to determine if they are non-reformist.[8] Do they reduce the power of the police and the prison system? Do they decrease resources for the prison-industrial complex, policing, and the military? Do they increase the power of grassroots organizations, especially those led by directly impacted populations? In regard to e-carceration, do these reforms enable Big Tech to grab more of our data? Do they expand the power and wealth of Big Tech? Of the surveillance state? These questions further mandate that a non-reformist reform should reduce the number of people who are incarcerated—including the e-carcerated—and mobilize people to fight for further systemic change. Some concrete examples might help clarify how this notion of reform relates to e-carceration.

THE PRACTICE OF NON-REFORMIST REFORM

We have noted that as the critique of mass incarceration grew in the 2010s, many policy makers and activists pushed to reduce jail populations through reducing or eliminating bail. Electronic monitoring was one of the first measures to emerge as a vehicle to decrease jail populations. Community Justice Exchange (CJE), a national abolitionist network of bail funds, opposed the introduction of such measures. Pilar Weiss, the executive director of CJE, contended that "if you are fighting for pretrial freedom systematically, you have to care about electronic monitoring. . . . You are fighting these conditions they put on release."[9] The Chicago Community Bond Fund (CCBF), a member of CJE, similarly rejected EM and looked for ways to fight it.

After years of work by CCBF and other organizations dedicated to ending cash bail, in 2017, Cook County chief judge Timothy Evans issued General Order 18.8A. This order aimed to ensure that no one remained in jail solely because they could not afford a money bond. This measure contributed to a great reduction in the jail population, from over 7,500 people to fewer than 5,800 in seventeen months. This was a significant, historic reform, but CCBF ensured that it became a *non-reformist* reform by gathering their own data to track the impact of 18.8A and using it to hold authorities accountable. To accomplish this, CCBF trained court watchers, who attended bond hearings and recorded the results. CCBF activists also gathered the stories of those who were released as a result of 18.8A. Their research showed that freeing people without cash bond had no significant impact on people reoffending or failing to make their court appearances. It also tracked the impact of individuals released on monitors. In the 2017 CCBF report *Punishment Is Not a Service*, the authors noted that many of the conditions of pretrial services and electronic monitoring "tend to replicate the punitive restrictions of incarceration rather than allowing individuals to maintain their rights before trial." In other words, the reform of electronic monitoring was creating new forms of incarceration. *Punishment Is Not a Service* particularly targeted the conditions of electronic monitoring as "often arbitrary and unnecessarily restrictive," frequently preventing people from "maintaining a job, caring for their children, interacting with their community and even receiving medical care." The report also highlighted the racial bias of the risk assessment tool used by the Cook County courts, noting that the chosen risk factors, such as previous arrests, simply further compounded "the injustices endured by Black, brown and poor Chicagoans" and reduced the lived experience of structural racism in Chicago to a data point.[10]

CCBF's work provides important examples of non-reformist reform. Had the bond fund merely pushed for reducing the jail population and nothing else, local authorities would have simply released people only to place them under strict programs of e-carceration. Such programs would have either landed them back in jail or had significant negative impacts on their quality of life, causing additional harm and trauma. Moreover, the uncontested expansion of electronic monitoring would have catalyzed further use of such technologies, widening the net of incarceration.

Exposing the shortcomings of reform requires follow-up and follow-through, which includes gathering data and collecting the stories of impacted people. CCBF carefully monitored the impact of these changes by mobilizing community members to become the watchdogs of the court process. Their follow-up included recording the stories of individuals like Lavette Mayes, who spent 121 days on an electronic monitor on pretrial release. In the end, Mayes accepted a plea bargain she did not want because the conditions of the monitor were imposing too many hardships on her children and family. As she described it, "my whole family was being incarcerated because of this."[11] CCBF's work acknowledged that people like Lavette Mayes had been directly impacted by both pretrial incarceration and e-carceration. They not only supported Mayes with money for bond, but provided her with a platform to tell her story to thousands of people. Hence, CCBF's abolitionist approach included both developing a framework of analysis and putting it into practice, constantly reflecting on their progress toward system transformation. In the words of Mariame Kaba, a mentor to many CCBF activists, "abolition is something that I, and everyone really, practice daily."[12] That daily practice means constant self-evaluation.

Determining the difference between non-reformist reform and reformist reform is not always easy. Debates over this issue have arisen in attempts to use legislation to challenge e-carceration. Because many of these technologies remain in operation, the question for abolitionists becomes a matter of strategy and tactics. Should they fight in the short run to regulate these technologies and reduce their harm? Or should they totally reject such reforms because they normalize the existence of these devices and the rights of the state and corporations to use them?

In a number of jurisdictions, activists have fought to eliminate a key weapon of e-carceration: the use of facial recognition software. Their argument has been that this technology has no positive use. This has resulted in the prohibition of the use of facial recognition software by city authorities in San Francisco and Somerville, Massachusetts. California, New Hampshire, and Oregon have all banned the use of facial recognition in police body cameras.[13] In 2021 King County, Washington, home to Seattle and two of the world's largest Big Tech companies, Microsoft and Amazon, became the first major county to ban use of facial recognition by all county departments, including the sheriff.[14] Part of the motivation for these restrictions has been research that revealed the inaccuracies of the software, especially when it comes to identifying Black people and women. But even if the software becomes more accurate, is there a use for it that will contribute to a safer and more just society? Activist Malkia Devich-Cyril has argued that this technology has its roots in "discredited pseudoscience and racist eugenics theories." In Devich-Cyril's view, facial recognition repeats the racist efforts by nineteenth-century European pseudoscientists who claimed Black people lacked intelligence because of the shape and contours of their skulls.[15] In the framing of this pseudoscience, a biological inferiority could provide rationalization for increased state violence and oppression. As the child of a Black Panther Party member, Devich-Cyril drew from their personal history to project how this technology could be used to identify and criminalize activists who participate in protests. Moreover, in seeking to track "perceived threats and criminal behavior,"[16] this technology also embodies an ableism that can easily criminalize people with intellectual disabilities, deafness, or mental health concerns.

However, in other instances, activists have opted to support measures to regulate technology as the only viable course of action. The POST Act of New York, which became law in 2020, compelled the New York Police Department commissioner to openly publish a use policy for each surveillance technology the department plans to use. Once the notice is published, the public will have a chance to submit any comments or concerns. The POST Act is a more moderate version of surveillance regulations passed in San Francisco and Oakland, which require police to get permission from the city council before obtaining new surveillance technologies. Albert Fox Cahn, executive director of the nonprofit Surveillance Technology Oversight Project, which fights against mass surveillance, was one of the POST Act's main advocates. Cahn argued that "without the POST Act, New Yorkers had no idea what tools our city was using to spy on our families and neighbors, and if you can't see a threat, you can't fight it."[17] While many reformers and some abolitionists supported the act, the organizers of the Stop LAPD Spying Coalition, a grassroots volunteer organization that fights against police surveillance, made a strong statement in opposition to this type of regulation: "Fuck the Police, Trust the People." They argued that rather than establishing any serious control over the police, legislation like the POST Act deepened the power of a "surveillance bureaucracy" comprised of lawyers, law enforcement, and elected officials, and undermined efforts by mobilized communities of color to develop alternatives to policing.[18] Their main argument was that "our people do not want to be surveilled, either illegally or legally." They referred to the surveillance apparatus as the "stalker state," an entity that not only gathered information but acted in ways that are highly intrusive and punitive toward marginalized populations.

Other technologies may present even more complicated challenges for abolitionists, and perhaps the most complicated of these is the cellphone. While cellphones offer an amazing degree of access to communication and information, as we have noted earlier, they have become a primary data-gathering technology for corporations and the state. Would an abolitionist perspective on cellphones consider them a tool of e-carceration and call for their abolition? Would abolition support the regulation of existing providers, or push for the establishment of alternative networks that could effectively operate outside the framework of the corporate and government surveillance state? Do alternative platforms featuring encryption, such as Signal, provide enough security to eliminate the surveillance threat of cellphones?

Another important abolitionist question is whether authorities have a right to any of our personal data or information. At the moment, most data sits on clouds controlled by major Big Tech companies. There is little accountability to the owners or generators of the data. In many instances, data may be sold to third parties. Such sales are usually to companies that target certain categories of people to market their goods or services. However, data may also be sold or shared for surveillance or law enforcement purposes, as ways to deepen the punishment of or control over the criminalized sector of the population. But even if that cloud were in the hands of a nonprofit or a state agency subject to strict oversight, without a complete transformation of government, that data could remain a force of e-carceration.

Other than ownership, a particularly challenging issue is the actual design of our communications devices. Currently, consumers have no real say in terms of limiting the capacity of their devices to capture certain data and be part of the punishment regime of e-carceration. In some instances, consumers can deactivate certain apps or functions, but overall, the frameworks of these devices are determined by Big Tech. An abolitionist vision of technology would ensure the design of communications devices that gives users absolute control.

Whether or not a reform is non-reformist will not always be a clear-cut matter. Abolition doesn't mean dogmatically applying the same rule in every situation. Rather, it necessitates understanding concepts like non-reformist reform and reflecting on how they relate to a particular set of circumstances, past, present, and future.

3. ABOLITION MEANS REJECTING CARCERAL FEMINISM

In a 2013 talk at the University of Chicago, Angela Davis highlighted where the struggle against mass incarceration intersects with the struggle against domestic and gender-based violence. She suggested that "people on the front lines against violence against women should also be on the front line of [prison] abolitionist struggles," while those opposed to "police crimes should be opposed to domestic—privatized—violence." She labeled this approach "abolition feminism."[19] A number of organizations and feminist thinkers have expanded on this thinking. Even as they recognize the need to hold people accountable for doing harm, many feminists, especially feminists of color, argue that extending past practices of mass criminalization and retribution only serve to strengthen the carceral state rather than address the fundamental underlying structural issues. Abolitionist organizer Mariame Kaba and other activists have rejected the reliance on the criminal legal system as a solution to gender-based violence. To refer to this approach, they deploy a term coined by feminist writer Elizabeth Bernstein—"carceral feminism."[20] Kaba amplified this notion with a now widely shared quote: "Prison is not feminist."[21]

In campaigning against e-carceration, abolitionists have run into considerable conflict with both law enforcement and carceral feminists who support the use of surveillance technology.[22] These groups often recommend the e-carceral technologies of bilateral electronic monitors and sex offender registries as part of a response to cases of gender-based or domestic violence. This exemplifies how supporters of e-carceration apply punitive technologies to a complex social problem.

The writings of criminologist Beth Richie and feminist activists from INCITE! Women, Gender Non-Conforming, and Trans people of Color Against Violence has highlighted how police responses to domestic violence incidents in communities of color often end up punishing the victim or bringing an unwanted culture of violence into a household or neighborhood.[23] In the words of INCITE!: "Police not only often fail to protect women of color and trans folks of color from interpersonal and community violence, they often perpetrate further violence against us, including when responding to calls for help."[24]

Judith Levine and Erica Meiners, in their pathbreaking analysis of gender and sexual violence, *The Feminist and the Sex Offender*, have decisively demonstrated the ineffectiveness of using criminal punishments such as e-carceration to address issues laden with race, gender, and class dynamics.[25] For example, as with electronic monitoring in general, no substantial body of evidence demonstrates that measures like sex offender registries contribute to public safety, especially in terms of reoffending. A 2018 study of the impact of sex offender registries after twenty years of implementation in New Jersey concluded that "no differences in recidivism" were noted between the people with sex offense convictions released before the implementation of the registry and those released after.[26] A study based on the federal Uniform

Crime Reporting Program data that looked at recidivism rates in regard to rapes in ten states showed the registry led to "no systematic influence on the number of rapes committed in these states as a whole."[27]

Although no proof exists of the registries' effectiveness, their public nature has resulted in a number of people on a registry being subjected to violent attacks through online tracking. In 2005, two men in Bellingham, Washington, who appeared on that state's publicly searchable sex offender registry were shot dead by Michael Anthony Mullen, who had found their names on the internet. Women, who make up about 7 percent of people on the registry, report receiving a disproportionate number of letters and other communications with sexually explicit comments and offers.[28] In at least fourteen states, there have been enough attacks on registrants to cause legislators to pass laws making it a crime to use registry information to harass, intimidate, or assault a registrant.[29]

ONE ABOLITIONIST RESPONSE

The story of Kristie Puckett-Williams highlights the abolitionist response to acts labeled as sex offenses. As a Black woman living with an addiction and an abusive male partner, Puckett-Williams was arrested in her hometown of Charlotte, North Carolina, in 2009. Puckett-Williams managed to work her way through a period of incarceration and turn her life around to become the coordinator for the Campaign for Smart Justice of the ACLU of North Carolina. Her experience on electronic monitoring convinced her that this technology fails to provide a solution to issues of gender-based violence. Her release from pretrial detention on EM sentenced her to go back into the house where she had suffered abuse. Under the restrictions of EM, there was no escape.

"When you look at violence, you're just looking at one part of a relationship," she said. "Restorative justice for me was for him to stop beating me. I still needed his financial contribution, needed him to protect me from other men, to love me in a way that didn't harm me. What we can't do in the name of safety is to keep locking people up."

She was particularly scathing about her EM experience.

> The monitor doesn't address the fundamental underlying problems that cause domestic violence. This is a social, political, and economic problem. We can't solve it with punishment.
>
> I don't believe people who perpetuate violence need to be locked up. It doesn't address the underlying situation of toxic masculinity and patriarchy. It does nothing about the way they use power and control as a way of coping with the conflict in their lives.

After her incarceration, Puckett-Williams worked for four years in a program for men who had a history of abusing women.

> I had to begin to see the humanity in them and expand upon that humanity. This was healing. But they also had to learn how toxic masculinity and white supremacy were the foundation of all this. I was always working to get them out of state control, out of the carceral state. They didn't know anything else. We didn't as a society offer them anything else.

She maintains that she had a "responsibility to hold them accountable but also to be compassionate and remain respectful. Society had labeled them as monsters." She connected it all back to her own previous situation. "I never wanted my abuser to be locked up. For me, once my basic needs were met, I was able to move toward the higher needs of being lawful and building relationships, but if my safety was threatened, I had to focus on surviving day to day."

In the end, the expansion of e-carceration in handling issues of gender-based and domestic violence forms a big part of Puckett-Williams's concern. "The monitor is a way for them to keep dehumanizing you without knowing you at all. With the spread of risk assessment, EM becomes another risk category. We should be working toward liberation, not incarceration."[30]

4. ABOLITION MEANS BUILDING THE POWER OF PEOPLE TO USE TECHNOLOGY

E-carceration is a distortion of the creative and liberating potential of technology. In imagining abolition, the technology we need to engage with most deeply is the internet. Never has there been a technology with more potential for liberation, or for building structures of sharing and collaboration. As technology activist Alfredo Lopez points out, "The internet is people, not the military or big business. The internet is the best method we have found to share ideas, but companies turn them into opportunities to advertise or militarize or control or punish. The struggle we have is to take it back."[31] Lopez co-founded the May First movement, a membership organization based in the United States and Mexico dedicated to democratizing technology. In an article in the online magazine *Radical Ecological Democracy*, May First reminded us that our computer is a box of wires and some machined parts that, when turned on, becomes "part of a network of 4.5 billion people, globally [where] we share information, ideas, activities and what's important to us." In May First's view, the computer "is the most remarkable project of communication the human race has ever engaged."[32]

In our present reality, the internet too often drowns us in toxic information—stories, tweets, memes, videos, gifs, plus whatever else helps keep us inside the boundaries of consumer capitalism. Accessing that toxic information is easy; wisdom and a nuanced understanding of the world are much harder to find. Still, many people have appropriated this technology for collaboration, community building, and fighting for social justice. They have constructed megaphones that at times allow people to share stories and experiences in ways we could never have dreamed of twenty years ago. But as a central tool in a racial capitalist society, the internet's overwhelming thrust is to keep us buying more products, and keep us believing capitalism is the greatest creation in human history—the only system worth having. The internet makes us believe that the measure of a person's worth lies in the value of their fortune or the number of followers and likes they have on Instagram or TikTok. In the existing internet reality, more people write product reviews than commentaries on climate change, nuclear weapons, systemic racism, or e-carceration. We know far more about the products that we buy or the sports teams that we love or hate than we do about our fellow human beings in other parts of the world or even in other neighborhoods of our own cities.

Yeshimabeit Milner, founder of Data 4 Black Lives, has helped alert us to the notion that "the Google search bar is a false oracle." In her calls to "Abolish Big Data," she argues that we need to "make data a tool for social change instead of a weapon of social oppression." Milner calls for the abolition of technologies such as facial recognition, biometric data collection, credit scoring, and risk assessment—essentially, the most harmful technologies of e-carceration and the surveillance state. Hamid Khan, key organizer of the Stop LAPD Spying Coalition, identifies as a "data abolitionist." He questions the rights of the state and corporations to mine our data. Khan cautions against the obsession for gathering data, especially in statistical form. "Data is a derivative of someone who is assessing our life . . . a numerical system rather than a human system." He argues that such an orientation is essentially creating a "road map for our own harm." "Our history is our truth," he adds, and data "invisibilizes that truth," even "stripping people of the ability to recognize their own truth."[33] The Stop LAPD Spying Coalition put these ideas into action in a multi-year campaign that culminated in 2019 with the city of Los Angeles cutting its contract with Palantir for predictive policing technology.[34] Some inventions of Big Tech, just as with nuclear weapons, have no positive function.

OUR DATA BODIES

Our Data Bodies (ODB) is one of the most important projects aimed at exploring ways that communities can take control of their own data. This project brings together community members in Detroit, Los Angeles, and Charlotte, North Carolina, to explore how data affected all aspects of people's lives. The term "data bodies" refers to the data our lives create in the present system of surveillance and e-carceration. ODB argues that these data bodies are "a manifestation of our relationships with our communities and institutions, including institutions of privilege, oppression, and domination."[35] In its grassroots education manual, the *Digital Defense Playbook*, ODB explains,

It's not just the individual; it's the information that's been generated about this individual and the systems that interact to make decisions about this individual, this individual's family, this individual's neighborhood—all the data's tentacles.[36]

ODB focuses on educating communities—especially Black, queer, and other marginalized populations—about how their daily lives leave a data trail that can be used to track and punish them and their communities. Through popular education and research in the target communities in their three cities, the ODB project works with people to imagine a different data world, where people and communities could control what data they generate and how it is used. One of the participants in a Detroit workshop, Ollie Mae, summarized her vision of a transformative use of data like this:

The changes I would make would be to have data that is intentional and targeted and centering people in the middle of those decisions. So, data would be created for the people and with people as opposed to on people and against people. Data would be done in a way that is an instrument and a tool to support their uplift and the uplift of their consciousness and the quality of their lives. It would be used to map and visualize so that people's understanding was centered in coming together and being their own solutionaries.[37]

The Detroit Community Technology Project (DCTP) is a key member of ODB. Detroiter Tawana Petty, a central leader of ODB and DCTP, connects the popular education on data bodies to resisting the growth of e-carceral technologies in Detroit. She advocates for applying a "racial lens" to fighting against surveillance in a city already invaded by hundreds of surveillance cameras under an urban plan called Project Green Light: "It's going to be much harder to convince not just Detroiters but the world that a Black city doesn't need to be surveilled." Petty places this vision in the context of a "deeper, longer conversation" that

{ requires a kind of organizing around anti-Black racism that often isn't comfortable to do even in social justice or liberal spaces. We try to get community members to think not just about the impact that their data has on them, but the impact that their data has on the decisions that affect their family, their neighborhood, and their city.[38] }

Another important example of building grassroots tech power is localized "mesh networks." These networks still make use of internet service providers, but they form a closed community, impenetrable to data snatchers, pop-up ad promotions, and mainstream cloud owners. They demonstrate ways for communities to build their organizing power and capacity to share resources. In the coming waves of disasters linked to climate change and political uprisings, such networks could become an alternative, secure means of communication. They would also be far less vulnerable to hackers and bots than mainstream networks since they share data through multiple pathways instead of relying on one central service provider.

LIBERATING THE INTERNET

The capacity to build mesh networks hinges on the ability to freely access the internet. In the last decade, a struggle over net neutrality has demonstrated how fragile popular access to the digital world is. The fundamental question underlying this issue is whether the internet is a right or a privilege. At stake in this debate is the question of whether tech companies should be permitted to structure internet access on the TV cable model, in which customers have different levels of access depending on how much they pay. A multi-year campaign driven by a coalition of nonprofits sprinkled with a few tech industry insiders managed to push the Federal Communications Commission (FCC) to pass a resolution in support of net neutrality in 2015. President Obama was a key supporter.

However, when Donald Trump became president, the person he appointed as chair of the FCC quickly moved to eliminate net neutrality. President Biden's appointment of Jessica Rosenworcel in 2021 to head the FCC signaled a shift back to federal support of net neutrality.

Net neutrality is an important step for abolitionists because it helps guarantee the capacity of social justice organizations and social movements to share their messages and build their networks. Without it, Big Tech companies would effectively block out the voices of people of color and other marginalized populations. As of 2019, five corporations controlled 90 percent of the media outlets in the United States.[39]

5. ABOLITION MEANS WRITING HISTORY FROM BELOW

Challenging e-carceration requires addressing history. The triumphal history of contemporary technology centers start-ups and the hothouse of ideas in Silicon Valley. Superheroes like Steve Jobs and Mark Zuckerberg are the stars of that show. We have seen the origin stories of electronic monitoring place the Harvard-based Gable brothers and Judge Jack Love in the lead roles. An abolitionist history of these technologies would be a history from below, one that includes the stories of seven-year-old Congolese boys mining the coltan for our cellphone capacitors for pennies an hour, and the perspectives of the youth used as experimental subjects by the Gable brothers for the first electronic monitors. The highly trained innovators and technical experts who we celebrate support not only the super-exploitation of labor, but incarceration, surveillance, and even armed invasions and killing. It is their call of duty, their default program.

Contemporary abolitionists are not the first people to take anti-capitalism seriously. Abolitionist thinking draws on the history of previous revolutionary and radical traditions. As Ruth Wilson Gilmore posits, abolition must be red, green, and international.[40] This means connecting to the traditions and philosophies of the historical and international Left and other liberation tendencies. These range from Marxism and the Black radical tradition, to feminism and queer theory, to African, Asian, and Latin American nationalisms and indigenous philosophies around the world as well as including many more tendencies in the socialist, communist, and anarchist realm; plus, of course, previous abolition paradigms and the visions of political prisoners. Rather than building from scratch, abolition draws from the lessons learned in previous political struggles and attempts to build revolutionary societies. In the process of transforming society in the twenty-first century and abolishing e-carceration, we will certainly face challenges and tensions. Perhaps one of the most challenging tensions rests between using the scale and efficiency afforded by technology and ensuring it doesn't serve the goals of profit-making and destruction. These technological challenges are new to anti-capitalist traditions.

To rise to these challenges requires a cohort of technology experts with a sensitivity to and a loathing for injustice. Their training should prepare them to produce technologies of liberation and constantly assess their role as anti-capitalist technologists. They should not be trained to produce techno-shackles that add more and more data to the clouds and convert more houses and neighborhoods into carceral space. Their training should prepare them to be accountable for the impact of what they produce not only in their own local communities but around the world. But the entire burden for creating technologies of liberation does not fall on the experts. As surveillance researcher and historian Simone Browne points out, individuals need to develop a "critical biometric consciousness," an awareness of the data contained in their own bodies and the ability to control that data.[41] "We continually have to challenge the system," she urges, "and not necessarily give in to the easy conveniences of these technologies."[42]

Challenges require not only individual consciousness but organization. For the National Council for Incarcerated and Formerly Incarcerated Women and Girls, challenging the system means taking a strong stance against electronic monitoring and other forms of e-carceration. Instead of opting for technological solutions, the National Council, which has chapters across the United States, focuses on building a national platform around three pillars: changing policy, building infrastructure at the local level to expand democratic structures like participatory budgeting and transformative justice, and conducting national campaigns to change the narrative around incarceration and other crucial issues. All of their efforts aim to center the role and voices of formerly incarcerated women and girls.

Andrea James, the executive director of the National Council, says that these three pillars are their way of "waging our war against prisons . . . until we move to a model of people led processes and self-governance. . . . We will build an alternative system in our country to meet the needs of our people." Alongside building local power, the National Council's vision also includes an internationalist component. They frequently visit Latin American and African countries to learn from the experience of their counterparts across the globe.

We began this book by focusing on the history of electronic monitoring devices, the technology most closely associated with the notion of e-carceration. But as the history of monitoring and other technologies has revealed, the boundaries of e-carceration extend way beyond black plastic devices informing a parole officer if their client is at home. Initially, the use of the term "e-carceration" may have seemed a bit extreme, but as we have connected the dots of these technologies and the extent to which they are exempt from popular control, labeling them as devices of incarceration becomes logical to those pursuing an abolitionist future. The term "e-carceration" highlights the urgency for social justice movements to see the threat posed by these technologies. We need to apply our imagination to how we can appropriate this technology and reset it in service of eliminating systems of oppression. We need to refocus technology toward organizations and solutions to address the mega problems of our era: climate change, militarization, the polarization of global wealth, the advance of the control of Big Data, and the growth of white supremacy.

This book started from a fundamental thesis: that electronic monitors are not an alternative to incarceration but an alternative form of incarceration. From there we have moved outward from the ankle shackle to e-carceration—a network of punitive and profit-extracting technologies. These technologies are not going to displace physical prisons, jails, and detention centers in the immediate future. Instead, they are building up a life of their own, carving out new territory for racial capitalism, the way imperialist powers kept extending their boundaries of conquest and expropriation. If we are to make abolition a reality, we need to fully understand the ways in which these paradoxical technologies can provide benefits and services to billions of people while simultaneously creating platforms, devices, and apps to surveil, control, and punish the criminalized sectors of society and beyond. As the freedom fighters of southern Africa have said for generations, "A luta continua" (The struggle continues).

ACKNOWLEDGMENTS

I first started researching electronic monitoring almost the minute they put that shackle on my leg in 2009. Along the way I have had support from many people to keep the struggle against e-carceration alive and to grow it into a book. I want to thank those who got me going in the early days, particularly people who donated to my 2013 Indiegogo fundraiser to provide funding to travel to California and Michigan to do interviews.

A number of people have been central to sustaining hope that the mantra of "It's better than jail" would one day be eradicated from discussions about electronic monitoring and e-carceration. I especially want to acknowledge the support I have received from Media-Justice since 2017, which enabled me to access their networks and learn from their work on surveillance and racial justice. I am especially grateful to radical liberation visionary Malkia Devich-Cyril, who welcomed me into MediaJustice and supported my fellowship at the Open Society Foundations. I am also thankful for the support that MediaJustice staffers Myaisha Hayes and Steven Renderos provided and their belief in the importance of the issue of e-carceration and digital prisons. I also express my gratitude to MediaJustice Comms folks Eteng Ettah and DJ Hudson for their timely, creative, and insightful work.

My connection to MediaJustice came about through folks at one of my local haunts, the Urbana-Champaign Independent Media Center, especially Danielle Chynoweth and Brian

Dolinar. Danielle was crucial in getting this project off the ground and building my proposal to the Open Society Foundations.

I am also grateful for people from a variety of organizations around the country who opened their doors to me. In Chicago that was the Chicago Community Bond Fund, Precious Blood Ministry of Reconciliation, Northside Transformative Law Center, and Lawndale Christian Legal Center. In California I connected with All of Us or None, Youth Justice Coalition, Fair Chance Project, and Center for Living and Learning; in Lansing, Michigan, NorthWest Initiative and CAPPS; and in New York, JustLeadershipUSA, JUST, and HOLLA.

Apart from these organizations, I was honored to be in community with many organizations and individuals who have taken up the struggle against e-carceration and have helped sharpen my knowledge and enhanced our collective understanding of these technologies. Special acknowledgment here goes to the Chicago Community Bond Fund again, particularly Sharlyn Grace, Matt McLoughlin, and Lavette Mayes; the Stop LAPD Spying Coalition, which keeps the abolition flame burning bright in the surveillance world; and the National Council for Incarcerated and Formerly Incarcerated Women and Girls, especially Andrea James, who saw through the fallacy of e-carceration from the beginning, and the dynamic Tiheba Bain. A special shout-out goes to all those who played an active role in fighting for the passage of HB 1115, which got through the Illinois assembly in 2019, and HB 386, which is now the only law in the United States requiring a state department of corrections to file a detailed annual report on electronic monitoring. Thanks to Patrice James, Sarah Staudt, Alan Mills, Chris Harrison, Monica Cosby, Gregg Gaither, Orlando Mayorga, Colette Payne, General Parker, Lindsey LaPointe, Isabel Beit, Ed Vogel, Nasir Blackwell, Michael Fore, Celia Colon, and Augie Torres. Maximum kudos on this legislation go to the sponsor of the HB 1115 and my local state representative, Carol Ammons.

I also want to single out the important role that my Champaign–Urbana organizational home, FirstFollowers Reentry Program, has had in keeping me grounded in the reality of mass incarceration and the challenges people face daily. It is one thing to read a story about the difficulties of being on a monitor, another thing to have to fight on behalf of someone on an ankle shackle to be allowed out of the house for two hours for a doctor appointment. For me, this research is not an academic matter but part of a battle for liberation. I am particularly in debt to Marlon Mitchell, Abdulhakeem Y. Salaam, James Corbin, Charles Davidson, Tamika Davis, Casandis Hunt, Kristina Khan, Anthony "Kee Kee" Minor, Regina Parnell, and Kevin "Snow" Williams for their constant support.

This book would not have been possible without the generosity of dozens of people, especially those who spent time on the ankle shackle or had loved ones on a shackle and agreed to be interviewed at various stages of this project. I apologize if I omitted anyone. They are: Aaron Hicks, Ali Sentwali, Alisha James, Angela Laureano, Annette Taylor, Ashleigh Carter, Augie Torres, Bruce Reilly, Chanel Rhymes, Chris Harrison, the Circles and Ciphers youth, Claudia Gonzalez, Coco Davis, Curtis Oats, Darrell Cannon, Deborah Howard-Sloan, Dorsey Nunn, Dustin Tirado, Edmund Buck, Emmanuel Andre, the late Ernest Shepard, Evan Okun, Father David Kelly, George Villa, Geri Silva, Hamid Khan, Henry Fante, Jean-Pierre Shackelford, Jenna Tomsky, Jerome Dillard, Jerry Freeman, Jobie Taylor, Johnny Page, Kent Shultz, Lark Mulligan, Maria Alexander, Lois DeMott, Maria Moon, Martha Shira, Maura Barry, Melissa Springs, Michael Alfères, Miguel Quezada, Molly Whitted, Monica Jahner, Pastor Jackson, Patsy Howells, Peggy West, Phillip Pierini, Rashanti McShane, Rebecca Ginsburg, Robert Smith, Sara Ferber, Sarah Hannah, Shalita Williams, Shaun Harris, Terry Rodriguez, Tiheba Bain, Teddy Williams, Timothy Williams, Topeka K. Sam, Tyshontae Williams, Veronica Williams, and Vincent Powell.

Another essential component in putting together a book project is people who share their own research knowledge and ideas. For me, these included Alfredo Lopez, Barbara Kessel, Bill Martin, Brenda Sanya, Chelsea Barabas, Cherise Fanno Burdeen, Chris Evans, Di Luong, Hamid Khan, Hannah Sassaman, Jacinta Gonzalez, Jindu Obiofuma, Judge Carla Baldwin, Kate Weisburd, Ken Salo, Mecke Nagel, Patrick Bond, Pilar Weiss, Shubha Bala, Simone Browne, Sunny Ture, and the foremost global authority on EM, Mike Nellis. I had timely assistance from a number of people on the nuts and bolts of my research: Anna Kurhajec, Tyler Camp, and Barbara Lacker-Ware. Then came the special type of colleagues who read my material and provided honest feedback instead of false praise. Thanks to Alison McDowell, Brendan McQuade, Daniel Gonzalez, and Erica Meiners.

I also must give thanks to the folks at The New Press, Diane Wachtell and Ellen Adler, who have been solidly behind me for years, to astute copy editor Brian Baughan, and zakia henderson-brown, who, like the best of editors offered lots of suggestions about structure, narrative, and everything else, which sometimes were disagreeable at first but in the end were right about 98 percent of the time. Your honesty and insight are much appreciated.

I could never have written this book without the ideological and spiritual direction from my comrades and mentors from my days in South Africa and Zimbabwe. Though they were not directly consulted for this project, the flame ignited by Mary Bassett, Moses Cloete, Laura Czerniewicz, Rick DeSatgé, Oupa Lehulere, the late Elaine Salo, Ighsaan Schroeder, and Mthetho Xhali still burns inside me nearly two decades after I was whisked away from Cape Town by the FBI.

For the past four years I have had the wonderful fortune to work side by side with one of the most principled and insightful people I have run across in my long journey. Emmett Sanders, who spent ninety days on a monitor after more than two decades in Illinois prisons, has been a tireless researcher and campaigner on this issue and has brought countless new perspectives to how we see this work in the context of fighting mass incarceration and realizing abolition.

The utmost gratitude of all goes to my family, the most vital source of inspiration. My mother, Barbara Kilgore, passed away in 2017 at age 104, but her spirit still energizes my notions of loyalty and unconditional love. My mother-in-law, Pat Barnes-McConnell, has been the rock on which our family has rested for over three decades. My sons, Lewis and Lonnie Barnes, and more recently my granddaughter, Celia, and her mother, Jordan Capik, have been an integral part of my path of moving out of the prison world into whatever normality exists in late-capitalist USA. But most of all, my gratitude and love goes to my partner, Terri Barnes, who is not only my most critical reader (how much do I loathe her truth-telling when she reads a chapter and says, "This isn't working for me at all"); without her critical eye, her encouragement when I wanted to surrender this book to the category of "good ideas for someone else to do," her tolerating the endless tales of e-carceral cruelty, I could never have reached completion. And her solidarity in this project is but the cap on years of support and love during years of incarceration and beyond.

NOTES

1: INTRODUCTION

1. J. Walsh, "America's Most Wanted: James Kilgore," January 26, 2002.

2. M. Taylor, "FBI Offers $20,000 for Last SLA Fugitive," *SFGate*, April 25, 2001.

3. Personal interview, August 10, 2017.

4. S. Zuboff, *The Age of Surveillance Capitalism: The Fight for a Human Future at the New Frontier of Power* (New York: PublicAffairs, 2018).

5. R. Gilmore, "Is Racism a Public Health Issue?," Center for the Study of Racism, Social Justice & Health, October 9, 2017.

6. J.B. Foster and R.W. McChesney, "Surveillance Capitalism," *Monthly Review*, July 1, 2014.

7. Cited in J. Weinel, *Inner Sound: Altered States of Consciousness in Electronic Music and Audio-Visual Media* (New York: Oxford University Press, 2018).

8. See the websites of Algorithmic Justice League, ajl.org; and Data 4 Black Lives, d4bl.org.

2: WHAT IS E-CARCERATION?

1. M. Alexander, "The Newest Jim Crow," *New York Times*, November 18, 2018.

2. M. Devich-Cyril, "Will You Harbor Me? To Fight Police Violence, Demand Digital Sanctuary," lecture, Personal Democracy Forum, June 9, 2017.

3. A. Kundnani, "What Is Racial Capitalism?," talk at the Havens Wright Center for Social Justice, University of Wisconsin-Madison, October 15, 2020.

4. C. Robinson, *Black Marxism: The Making of the Black Radical Tradition* (Chapel Hill: University of North Carolina Press, 1983).

5. R.D.G. Kelley, "What Is Racial Capitalism and Why Does It Matter?," lecture, University of Washington, November 16, 2017.

6. For an explanation of risk assessment, see M. Henry, "Risk Assessment Explained," *The Appeal*, December 14, 2019; see also J. Angwin et al., "Machine Bias," ProPublica, May 23, 2016.

7. E. Fabris, *Tranquil Prisons: Chemical Incarceration Under Community Treatment Orders* (Toronto: University of Toronto Press, 2011).

8. J. Jouvenal, "Facial Recognition Used to Identify Lafayette Square Protestor Accused of Assault," *Washington Post*, November 2, 2020.

9. J. Vincent, "NYPD Used Facial Recognition to Track Down Black Lives Matter Activist," *The Verge*, August 18, 2020.

10. D. West, "Digital Fingerprints Are Identifying Capitol Rioters," Brookings Institution, January 19, 2020.

11. J. Cox, "Leaked Location Data Shows Another Muslim Prayer App Tracking Users," *Vice*, January 11, 2021.

12. M. Alexander, *The New Jim Crow: Mass Incarceration in the Age of Colorblindness* (New York: The New Press, 2010).

13. B. Obama, "Weekly Address: Building a Fairer and More Effective Criminal Justice System," The White House, Office of the Press Secretary, April 23, 2016.

14. D. Roberts, "Eric Holder Unveils New Reforms Aimed at Curbing US Prison Population," *The Guardian*, August 12, 2013.

15. D. Dagan, "Right-Wing Prison Reform," *HuffPost*, May 21, 2014.

16. J. Kilgore, "Repackaging Mass Incarceration," *CounterPunch*, June 6, 2014.

17. "The GEO Group Closes $415 Million Acquisition of B.I. Incorporated, *Business Wire*, February 11, 2011.

18. Quoted in D. Kupfer, "The New Surveillance State," *The Progressive*, June 1, 2019.

19. R. Benjamin, Presentation to Our Tech Futures Conference, online event, June 1, 2021.

20. R. Cooke, "A Brief History of Quantitative Risk Assessment," Resources for the Future, Summer 2009, media.rff.org; P. Odih, *Advertising in Modern and Postmodern Times* (New York: Sage, 2007).

21. C. O'Neil, *Weapons of Math Destruction: How Big Data Increases Inequality and Threatens Democracy* (New York: Penguin, 2016); Angwin et al., "Machine Bias"; Community Justice Exchange, *An Organizer's Guide to Confronting Pretrial Risk Assessment Tools in Decarceration Campaigns*, December 2019.

22. R. Benjamin, *Race After Technology* (New York: Polity Press, 2019).

23. "About the Public Safety Assessment: How It Works," Advancing Pretrial Policy and Research, n.d.

24. T. McCoy, "Eviction Isn't Just About Poverty. It's Also About Race—and Virginia Proves

It," *Washington Post,* November 10, 2018; M. Singletary, "Credit Scores Are Supposed to Be Race-Neutral. That's Impossible," *Washington Post,* October 16, 2020.

25. S. Garfinkel, "A Peek at Proprietary Algorithms," *American Scientist* 105, no. 6 (2017): 326.

26. M. Henry, "Risk Assessment: Explained," *The Appeal,* December 14, 2019.

27. Pew Trust, "Use of Electronic Offender-Tracking Devices Expands Sharply," issue brief, September 7, 2016.

28. The original use is J. Kilgore, "Electronic Monitoring Is Not the Answer: Critical Reflections on a Flawed Alternative," MediaJustice, October 2015, but it was also used by M. Alexander, "The Newest Jim Crow," *New York Times,* November 8, 2018.

29. B. Green and C. Rigano, "Specialized Smartphones Could Keep Released Offenders on Track for Successful Reentry," National Institute of Justice, Washington, DC, April 20, 2020.

30. K. Wiggers, "Problematic Study on Indiana Parolees Seeks to Predict Recidivism with AI," *The Machine,* August 14, 2020.

31. Anna Altman, "Mommy and Data," *The New Republic,* January 14, 2019. The term "Femtech" is controversial with authors such as Megan Capriccio and Olivia Goldhill, who argue that it classifies women as a "niche sub-category." See M. Capriccio, "Femtech: Controversial or Necessary?," Medium,

November 20, 2019.

32. J. Richmond, "The New Year of Optimism for Femtech," *Forbes,* December 31, 2016.

33. E. Jaramillo, "Femtech in 2019: 13 Trends and Highlights in Women's Health Technology," *Forbes,* December 17, 2019.

34. "The Microchip—One Year Later, Where Are They?" Three Square Market, news release, July 26, 2018.

35. I. Davidovic, "Should We Be Worried by Ever More CCTV Cameras?," BBC News, November 18, 2019.

36. T. McCue, "Home Security Cameras Market to Surpass $9.7 Billion by 2023," *Forbes,* January 31, 2019.

37. AIT News Desk, "Top 10 Countries and Cities by Number of CCTV Cameras," AIthority, December 5, 2019.

38. A. Regalado, "Who Coined 'Cloud Computing'?," *MIT Technology Review,* October 31, 2011.

39. V. Sahu, "Top 6 Cloud Service Providers Who'll Dominate the Cloud War," TechAhead, January 27, 2020.

40. MediaJustice, "Civil Rights Groups Urge Congress to Act to Expose FBI Surveillance of Black Activists," news release, September 17, 2019.

41. B. Fearnow, "FBI Ranks 'Black Identity Extremists' Bigger Threat Than Al Qaeda, White Supremacists: Leaked Documents," *Newsweek,* August 8, 2019.

42. B. Tau, "FBI Abandons Use of Term

'Black Identity Extremism,'" *Wall Street Journal*, July 23, 2019; MediaJustice, "FBI Misled Congress: Black Activists Still Under Investigation by New and Old Extremist Designations," news release, June 17, 2020.

43. D. Roberts and J. Vagle, "Racial Surveillance Has a Long History," *The Hill*, January 4, 2016.

44. D. Roberts, "Digitizing the Carceral State," *Harvard Law Review*, no. 132 (2019): 1700.

45. See G. Greenwald, *No Place to Hide: Edward Snowden, the NSA, and the US Surveillance State* (New York: Metropolitan, 2014); J. Assange and A. O'Hagan, *Julian Assange: The Unauthorized Autobiography* (Edinburgh: Canongate, 2011); J. Assange, *The WikiLeaks Files: The World According to US Empire* (New York: Verso, 2015).

46. R. Esguerra, "Google CEO Eric Schmidt Dismisses the Importance of Privacy," Electronic Frontier Foundation, December 10, 2009.

47. A. Rusbridger, J. Gibson, and E. MacAskill, "Edward Snowden: NSA Reform in the US Is Only Beginning," *The Guardian*, May 22, 2015.

48. A. Abdo, "You May Have 'Nothing to Hide' but You Still Have Something to Fear," ACLU, August 2, 2013.

49. A. Roberts, "Digitizing the Carceral State," 1700.

50. V. Eubanks, *Automating Inequality: How High-Tech Tools Profile, Police, and Punish the Poor* (New York: St. Martin's Press, 2018).

51. Roberts, "Digitizing the Carceral State," 1697.

52. W. Poster, "Racialized Surveillance in the Digital Service Economy," in *Captivating Technology: Race, Technoscience, and the Carceral Imagination*, ed. R. Benjamin (Durham, NC: Duke University Press, 2019).

53. N. Hinojos, "Criminalization of American Indians in the US Explored During Lecture," *Daily Sundial*, March 23, 2015; R. Dunbar-Ortiz, *An Indigenous Peoples' History of the United States* (Boston: Beacon Press, 2019).

54. S. Browne, *Dark Matters: On the Surveillance of Blackness* (Durham, NC: Duke University Press, 2015).

55. Ibid.

56. Sundown Towns: A Hidden Dimension of American Racism website, https://sundown.tougaloo.edu/sundowntowns.php.

57. "Hall, Gus" Our Campaigns website, n.d.

3. MONITORING: BORN IN THE PUNISHMENT PARADIGM

1. R.S. Gable and R.K. Gable, "Strategies for Intervention," *Perspectives: The Journal of the American Probation and Parole Association* 31, no. 1 (Winter 2007): 25–28.

2. See, for example, E. Anderson, "The Evolution of Electronic Monitoring," NPR, May 24, 2014.

3. Gable and Gable, "Strategies for Intervention."

4. R.L. Schwitzgebel, "A Belt from Big Brother," *Psychology Today*, April 1969, p. 47.

5. R. Gable, "Electronic Monitoring of Criminal Offenders," https://rgable.wordpress.com/.

6. R. Gable, "Looking Back: Tagging—An Oddity of Great Potential," *The Psychologist* 24, no. 11 (2011): 866–67.

7. R. Schwitzgebel and R. Bird, "Methods and Designs: Sociotechnical Design Factors in Remote Instrumentation with Humans in Natural Environments" *Behavior Research Methods and Instruments* 2, no. 3 (1970): 99–105.

8. C. Piller, "Probe Uncovers Strip Searches, Chains and Racism at Prisons," *Sacramento Bee*, May 9, 2010.

9. G. Beato, "The Lighter Side of Electronic Monitoring," *Reason*, May 24, 2012.

10. E. Cummins, *The Rise and Fall of California's Radical Prison Movement* (Stanford, CA: Stanford University Press, 1994); G. Felber, *Those Who Know Don't Say* (Chapel Hill: University of North Carolina Press, 2020).

11. "Soledad Brother: The Prison Letters of George Jackson," History Is a Weapon website.

12. G. Jackson, *Blood in My Eye* (1971; repr., Baltimore: Black Classic Press, 1996).

13. H.B. Franklin, ed., *Prison Writing in 20th-Century America* (New York: Penguin, 1998).

14. Abu-Jamal has spent much of his time in prison on death row. An international campaign to free him and proclaim his innocence has not managed to reverse the court verdict.

15. Attica Brothers, "The 31 Demands Raised by the Attica Brothers of September 9, 1971," listed on Encyclopedia.com.

16. Cited in Process Editors, "Organizing the Prisons in the 1960s and 1970s: Part One, Building Movements," *Process* (blog), September 20, 2016.

17. Process Editors, "Organizing the Prisons."

18. United Prisoners Union, "United Prisoners Bill of Rights," San Francisco, 1970.

19. Process Editors, "Organizing the Prisons."

20. Morales v. Schmidt, 340 F. Supp. 544 (W.D. Wis. 1972).

21. Prison Construction Plans and Policy, "Hearings Before the Subcommittee on Courts, Civil Liberties, and the Administration of Justice of the Committee on the Judiciary," House of Representatives, Ninety-fourth Congress, First Session, July 28 and 30, 1975, p. 2.

22. R. Martinson, "What Works? Questions and Answers About Prison Reform," *Public Interest*, no. 35 (Spring 1974): 22–54.

23. J. Miller, "The Debate on Rehabilitating Criminals: Is It True That Nothing Works?," *Washington Post*, April 23, 1989.

24. R. Corbett and G. Marx, "Critique: No Soul in the New Machine: Technofallacies in the New Electronic Monitoring Movement," *Justice Quarterly* 9, no. 3 (1991): 399–414.

25. J. Forman, *Locking Up Our Own: Crime and Punishment in Black America* (New York: Farrar, Straus and Giroux, 2017).

26. R. Gable, "Electronic Monitoring of Criminal Offenders."

27. Schwitzgebel, "Belt from Big Brother," 65.

28. Gable and Gable, "Strategies for Intervention," 28.

29. R. Gable, "The Ankle Bracelet Is History: An Informal Review of the Birth and Death of a Monitoring Technology," *Journal of Offender Monitoring* 27, no. 1 (2014): 4.

30. As of April 2021, Pride remained in existence, largely as a provider of probation services and EM for DUIs. On its website, it bills itself as one of the first "private probation agencies" in the United States. "Pride Integrated Services, Inc.," aboutpride.org/Probation.aspx.

31. Gable, "The Ankle Bracelet Is History."

32. M. Renzema and D. Skelton, "Trends in the Use of Electronic Monitoring: 1989," *Journal of Offender Monitoring* 3, no. 3 (Summer 1990): 12–19.

33. J. Cullen, "The History of Mass Incarceration," Brennan Center for Justice, July 20, 2018.

34. D. Gutman, "What Happened to the Computer Revolution?," *Commodore Magazine*, September 1987.

35. Quoted in Corbett and Marx, "Critique."

36. Editors, "The 1999 Electronic Monitoring Survey," *Journal of Offender Monitoring* 12, no. 4 (Fall 1999).

37. "About SCRAM Systems," SCRAM Systems website, scramsystems.com/our-company/about-us; B. Barton, "Secure Continuous Remote Alcohol Monitoring Technology: Evaluability Assessment," National Institute of Justice, n.d.

4: BUILDING THE MYTH OF ELECTRONIC MONITORING: NOT A "SHRED OF DATA"

1. J. Kilgore, "Electronic Monitoring: A Survey of the Research for Decarceration Activists," *Challenging E-Carceration* (blog).

2. B. Matthews, "Corrections, Rehabilitation and Criminal Justice in the United States, 1970–Present," *Eastern Kentucky University Corrections* (blog), February 3, 2015.

3. J. Lee, "Putting Parolees on a Tighter Leash," *New York Times*, January 31, 2002.

4. Quoted in E. Anderson, "The Evolution of Electronic Monitoring Devices," NPR, May 24, 2014.

5. D. Matthews, "Prisons Are Terrible, and There's Finally a Way to Get Rid of Them," *Vox*, June 27, 2014.

6. S. Yeh, "The Electronic Monitoring Paradigm: A Proposal for Transforming Criminal Justice in the USA," *Laws*, March 2015.

7. "Offender Monitoring Solution Improves Efficiencies and Cuts Costs," Sierra Wireless website, accessed February 20, 2021.

8. SuperCom, "SuperCom Launches New

$1.2 Million National Electronic Monitoring Project in Europe," news release, December 1, 2020.

9. R. Swan, "Jail to Go: Ankle Bracelets Could Be the Next Great Law Enforcement Tool, If the City Doesn't Get Defeated by Data," *SF Weekly*, May 21, 2014.

10. Georgia Code, Chapter 7, Article 2, Part 1 16-7-29.

11. E. Erez and P. Ibarra, "Electronic Monitoring of Domestic Violence Cases—a Study of Two Bilateral Programs," *Federal Probation* 68, no. 1 (2004): 15–20.

12. For a summary of her findings each year, see "Offender Supervision with Electronic Technology," Bureau of Justice Assistance, 2009, p. 17.

13. Pew Trust, "Use of Electronic Offender-Tracking Devices Expands Sharply," issue brief, September 7, 2016.

14. N. Ghandnoosh, "US Prison Population Trends: Massive Buildup and Modest Decline," Sentencing Project, September 17, 2019.

15. My efforts to obtain that information from Pew brought no response.

16. Private conversation with Mike Nellis, a renowned EM expert in the United Kingdom, February 3, 2021. As of this writing, the Vera Institute is compiling a national census of electronic monitoring devices by combining publicly released figures with projections from counties and states that either do not reveal or do not record EM census data.

17. P. St. John, "Probation Officials Concede Failures in GPS Tracking of Felons," *Los Angeles Times*, February 25, 2014.

18. M. Koran, "Lost Signals, Disconnected Lives," *Wisconsin Watch*, March 24, 2013.

19. R. Vetterkind, "State GPS Has Huge Problems," *Urban Milwaukee*, March 7, 2018.

20. "5 Investigates: Faulty GPS Monitoring Devices Being Replaced," WCVB, July 7, 2016.

21. Kofman, "Digital Jail: How Electronic Monitoring Drives Defendants into Debt," ProPublica, July 3, 2019.

22. O. Solon, "Digital Shackles: The Unexpected Cruelty of Ankle Monitors," *The Guardian*, August 28, 2018. Note that the article refers to Mr. Sentwali by his government name of Willard Birts.

23. R. Vetterkind, "Homeless Offenders Create Gaps in Wisconsin's GPS Monitoring System," *Wisconsin Watch*, March 4, 2018.

24. S. Balasubramanyam, "Electronic Monitoring Technology Must Be Regulated," *Law360*, August 18, 2019.

25. J. Petersilia, "Looking Back to See the Future of Prison Downsizing in America," Keynote Address to National Institute of Justice Conference, Arlington, VA, June 19, 2012.

26. J. Belur et al., "A Systematic Review of the Effectiveness of the Electronic Monitoring of Offenders," University College London, Department of Security and Crime Science, June 2017.

27. S. Aos, M. Miller, and E. Drake,

"Evidence-Based Public Policy Options to Reduce Future Prison Construction, Criminal Justice Costs and Crime Rates," Washington State Institute for Public Policy, October 2006.

28. For a more detailed analysis of the Bales report and other EM research, see J. Kilgore, "Electronic Monitoring: A Survey of the Research for Decarceration Activists," in "Key Resources" on the Challenging E-Carceration website.

29. A. Chabira, "A Routine Police Stop Landed Him on California's Gang Database. Is it Racial Profiling?," *Los Angeles Times*, May 9, 2019.

30. Office of Juvenile Justice and Delinquency Prevention, "Model Programs Guide Literature Review: Home Confinement and Electronic Monitoring," October 2014.

31. K. Sainju et al., "Electronic Monitoring for Pretrial Release: Assessing the Impact," *Federal Probation*, December 2018, pp. 3–15; K. Wolff et al., "The Impact of Location Monitoring Among US Pretrial Defendants in the District of New Jersey," *Federal Probation* 81, no. 3 (2017): 8–14.

32. National Immigrant Justice Center et al., *The Real Alternatives to Detention*, June 2019.

33. M. Alper and M. Durose, "Recidivism of Sex Offenders Released from State Prison: A 9-Year Follow-Up (2005–14)," U.S. Department of Justice, Bureau of Justice Statistics, May 2019.

34. W. Sawyer, "BJS Fuels Myths About Sex Offense Recidivism, Contradicting Its Own Data," Prison Policy Initiative, June 6, 2019.

35. Author interviews with Janice Bellucci, July 29, 2014; Frank Lindsay, August 5, 2014; Aaron Hicks, July 25, 2018.

36. S. Yoder, "Why Sex Offender Registries Keep Growing Even as Sexual Violence Rates Fall," *The Appeal*, July 3, 2018.

37. Cited in Yoder, "Why Sex Offender Registries Keep Growing."

38. Estimates of electronic monitoring costs derived from EM contracts with providers, made available by Freedom of Information Act requests from departments of corrections in Illinois, California, North Carolina, Iowa, and Indiana. Estimates of incarceration costs derived from the Vera Institute of Justice report series "The Price of Prisons"; S. Rayford, "These States Have the Highest Cost per Prisoner," *Los Angeles Times*, May 3, 2016; Justice Policy Institute, "Sticker Shock 2020: The Cost of Youth Incarceration," July 2020.

39. C. Mai and R. Subramanian, *The Price of Prisons: Examining Spending Trends, 2010–15*, Vera Institute of Justice, May 2017.

40. Sanders was a researcher on the Challenging E-Carceration Project of Media Justice, for which the author is founder and director.

41. Interview with the author, December 30, 2020.

42. Kofman, "Digital Jail."

43. M. Menendez and L. Eisen, *The Steep Costs of Criminal Justice Fees and Fines*, Brennan Center for Justice, November 2019.

44. J. Shapiro, "Measures Aimed at Keeping People Out of Jail Punish the Poor," NPR, May 24, 2014.

45. J. Kilgore and E. Sanders, "Lawsuit Confronts Extortion of Prisoners by Electronic Monitoring Firm," *Truthout*, August 6, 2018.

46. E. Murphy, "Paradigms of Restraint," *Duke Law Journal* 57 (2007): 1323–61.

47. K. Weisburd, "Monitoring Youth: The Collision of Rights and Rehabilitation," *Iowa Law Review* 101 (2015): 297–341.

48. B. Feuchter, "Criminal Law - Home Alone: Why House Arrest Doesn't Qualify for Presentence Confinement Credit in New Mexico—State v. Fellhauer," *New Mexico Law Review* 28, no. 3 (1998): 519–33.

49. State of Iowa v. Brett Calvin Hensley, Supreme Court of Iowa, Case no. 16-2178, filed May 4, 2018.

50. U.S.C. § 3585(b); Fraley v. U.S. Bureau of Prisons, 1 F.3d 924 (9th Cir. 1993).

51. Commonwealth v. Dixon, 1633 MDA 2016 (May 1, 2017).

52. Trial order, Merced, 2002 WL 34401528 (No. 2256-02), cited in C. Arnett, "From Decarceration to E-Carceration," *Cardozo Law Review* 41, no. 2 (2019), http://cardozolawreview.com/from-decarceration-to-e-carceration/.

53. State v. Duhon, 2005-NMCA-120, 138 N.M. 466, 122 P.3d.

54. This information is gathered from interviews and conversations with many people on EM as well as the author's work in the First-Followers Reentry Program in Illinois where he encountered many clients with those EM restrictions.

55. Precious Blood Ministry et al., "Letter in Support of HB 1115," January 30, 2019.

56. Chris Harrison, Testimony to Illinois State Assembly Judiciary-Criminal Committee, March 26, 2019.

57. P. James, "Once People Have Served Their Time in Prison, They Should Be Free," Shriver Center on Poverty Law, May 21, 2019.

58. K. Lerner, "Illinois Loosened Ankle Monitor Restrictions, but Advocates Say It's Too Soon to Celebrate," *The Appeal*, October 18, 2019.

59. The details on implementation have been gleaned from the author's many conversations with people on EM, personnel involved in reentry programs that service people on the monitor, and through the investigative efforts of members of the Illinois Coalition to Challenge Electronic Monitoring, especially Patrice James, director of community justice for the Shriver Center on Poverty Law, and Sarah Staudt, senior policy analyst for the Chicago Appleseed Fund for Justice. The mandated change in hours for movement appears in Memo from Craig Findley to the Director and Chief of Parole for the Illinois Department of Corrections, "Changes to Conditions of Release and Compliance Reporting," July 15, 2019.

60. State of North Carolina v. Torrey Grady, filed August 16, 2019.

61. Buting, Williams and Stilling, S.C., "Federal Lawsuit Seeks to Halt Wisconsin's Lifetime GPS Monitoring," buting.com, April 5, 2019.

62. Personal interview with the author, February 5, 2021.

63. Arnett, "From Decarceration to E-Carceration."

64. Response to Freedom of Information Act request to Massachusetts Parole Board, July 2017.

65. Anonymous interviewee, January 16, 2018.

66. Chicago Community Bond Fund, "No More Shackles: Arguing Against Pretrial Electronic Monitoring," video, 2019.

67. Presentation at "Electronic Monitoring and Surveillance in America," public forum, National Council for Incarcerated and Formerly Incarcerated Women and Girls, Yale University Law School, March 14, 2019.

68. Joint interview of Emmanuel Andre with Emmett Sanders, July 7, 2017.

69. Council of Europe, Committee of Ministers, "Recommendation (2014) 4 of the Committee of Ministers to Member States on Electronic Monitoring," February 19, 2014.

70. J. Kilgore, "Meet Mike Nellis, Global Expert on Electronic Monitoring," Challenging E-Carceration website, February 7, 2019.

71. Center for Media Justice, "Guidelines for Respecting the Rights of Individuals on Electronic Monitoring," March 22, 2018.

72. Renzema and Mayo-Wilson, "Can Electronic Monitoring Reduce Crime?" *Journal of Experimental Criminology* 1 (2005), 215–37.

5: THE "WAYWARD TECHNOLOGY": BUSTING THE MYTH OF ELECTRONIC MONITORING

1. M. Koran, "State's GPS Monitoring of Offenders Raises Concerns," *The Cap Times*, March 24, 2013.

2. Personal interview with the author, August 20, 2012.

3. Ashoka, "Welcome Change: Why We Need Data for Black Lives," video interview with Yeshimabeit Milner, YouTube, September 2, 2020.

4. S. Hartman, *Scenes of Subjection: Terror, Slavery, and Self-Making in Nineteenth-Century America* (New York: Oxford, 1997).

5. Arnett, "From Decarceration to E-Carceration," *Cardozo Law Review* 41, no. 2 (2019), http://cardozolawreview.com/from-decarceration-to-e-carceration.

6. Interviewers for Challenging E-Carceration included Emmett Sanders, Monica Cosby, and Chris Harrison. Other research work was done by Barbara Lacker-Ware, Tyler Camp, Jindu Obiofuma, and Anna Kurhajec.

7. We compiled a bibliography on electronic monitoring in 2018 as well as writing two articles surveying the existing literature. These are available on the "Key Resources" page of the Challenging E-Carceration website.

8. Author communication with Charles Kelley, Marion County Corrections, March 11, 2019; A. Kofman, "Digital Jail."

9. F. Hussein, "GPS Ankle Bracelet Company Booming in Indy," *IndyStar*, December 16, 2016.

10. Track Group, Inc., "Track Group Reports Fiscal 2019 Financial Results," news release, January 13, 2020.

11. ACLU Indiana, "Electronic Monitoring Overreliance in Marion County," May 6, 2020.

12. K. Turnbaugh, "Electronic Monitoring," *The Compiler* (Winter/Spring 1995).

13. See, for example, the Bond Fund's 2017 report, *Punishment Is Not a Service*, which heavily critiques the use of pretrial monitors in Cook County.

14. Jail population figures from Cook County Sheriff's website.

15. M. Hendrickson, "Cook County Sheriff's Office Runs Out of Electronic Monitoring Bracelets," *Chicago Sun-Times*, May 7, 2020.

16. J. McKim, "Electronic Shackles: Use of GPS Monitors Skyrockets in Massachusetts Justice System," GBH News, August 10, 2020.

17. Joshua Sabatini, "Number of Inmates Released on Electronic Monitoring Triples Following Bail Ruling," *San Francisco Examiner*, March 20, 2019.

18. K. Weisburd, "The Operation of Electronic Monitoring in the United States," draft report, 2021.

19. M. Hennessy-Fiske, "Immigrants Object to Growing Use of Ankle Monitors After Detention," *Los Angeles Times*, August 2, 2015. Total counts of ankle monitors are occasionally enhanced by a leak from a major EM player. BI, the largest electronic monitoring company in the U.S., in 2018 let it slip on its website that it claimed to have 144,000 people under electronic surveillance. It quickly took the post down.

20. P. Conway, "The 2002–03 Survey of Electronic Monitoring," *Journal of Offender Monitoring* 15, no. 1 (2002): 5–13.

21. Unpublished data gathered by Challenging E-Carceration project.

22. EC M&A website, "Sentinel Offender Services Acquires G4S Justice Services," https://ec-ma.com/.

23. J. Kilgore, "Electronic Monitors: How Companies Dream of Locking Us in Our Homes," *In These Times*, April 23, 2018.

24. U.S. Securities and Exchange Commission, Form 20-F for SuperCom, 2016.

25. Pew Research, 2015, op. cit.

26. Personal interview with the author, January 18, 2021.

27. Personal interview with the author, January 19, 2021.

28. "First 90 Days of Prisoner Resistance to COVID-19: Report on Events, Data and Trends," *Perilous Chronicle*, November 12, 2020.

29. Quoted in "First 90 Days of Prisoner Resistance to COVID-19."

30. Quoted in SNN Network, "SuperCom Discusses Leveraging Compliance Technology to Combat the Spread of Coronavirus," video interview, YouTube, April 8, 2020.

31. Personal interview, April 24, 2018.

32. Personal interview, December 30, 2020.

33. J. Pagonakis, "Wrongly Convicted Cleveland Man, Forced to Wear Ankle Monitor, Wants Ohio Law Changed," Cleveland News 5, April 5, 2018.

34. Personal conversation with activists of Youth Justice Coalition, October 14, 2017.

35. Other researchers include the Chicago Community Bond Fund, Aaron Cantu, Chaz Arnett, Kate Weisburd, The Samuelson Clinic, Puck Lo, and Lauren Kilgour.

36. Personal conversations with the author, 2017–18.

37. *Leave It to Beaver* was a 1950s TV comedy revolving around the very white Cleaver family and their wholesome life in the white world of suburbia.

38. Weisburd, "Operation," op. cit.

39. Personal interview, July 7, 2017.

40. Personal interview, July 7, 2017.

41. University of California, Berkeley, School of Law et al., *Electronic Monitoring of Youth in the California Justice System*, 2017.

42. Personal interview, January 17, 2019.

43. Personal interview, July 18, 2017.

44. Chicago Community Bond Fund, *Punishment Is Not a Service*, 2017.

45. Personal interview with the author, May 3, 2021.

46. Hearing Before Illinois House Judiciary Committee, February 22, 2019.

47. "LCLC and EM," unpublished report, September 2017.

48. J. Kilgore, "Coco Davis: They Monitored Her Uncle After He Had Died," Medium, June 8, 2018.

49. Personal conversation with the author, May 3, 2021.

50. Kathryn O. Greenberg Law Clinic et al., "Immigration Cyber Prisons: Ending the Use of Electronic Ankle Shackles," Research Report, June, 2021.

51. J. Kilgore, "Michael Robinson: The Wounds of an Ankle Shackle," *Challenging E-Carceration* (blog), January 31, 2020.

52. Cantu, "When Innocent Until Proven Guilty Costs $400 a Month—and Your Freedom," *Vice*, May 28, 2020.

53. Presentation at "Electronic Monitoring and Surveillance in America," public forum, National Council for Incarcerated and Formerly Incarcerated Women and Girls, Yale University Law School, March 14, 2019.

54. Cited in M. Lefkowitz, "Ankle Monitors Could Stigmatize Wearers, Research Says," Phys.org, June 18, 2020.

55. Mohawk Johnson (@MohawkJohnson), Twitter, January 9, 2021.

56. Personal interview, October 17, 2019.

57. This information draws on two personal interviews with Jerry Freeman, one by Emmett Sanders, April 12, 2019, and one by the author, April 23, 2019.

58. Personal interview, October 17, 2019.

59. "Deadnaming" refers to the degrading practice of calling a transgender person by the name they used before they transitioned.

60. Quoted in Media Justice, "Racism, Transphobia and Electronic Monitoring," *#NoDigitalPrisons* (blog), September 27, 2019.

61. For overview of the issue, see J. Rohrlich, "US Parole System Fraught with Allegations of Sexual Abuse," *Quartz*, February 21, 2020; for Illinois case, see "Ill. Probation Officer Guilty of Sex with Parolee," Corrections1, May 6, 2011.

62. "Demonstrating the Sex-Offender Exclusion Zones Undermine Efforts to Protect

Children," Prison Policy Initiative, n.d.

63. S. Valiente, "Welcome to Miracle Village," The Marshall Project, January 26, 2015.

64. J. Anderson, "Chicago 400 Alliance Shares the Difficulty of Finding Housing While on a Conviction Registry," *North by Northwestern*, October 29, 2020.

65. J. Brand, "The Criminalization of Homelessness Explained," *The Appeal*, June 29, 2018.

66. A. Cross et al., *Jail Incarceration in Wayne County, Michigan, 2018–19*, Vera Institute, 2021.

67. Freedom of Information Act request, July 2018.

68. Report to Budget and Finance Committee of San Francisco Board of Supervisors, October 30, 2020.

69. Data from Ohio and Kansas obtained from Freedom of Information Act requests to state departments of corrections.

70. Kathryn O. Greenberg Law Clinic et al. "Immigration Cyber Prisons: Ending the Use of Electronic Ankle Shackles, Research Report, June, 2021.

71. L. Mack, "Electronic Monitoring Hurts Kids and Their Communities," Juvenile Justice Information Exchange, October 24, 2018.

72. M. Alexander, "The Newest Jim Crow," *New York Times*, November 8, 2018.

73. Personal interview with the author, Inglewood, CA, August 18, 2014.

74. Quote from speech at rally for Meek Mill, Philadelphia, June 18, 2018.

75. Hall, "Unapologetic in Our Visions for Liberation: A Conversation with Arissa Hall," *#NoDigitalPrisons* (Medium blog series), August 27, 2020.

76. Personal interview with the author, July 4, 2018.

6: IMMIGRATION AND ELECTRONIC MONITORING: SMART-LINKS AND GEO-FENCES

1. National Immigration Project, Immigrant Defense Project, and Mijente, *Who's Behind ICE? The Tech and Data Companies Fueling Deportations*, 2018.

2. M. Zaveri and C. Hauser, "Mississippi Plants Knowingly Hired Undocumented Workers, ICE Says," *New York Times*, August 15, 2019.

3. A. Goodman, "Mississippi ICE Raids Targeted Workers Who Fought for Better Conditions," *Truthout*, August 9, 2019.

4. S. Eaton, "How Undocumented Workers Skirt Job Paperwork Requirements," Cleveland.com, January 30, 2019.

5. Personal interview with the author, January 19, 2021.

6. Personal interview with the author, August 15, 2019.

7. J. Gonzalez, Presentation to Our Tech Futures Conference, online event, June 1, 2021.

8. Quoted in "Braceros: History, Compensation," *Rural Migration News* 12, no. 2 (2006).

9. E. Blakemore, "The Largest Deportation in American History," History.com, June 18, 2019.

10. Bureau of Agricultural Economics, *Agricultural Situation* 31, no. 1 (1947).

11. UCLA Bracero History Archive, "About" and "History," braceroarchive.org.

12. J. Burnett, "The Bath Riots: Indignity Along the Mexican Border," NPR, February 2, 2006.

13. "Jose Carmon," UCLA Bracero History Archive.

14. J. Kim, "The Political Economy of the Mexican Farm Labor Program," *Aztlán* 29, no. 2 (2004): 13–55.

15. "Table 39. Aliens Removed or Returned: Fiscal Years 1892 to 2015," Yearbook of Immigration Statistics, Department of Homeland Security, 2015; K. Lytle- Hernandez, "UCLA Faculty Voice: Largest Deportation Campaign in US History Is No Match for Trump's Plan," *UCLA Newsroom*, March 23, 2017.

16. K. Lytle-Hernandez, "Largest Deportation Campaign in History Is No Match for Trump's Plan," The Conversation, March 8, 2017.

17. J. Jeer, "Operation Wetback Revisited," *The New Republic*, April 25, 2016.

18. Office of the Inspector General, "Operation Gatekeeper: An Investigation into Allegations of Fraud and Misconduct," Department of Justice, July 1998.

19. IDENT is in the process of being replaced by the Homeland Advanced Recognition Technology (HART) system, which is projected to handle 180 million biometric transactions by 2022. In addition to fingerprints, HART will gather facial profiles and DNA, and use databases to analyze people's relationship patterns. See J. Lynch, "HART: Homeland Security's Massive New Database Will Include Face Recognition, DNA, and Peoples' 'Non-obvious Relationships,'" Electronic Frontier Foundation, June 7, 2018; and Thales Group, "DHS's Automated Biometric Identification System IDENT—the Heart of Biometric Visitor Identification in the USA," n.d.

20. Ong Hing, "The Racism and Immorality of the Operation Gatekeeper Trap," *Border Criminologies* (blog), Oxford University, April 13, 2015.

21. Immigration Act of 1882, 47th Congress, 1st Sess., chap. 376.

22. See L. Fusao Inada, ed., *Only What We Could Carry: The Japanese American Internment Experience* (Berkeley, CA: Heyday Books, 2000).

23. "Unlocking Liberty: A Way Forward for U.S. Immigration Detention Policy," Lutheran Immigration and Refugee Service, 2011.

24. S. Gamboa, "House Approves U.S. Mexican Border Fence," Associated Press, September 14, 2006; W. Ewing, "Looking for a Quick Fix: The Rise and Fall of the Secure Border Initiative's High-Tech Solution to Unauthorized Immigration," Immigration Policy Center, April 15, 2010.

25. National Immigration Forum, "What Is Operation Streamline?," September 1, 2020.

26. E.A. Carson, "Prisoners in 2011," U.S. Department of Justice, Bureau of Justice Statistics, Washington, DC, December 2012.

27. M. Fisher, "After SBInet—the Future of Technology on the Border," Testimony Before

U.S. House Committee on Homeland Security, March 15, 2011.

28. "ICE Contract w/BI Incorporated for Electronic Monitoring/Alternatives to Detention Program, 2009 to 2014," *Prison Legal News*, July 20, 2009.

29. A. Panjwani, "ICE Digital Prisons: The Expansion of Mass Surveillance as ICE's Alternative to Detention," Just Futures Law and Mijente Report, May 2021.

30. New York Civil Liberties Union v. US Immigration and Customs Enforcement, case 1:18-cv-11557, filed December 11, 2018, in United States District Court for Southern District of New York.

31. D.R. Jones, "A Racist Trump Declares War on Immigrants of Color," Community Service Society of New York, August 22, 2019.

32. A. Hamilton, "Palantir CEO Alex Karp Claims the Company's Tech Is Used to Target and Kill Terrorists," *Business Insider*, May 26, 2020.

33. T. Hatmaker, "Palantir Wins $800 Million Contract to Build the US Army's Next Battlefield Software System," *TechCrunch*, March 27, 2019.

34. "EPIC v. CBP (Analytical Framework for Intelligence) Electronic Privacy Information Center, n.d.; Department of Homeland Security Privacy Office, "2015 Data Mining Report to Congress," February 2016.

35. P. Edge, "Privacy Impact Assessment for ICE Investigative Case Management," Department of Homeland Security, June 16, 2016.

36. S. Woodman, "Palantir Provides the Engine for Donald Trump's Deportation Machine," *The Intercept*, March 2, 2017.

37. J. Kilgore, "The Future of Immigration Enforcement and Surveillance," interview with Daniel Gonzalez, Medium.com, September 4, 2019.

38. Federal News Network Staff, "OMB Announces 'Cloud First' Policy for Agencies," Federal News Network, November 23, 2010.

39. P. Goldstein, "ICE Makes Headway on Its Cloud Migration," *FedTech*, January 9, 2019.

40. National Immigration Project et al., *Who's Behind ICE?*

41. J.V. Cuffari, "CBP Has Improved Southwest Border Technology, but Significant Challenges Remain," DHS Office of the Inspector General, February 2021.

42. "Fact Sheet: The Dangers of a Tech Wall," Mijente and Just Futures Law, 2021.

43. Ibid.

44. A. Ahlawat, Presentation to Our Tech Futures Conference, online convening organized by Mijente and Just Futures Law, June 3, 2021.

45. V. Eubanks, *Automating Inequality: How High-Tech Tools Profile, Police, and Punish the Poor* (New York: St. Martin's Press, 2018).

46. United States District Court for the Southern District of Mississippi, "Application for a Search Warrant," for the search of Koch Foods, August 5, 2019, Case 3:19-mj-00205-LRA Document 1.

47. Jacobsen, *The First Platoon: A Story of Modern War in the Age of Identity Dominance* (New York: Dutton, 2021), p. 17.

48. National Immigration Project et al., *Who's Behind ICE?*; personal interview with the author, January 19, 2020.

49. Quoted from "Privacy Impact Statement by Falcon-SA," in Mijente, "Breaking: Palantir's Technology Used in Mississippi Raids Where 680 Were Arrested," October 4, 2019.

50. Goodman, "Mississippi ICE Raids Targeted Workers."

51. Public charge was defined in the *Federal Register* on August 14, 2019, as an "alien who received one or more public benefits for more than 12 months in the aggregate within any 36-month period."

52. A. Glaser and W. Oremus, "A Collective Aghastness," *Slate*, June 28, 2018.

53. Charlotte and Dave Willner, "Reunite an Immigrant Parent with Their Child," fundraiser for RAICES, June 16, 2018.

54. S. Frankel, "Microsoft Employees Protest Work with ICE, as Tech Industry Mobilizes over Immigration," *New York Times*, June 19, 2018.

55. National Immigration Project et al., *Who's Behind ICE?*, 1.

56. T. Vazquez, "Advocates of Color Are Creating Alternatives to Detention for LGBTQ Migrants," Rewire News Group, August 7, 2019.

57. O. Tometi and C. Lipscombe, "What the Shooting of Alfred Olango Says About the State of Black Refugees in the U.S." *Time*, October 18, 2016.

58. U.S. Immigration and Customs Enforcement, "IDENT/IAFIS Interoperability Statistics," May 23, 2011.

59. "Removals Under the Secure Communities Program," Transactional Records Access Clearinghouse (TRAC), 2019.

60. Leadership Conference Education Fund, "Illinois Becomes First State to Withdraw from Secure Communities," May 5, 2011.

61. S. Browne, *Dark Matters: On the Surveillance of Blackness* (Durham, NC: Duke University Press, 2015), 128.

62. Personal interview with the author, September 16, 2019.

63. Personal interview, January 19, 2021.

7: THE PANDEMIC AND THE GROWTH OF E-CARCERATION

1. N. Klein, "How Big Tech Plans to Profit from the Pandemic," *The Guardian*, May 13, 2020.

2. Data for Black Lives, Full report of D4BL COVID-19 Movement Roundtable, cited in "We Will Not Allow the Weaponization of COVID-19 Data," *Yeshi* blog, Medium.com, May 18, 2020.

3. Conversation with the author, February 5, 2021.

4. S. Biddle, "Coronavirus Monitoring Bracelets

Flood the Market, Ready to Snitch on People Who Don't Distance," *The Intercept*, May 25, 2020.

5. Personal interview with the author, March 25, 2020.

6. L. Lerner, "Study: Nearly 16% of Illinois COVID-19 Cases Linked to Spread from Chicago Jail," *UChicago News*, June 5, 2020; M. Silver, "Milwaukee County Takes Steps to Reduce Number of Inmates During Coronavirus Pandemics," WUOM 89.7, May 1, 2020.

7. MediaJustice, "COVID-19: Release People from Prisons and Jails Without Electronic Monitoring," MediaJustice website, n.d.

8. Department of Homeland Security, US Immigration and Customs Enforcement, "Detention Management," May 8, 2021.

9. T. Walters, "Critics Decry Surveillance App That Tracks Undocumented Immigrants," *The Gotham Grind* (Medium publication), October 22, 2019.

10. Personal conversations with several individuals under supervision of the Illinois Department of Corrections (IDOC) and an IDOC official, all of whom preferred to remain anonymous.

11. T. DeMio, "Akron to Put 1,000 People on GPS," *Beacon Journal*, June 1, 2020.

12. Telmate website, telmate.com.

13. M. Osberg and D. Mehrotra, "When Your Freedom Depends on an App," *Gizmodo*, April 27, 2020.

14. From Acivilate website, acivilate.com.

15. Personal phone interview with the author, June 9, 2020.

16. A. Aziz, "The Power of Purpose: How Promise Is Using Technology to Solve the Epidemic of Mass Incarceration," *Forbes*, March 18, 2020.

17. "Libre by Nexus to Stop Using Body Affixed GPS Devices and Will Reapportion GPS Costs to Provide Free Healthcare to All Libre Clients," Libre by Nexus website.

18. *Dismantling Injustice* podcast, episode 12: "Breaking the Shackles with Amaha Kassa"; Donovan's apparent transformation didn't totally convince immigrant rights organizers in New York State. Anchored by African Communities Together and the Brooklyn Community Bail Fund, they launched the Break the Shackles campaign in 2019 to push for the passage of the Protect Immigrant New Yorkers Act to ban the use of electronic monitors by private companies that paid the bond to release individuals from immigration detention.

19. Kilgore, interview with Daniel Gonzalez.

20. SNN Network, "SuperCom Discusses Leveraging Compliance Technology to Combat the Spread of Coronavirus," video interview with Ordan Trabelsi, YouTube, April 8, 2020.

21. A. Greenberg, "Does Covid-19 Contact Tracing Pose a Privacy Risk?," *WIRED*, April 17, 2020.

22. "Crush COVID RI," Rhode Island State Department of Health website, n.d.

23. P. Mozur, R. Zhong, and A. Krolik, "In Coronavirus Fight, China Gives Citizens a

Color Code with Red Flags," *New York Times*, March 1, 2020.

24. "Intensified Surveillance in Containment Zones: COVID-19 Lockdown," *DD News*, May 2, 2020; A. Dey, "Delhi: Amid 4th Covid Wave, Districts Intensify Micro Containment Zone Strategy," *Hindustan Times*, April 9, 2021.

25. World Health Organization, "Scientific Brief," April 24, 2020.

26. N. Kofler and F. Baylis, "Ten Reasons Why Immunity Passports Are a Bad Idea," *Nature*, May 21, 2020.

27. "COVID-19 Response," Republic of Korea, Central Disaster Management Headquarters, February 25, 2020.

28. Illinois News Bureau, "Safer Illinois App Available for Faculty Members, Staff, Students," news release, August 13, 2020.

29. C. Cauguiran, "University of Illinois 'Safer Illinois' App Could Notify Users of Covid-19 Exposure in Minutes," ABC 7 Chicago, August 20, 2020.

30. Rokwire Editorial Team, "The Human Element: How the Need for Voluntary Adoption Changed Every Aspect of the Illinois Reopening Plan," Rokwire.org, August 17, 2020.

31. N. Broda, "Oakland University Asking Students, Staff to Wear 'BioButton' to Track COVID-19 Symptoms," *Oakland Press*, August 9, 2020.

32. P. Madhukar, "The Hidden Costs of High-Tech Surveillance in Schools," Brennan Center for Justice, October 17, 2019.

33. T. Sharma and M. Bashir, "Use of Apps in the Covid-19 Response and the Loss of Privacy Protection," *Nature Medicine*, May 26, 2020.

34. Data for University of Illinois from Data-USA, "COVID-19 in Numbers: University of Illinois at Urbana-Champaign."

35. Data for state of Illinois from US Census Bureau, "Quick Facts Illinois."

36. "What Is Rokwire?" Rokwire.org, n.d.

37. E. Schmidt, "Chinese Tech Landscape Overview," presentation to conference of National Security Commission on Artificial Intelligence, May 2019.

38. Amazon.com, "Amazon.com Announces Second Quarter Results," news release, July 30, 2020; "Facebook Reports 2nd Quarter 2020 Results," news release, July 30, 2020; J. Bursztynsky, "Apple Becomes First US Company to Reach a $2 Trillion Market Cap," CNBC, August 19, 2020.

39. K. Wiese, "Amazon's Profit Soars 220 Percent as Pandemic Drives Shopping Online," *New York Times*, April 29, 2021.

40. J. Stanley, *Temperature Screening and Civil Liberties During an Epidemic*, ACLU, May 19, 2020.

41. Human Rights Watch, "Mobile Location Data and Covid-19," hrw.org, May 13, 2020.

42. "Regulation 2016/679 of the European Parliament and of the Council," EUR-Lex, April 27, 2016.

43. D. Leprince-Ringuet, "GDPR: Fines Increased by 40% Last Year and They're About to Get a Lot Bigger," *ZDNet*, January 19, 2021.

44. "M. Rosemain, "French Watchdog Fines Google, Amazon for Breaching Cookie Rules,"

Reuters, December 10, 2020.

45. Quoted in D. James, "This Groundbreaking New Tool Reveals the Truth About Covid-19, *Essence*, June 10, 2020.

46. T. Wright, "Electronic Monitoring Isn't Helping People on Parole, It's Sending Them Back to Prison," *In These Times*, October 10, 2018.

8: CAMDEN, NJ, AND THE "SILICON VALLEY WAY OF DOING POLICING"

1. M. Boren et al., "Obama Lauds Policing in Camden, Holds It Out as Model," *Philadelphia Inquirer*, May 18, 2015; J. Gardner, "Camden County Police to Receive Catholic Charities Award," Diocese of Camden blog, n.d.

2. Personal conversation with the author, February 17, 2021.

3. K. Landergan, "The City That Really Did Abolish the Police," *Politico*, June 12, 2020.

4. Personal interview with the author, February 21, 2021.

5. B. Williams, NBC Nightly News, March 7, 2013.

6. W. Whitman, "I Dreamed in a Dream," from *Leaves of Grass*, Walt Whitman Archive, whitmanarchive.org.

7. New York Shipbuilding Corporation, "The Story of 'New York Ship,'" newyorkship .org.

8. B. McQuade, *Pacifying the Homeland: Intelligence Fusion and Mass Supervision* (Oakland: University of California Press), loc 176.

9. Vera Institute, "Incarceration Trends in New Jersey," 2018.

10. U.S. Census Bureau, "Quick Facts, Camden City, New Jersey."

11. P. Cole, "Camden, N.J., a Study in the Fate of Cities That Lose Industries," *Chicago Tribune*, August 25, 2000.

12. "Camden, N.J., Ranked Most Dangerous City in U.S.," *Washington Post*, November 22, 2005.

13. K. Fahim, "An Inside Look at Violence in Camden," *New York Times*, February 9, 2008.

14. "New Perspectives," *Newsweek*, January 9, 2005.

15. K. King, "The Power Broker Behind Camden, N.J.'s Upswing," *Wall Street Journal*, July 9, 2018.

16. A. Saul, "Let's Not Forget the Complicated History Behind Camden's Transformed Police," *MinnPost*, July 2, 2020.

17. R. Miller, "Camden Is Not a Blueprint for Disbanding the Police," *Salon*, June 13, 2020.

18. M. Maciag, "Why Camden, N.J., the Murder Capital of the Country, Disbanded Its Police Force," Governing.com, June 2014.

19. A. Steele, "Camden County Police Chief Scott Thomson Gets Raise," *Philadelphia Inquirer*, March 20, 2015.

20. "Policing in Camden Has Improved but Concerns Remain," ACLU website, May 18, 2015.

21. A. McNeil, "Camden Launches First 'Virtual Neighborhood Watch,'" *Daily Journal*, May 2, 2014.

22. McQuade, *Pacifying the Homeland*, loc 3518.

23. C. Friedersdorf, "The Surveillance City

of Camden, New Jersey," *The Atlantic*, December 12, 2013.

24. S. Rodas, "How Camden PD Plans to Use Artificial Intelligence to Help Anticipate Shootings," TAPinto.net, January 23, 2020.

25. Department of Homeland Security, *Advancing the Homeland Security Information Sharing Environment: A Review of the National Network of Fusion Centers*, 2019.

26. New Jersey Office of Emergency Management, Fall Bulletin, 2008.

27. R. Everett, "Camden, N.J, Police Use AI for Proactive Policing," *Government Technology*, February 19, 2020.

28. Department of Justice, "Department of Justice Announces Camden, N.J., as Selected City for New Violence Reduction Network," news release, September 29, 2014.

29. Delaware Valley Intelligence Center website.

30. M. Smith and R. Austin, "Launching the Police Data Initiative," White House Media Release, May 18, 2015.

31. McQuade, *Pacifying the Homeland*.

32. A. Bellano, "Camden Among Seven Cities Nationally Targeted in Sweep of Violent Crime Suspects," Patch.com, April 16, 2015.

33. T. Darragh, "Hundreds of Fugitives Picked Up in N.J. in U.S. Marshals' Sweep," NJ.com, March 24, 2016.

34. B. McQuade, "The Demilitarization Ruse," *Jacobin*, May 24, 2015.

35. Department of Justice, "Department of Justice Announces Camden, N.J., as Selected City."

36. Cited in B. McQuade, "The Camden Police Department Is Not a Model for Policing in the Post–George Floyd Era," *The Appeal*, June 12, 2020.

37. McQuade, *Pacifying the Homeland*, p. 162.

38. J. Hoban and B. Gourlie, "Training Camden: 3 Steps to Creating a Protector Culture," Police1.com, June 9, 2020.

39. Landergan, "The City That Really Did Abolish the Police."

40. J. Brady, "Obama: Camden, N.J., Police a Model for Improving Community Relations," *All Things Considered*, NPR, May 22, 2015.

41. Not in Our Town, "Camden's Turn," YouTube, August 28, 2020.

42. Ibid.

43. McQuade, "The Demilitarization Ruse."

44. "Opportunity Zones," Camden County website, n.d.

45. Subaru U.S. Media Center, "Subaru of America Celebrates New Headquarters in Camden, NJ with Grand Opening Ceremony," news release, April 27, 2018.

46. J. Walsh, "On the Waterfront: American Water Opens Camden Headquarters," *Courier Post* online, December 4, 2018; A. Zoppo, "What $260 Million in Tax Breaks Buys in Camden: Vast Holtec Campus," *Philadelphia Inquirer*, September 7, 2017.

47. H. Gillette, "Hope Boosted for 'Eds and Meds' in Camden," *Newsworks*, WHYY, April 7, 2014.

48. L. Nichols, "Philadelphia 76ers Open Training Facility in Camden," NJ.com, September 23, 2016.

49. Cited in D. Lampariello, "In Camden, N.J., Crime Plummeted After Police Was 'Disbanded,'" Fox5 News, June 15, 2020.

50. J. Shaw, "Violent Crime Has Dropped in Camden, but Homicides Are Up Slightly," *Inquirer*, January 3, 2020.

51. TAPinto Camden Staff, "Camden County Police Host U.S. DOJ Conference on Technologies Usage," TAPinto.net, June 6, 2019.

52. A. Rao, "These New Jersey Cities Reformed Their Police—What Happened Next?," *The Guardian*, June 26, 2020.

53. Ibid.

54. S. Fussell, "What Disbanding the Police Really Meant in Camden, New Jersey," *WIRED*, July 1, 2020.

55. I. Derysh, "Is Camden a Model for Police Reform? Activists Who Live There Don't Think So," *Salon*, July 3, 2020.

56. "Camden City, NJ," Departments at Rutgers-Camden, dept.camden.rutgers.edu.

9: E-CARCERATION, SETTLER COLONIALISM, AND THE OPEN-AIR PRISON

1. Interview in *Gaza Fights for Freedom* (dir. A. Martin, 2019).

2. T. Gash, "Forget Prisons, the Future of Punishment Will Be Virtual," *WIRED*, February 10, 2020.

3. The estimate of decrease in the incarcerated population combined the 2020 Department of Justice Census, "Prisoners in 2019," with an estimated count of prison populations done by the Vera Institute of Justice, "People in Jail and Prison in 2020." The DOJ figures showed a fall in prison population of about 10 percent from 2009 to 2019. The Vera count showed a 14 percent decrease in population in prisons and jails from the end of 2019 until the end of 2020. My figures also took into account the 2020 report from the Prison Policy Initiative, "The Whole Pie," which showed a total of nearly 2.3 million people in all state and federal prisons, local jails, immigrant detention centers, state psychiatric hospitals, Indian Country jails, military prisons, civil commitment centers, and prisons in U.S. territories.

4. "Correctional Population in the United States, 2017–18," U.S. Department of Justice, Bureau of Justice Statistics; N. Ghandnoosh, "Can We Wait 75 Years to Cut the Prison Population in Half?," Sentencing Project, March 8, 2018.

5. "The Most Significant Criminal Justice Policy Changes from the COVID-19 Pandemic," Prison Policy Initiative, May 18, 2021.

6. Ibid.

7. C. Richardson, "Joseph 'Jazz' Hayden Says NYPD Hits Sour Note with Uptown Stop-and-Frisks," *New York Daily News*, September 13, 2012.

8. Personal interview with the author.

9. H. Jacobs, "These Maps Show What the Gaza Invasion Would Look Like in Major U.S. Cities," *Business Insider*, July 25, 2014.

10. M. Plitnick, "Biden Must Face the Facts: Israel Is an Apartheid Regime," *The Nation*, January 21, 2021.

11. Y. Rabkin, "Demystifying Zionism," *Canadian Dimension*, September 2009.

12. Y. Litvin, "The Zionist Fallacy of 'Jewish Supremacy,'" *Al Jazeera*, January 9, 2019.

13. W. Cleveland, *A History of the Modern Middle East* (Boulder, CO: Westview, 2004), 228.

14. "The Nakba Did Not Start or End in 1948," *Al Jazeera*, May 23, 2017.

15. Ibid.

16. The framing of the notion of Israeli occupation is spelled out in the "Statement of the Special Rapporteur on the Human Rights Situation in the Palestinian Territory Occupied Since 1967 on the role of the EU with regards to the looming Israel annexation of parts of the Palestinian West Bank."

17. "List of Military Checkpoints in the West Bank and Gaza Strip," Israeli Information Center for Human Rights in the Occupied Territories, September 25, 2019.

18. Report of the independent commission of inquiry established pursuant to Human Rights Council S-21/1on the 2014 Gaza Conflict, A/HRC/29/52.

19. UN News, "Israel-Palestine: Political Solution Only Was to End 'Senseless' Cycles of Violence," May 27, 2021.

20. "Gaza Crisis: Toll of Operation in Gaza," BBC News, September 1, 2014.

21. N. Chomsky, "'Exterminate the Brutes': Gaza 2009," in N. Chomsky and I. Pappe, *Gaza in Crisis: Reflections on Israel's War Against the Palestinians* (Chicago: Haymarket, 2010).

22. Associated Press, "Gaza Is 'Open-Air Prison'? UN Humanitarian Chief," *NWorld*, March 12, 2010.

23. "Israel and Occupied Palestinian Territories," Amnesty International, 2020.

24. A. Simmons, "Life in the Gaza Strip—a Cauldron of Deficit, Despair and Desperation," *Los Angeles Times*, February 8, 2018.

25. D. Estrin, "Desperation in Gaza, Where over Half of Work Force Is Unemployed," NPR, December 29, 2018; Ibid.

26. A.N. Farzan et al., "How Conflict, Blockades and History Have Shaped the Geography of Gaza," *Washington Post*, May 14, 2021.

27. United Nations Relief and Works Agency, "Where We Work: Gaza Strip," December 2019.

28. Ibid.

29. M. Gaylard, *Gaza in 2020: A Liveable Place?*, United Nations, August 2012.

30. "The Global Surveillance Industry," report by Privacy International, 2016.

31. Ibid.

32. I.B. Zion, "As Attack Drones Multiply, Israeli Firms Develop Defenses," Associated Press, September 26, 2019.

33. A. Kane, "How Israel Became a Hub for Surveillance Technology," *The Intercept*, October 17, 2016.

34. "Israel's Occupation: 50 Years of Dispossession," Amnesty International, amnesty.org.

35. L. Alsaafin, "The Colour-Coded Israeli ID System for Palestinians," *Al Jazeera*, November 18, 2017.

36. D. Estrin, "Israel Uses Controversial Technology to Screen Palestinians in the West Bank," NPR, August 21, 2019.

37. "Elbit Deploys Third Integrated Fixed Tower in the US," *Israel Defense*, July 2, 2018; "Globalized Gaza: How Tech, Surveillance and Policing Flow from Occupied Palestine to the US Border," in *It's Going Down*, podcast, November 22, 2019.

38. W. Parrish, "The U.S. Border Patrol and an Israeli Military Contractor Are Putting a Native American Reservation Under 'Persistent Surveillance," *The Intercept*, August 25, 2019.

39. D. Arkin, "Pressing on the Screen: DAP 750 Is Bound to Transform Land Maneuvers," *IsraeliDefense*, November 15, 2020.

40. A. Ziv, "This Israeli Face-Recognition Startup Is Secretly Tracking Palestinians," *Haaretz*, July 15, 2019.

41. Associated Press, "Israel Used Calorie Count to Limit Gaza Food During Blockade, Critics Claim," *The Guardian*, October 17, 2012.

42. Ibid.

43. "Israel Reverses Punitive Restrictions Imposed in Recent Weeks, Including Its Ban on Entry of Fuel into Gaza but Leaves the 'Regular' Closure in Place," ReliefWeb, September 1, 2020.

44. H. Tawil-Souri, "Digital Occupation: Gaza's High-Tech Enclosure," *Journal of Palestinian Studies* 41, no. 2 (2012).

45. Ibid.

46. Cited in R. Abou Jalal, "How Gazans Are Dealing with the Internet Crisis," *Al-Monitor*, July 7, 2017.

47. "A Threshold Crossed: Israeli Authorities and the Crimes of Apartheid and Persecution," Human Rights Watch Report, April 27, 2021.

48. "13 Years of Illegal Closure with Impunity," ReliefWeb, July 20, 2020.

49. Cited in "13 Years of Illegal Closure with Impunity."

50. R. Dunbar-Ortiz, *An Indigenous Peoples' History of the United States* (Boston: Beacon Press, 2019).

51. L. Lin and N. Purnell, "A World with a Billion Cameras Watching You Is Just Around the Corner," *Wall Street Journal*, December 6, 2019.

52. R. Molla, "How Amazon's Ring Is Creating a Surveillance Network with Video Doorbells," *Vox*, January 28, 2020.

53. MediaJustice, "MediaJustice Responds to Report on Amazon Ring's Racist Culture and Police Partnerships," news release, December 9, 2019.

54. Ibid.

55. S. Fussell, "When Private Security Cameras Are Police Surveillance Tools," *Wired*, August 11, 2020.

56. Speri, "Stop-and-Frisk Never Really Ended. Now It's Gone Digital," *The Intercept*, October, 13, 2020.

57. Personal conversation with the author, July 21, 2020.

58. M. Schenwar and V. Law, *Prison by Any Other Name* (New York: The New Press, 2020).

59. Ibid.

60. N. Walrath, "Pacifying the Moral Economies of Poverty in an Era of Mass Supervision: An Interview with Brendan McQuade," Hampton Institute, September 19, 2019.

61. Stop LAPD Spying Coalition, "Fuck the

Police, Trust the People," June 2020; Hamid Khan, personal interview with the author, March 13, 2021.

62. A. Panjawani, "Ice Digital Prisons: The Expansion of Mass Surveillance as ICE's Alternative to Detention," Report for Mijente and Just Futures Law, May 2021.

63. Personal interview with the author, October 14, 2020.

64. L. Ben-Moshe, *Decarcerating Disability: Deinstitutionalization and Prison Abolition* (Minneapolis: University of Minnesota Press, 2020), 111.

10: DATA PROFITEERING FROM THE BODIES OF THE CRIMINALIZED

1. Cited in T. Scott, "Impact Investing and Venture Philanthropy's Role in Sowing the Seeds of Financial Opportunity," *Truthout*, June 10, 2017.

2. Quoted in A. Parmar, "Welcome to Surveillance Capitalism," *The Montclarion*, September 30, 2020.

3. I. Bernard, "The *Zong* Massacre," *Black Past*, October 11, 2011.

4. Z. Kish and J. Leroy, "Bonded Life: Technologies of Racial Finance from Slave Insurance to Philanthrocapital," *Cultural Studies* 29, nos. 5–6 (2015): 13.

5. Ibid.

6. J. Webster, "The *Zong* in the Contest of the Eighteenth-Century Slave Trade," *Journal of Legal History* 28, no. 3 (2007).

7. "Burden" (also "burthen"), a maritime term from the seventeenth to the nineteenth century, was used as a way to measure the cargo capacity of ships. One burden is approximately equal to 0.7 ton.

8. Webster, "The *Zong* in the Contest."

9. J. Oldham, "Insurance Litigation Involving the *Zong* and Other British Slave Ships, 1780–87," *Journal of Legal History* 28, no. 3 (2007).

10. Just Futures Law, "Does ICE Have My DMV Data?," webinar, March 10, 2020.

11. "Secure Our Data: Protecting the Privacy of Pennsylvania Residents and Drivers," Driving PA Forward, 2020.

12. R. Morin, "Rising Share of Americans See Conflict Between Rich and Poor," Pew Research Center, January 11, 2012.

13. B. White, "Why the Rich Are Freaking Out," *Politico*, January 30, 2014.

14. J. Toonkel, "Analysis: Wall Street Sees Social-Impact Bonds as a Way to Do Good and Do Well," Reuters, November 12, 2013.

15. C. Loomis, "The $600 Billion Challenge," *Fortune*, June 16, 2010.

16. T. Neilson, "10 Reasons Why the Giving Pledge Will Reshape Philanthropy," *Huffington Post*, December 10, 2010.

17. "Pay for Success: An Opportunity to Find and Scale What Works," The White House Office of Social Innovation and Civic Participation website, n.d.

18. "Spreading Gospels of Wealth," *The Economist*, May 19, 2012.

19. "Peterborough," Social Finance website, socialfinance.org.

20. E. Disley et al., "Lessons Learned from the Planning and Early Implementation of the Social Impact Bond at HMP Peterborough," RAND Corporation Technical Report, 2011, p. 12.

21. "World's First Social Impact Bond in UK Cuts Recidivism and Rewards Investors," Apolitical website, October 31, 2017.

22. "Social Impact Bond Project at Rikers Island," MDRC website, n.d.; D. Cohen and J. Zelnick, "What We Learned from the Failure of the Rikers Island Social Impact Bond," *Nonprofit Quarterly*, August 7, 2015.

23. N. Popper, "Success Metrics Questioned in School Program Funded by Goldman," *New York Times*, November 3, 2015.

24. I. Boggild-Jones and E. Gustaffson-Wright, "A Global Snapshot: Impact Bonds in 2018," Brookings Institution website, n.d.

25. G. Berlin, "Learning from Experience: A Guide to Social Impact Bond Investing," MDRC Report, 2016, p. 15.

26. M. Eldridge and K. Walker, "Principles for Selecting PFS Outcome Metrics," Urban Institute, June 7, 2016.

27. See, for example, Editorial Board, "Catch a Cold: Go to Prison," *Los Angeles Times*, November 26, 2013.

28. R. King and B. Elderbroom, *Improving Recidivism as a Performance Measure*, Urban Institute, Justice Policy Center, October 2014.

29. J.K. Roman, "Solving the Wrong Pockets Problem," Urban Institute, September 2015.

30. D. Dawkins, "Buffett, Gates and the Giving Pledge: Trust Issues for Billionaire Philanthropists," *Forbes*, October 29, 2019.

31. W. Megginson, *The PB Report 2015/2016*, Privatization Barometer, p. 1.

32. J. Netter and W. Megginson, "From State to Market: A Survey of Empirical Studies on Privatization," *Journal of Economic Literature* 39, no. 2 (2001): 321–89.

33. Urban Institute, "What Is Pay for Success (PFS)?," December 12, 2017.

34. M. Roy, N. McHugh, and S. Sinclair, "A Critical Reflection on Social Impact Bonds," *Stanford Social Innovation Review*, May 1, 2018.

35. C. Rhodes and P. Bloom, "The Trouble with Charitable Billionaires," *The Guardian*, May 24, 2018.

36. V. Eubanks, *Automating Inequality: How High-Tech Tools Profile, Police, and Punish the Poor* (New York: St. Martin's Press, 2018), 188.

37. W. Christl, "Corporate Surveillance in Everyday Life," *Cracked Labs*, Vienna, 2017.

38. D. Harvey, *A Short History of Neoliberalism* (Oxford: Oxford University Press, 2007).

39. Samson v. California, 547 U.S. 852.

40. J. Horowitz and C. Utada, "Community Supervision Marked by Racial and Gender Disparities," Pew Research Center, December 6, 2018.

41. Hispanic is an ethnic category used by the U.S. Department of Justice and the U.S. census to apply to anyone who self-identifies as Hispanic. Many people who are officially classified as Hispanic may prefer other categories such as Latinx or Latino/a, but Hispanic is the statistical category used by the U.S. government.

42. J. Eaglin and D. Solomon, *Reducing Racial and Ethnic Disparities in Jails: Recommendations for Local Practice*, Brennan Center for Justice, 2015.

43. Kish and Leroy, "Bonded Life."

44. "Do No Harm," American Anthropological Association website, November 1, 2012.

45. Better Than Cash Alliance website, betterthancash.org.

46. Ibid.

47. E. Larsen, "Fact Check: Do Millions of Americans Not Have Government Photo ID?," *Conservative Daily News*, December 2, 2018; S. Horwitz, "Getting a Photo ID So You Can Vote Is Easy, Unless You're Poor, Black, Latino or Elderly," *Washington Post*, May 23, 2016.

48. ACLU, "National Identification Cards: Why Does the ACLU Oppose a National I.D. System?," n.d.

49. Electronic Frontier Foundation, "Mandatory National IDs and Biometric Databases," n.d.

50. N. Kobie, "The Complicated Truth About China's Social Credit System," *WIRED*, June 7, 2019.

51. D. Harvey, *A Brief History of Neoliberalism* (New York: Oxford University Press, 2007).

52. C. Collins et al., "The Giving Pledge at 10: A Case Study in Top Heavy Philanthropy," Institute for Policy Studies, briefing paper, August 3, 2020.

11: ABOLITION AND CHALLENGING E-CARCERATION

1. M. Abu-Jamal, "From One Struggle to Another: Lessons from the First Abolition Movement," Abolition for the People Series, Medium.com, October 26, 2020.

2. Yeshi, "We Will Not Allow the Weaponization of COVID-19 Data," *Yeshi* blog, Medium.com, May 18, 2020.

3. Stop LAPD Spying Coalition, "Police State and Our Journey Toward Abolition," webinar, January 17, 2021.

4. F. Moten and S. Harney, "The University and the Undercommons: Seven Theses," *Social Text* 79, vol 22, no. 2 (2004): 101, 114.

5. T. Sonnemaker, "Google Will Pay $2.6 Million to Workers over Claims Its Hiring and Pay Practices Were Biased Against Women and Asians," *Business Insider*, February 1, 2021; S. Noble, "Google Has a Striking History of Bias Against Black Girls," *Time*, March 26, 2018.

6. "Community Defense: Sarah T. Hamid on Abolishing Carceral Technologies," *Logic*, no. 11, August 31, 2020.

7. C.L.R. James, *The Future in the Present: Selected Writings* (London: Allison and Busby, 1977).

8. See M. Stahly-Butts, "Beyond 'Criminal Justice Reform': Conversations on Police and Prison Abolition," presentation, NYU Review of Law and Social Change Conference, October 14, 2016; M. Stahly-Butts and R. Herzing, "Abolition Is Liberation," presentation, Portland Institute for Contemporary Art, November 23, 2019; A. Mische, "Between Disruption and Coordination: Building Insider-Outsider Strategies," *Peace Policy*, September 15, 2020. See also J. Duffy Rice and C. Smith, "Episode 20: Mariame Kaba and Prison Abolition," in *Justice in America*, podcast, March 20, 2019; D. Spade, "The Queer and Trans Fight for Liberation— and Abolition," *Abolition for the People* (Medium publication), 2020.

9. Personal interview with the author, January 8, 2021.

10. Chicago Community Bond Fund, *Punishment Is Not a Service*.

11. K. Lerner, "As States Look to Cut Jail Populations, Electronic Miniature Prisons Are on the Rise," *The Appeal*, February 28, 2019.

12. J. Duda, "Towards the Horizon of Abolition: A Conversation with Mariame Kaba," *The Next System Project*, November 9, 2017.

13. S. Crawford, "Facial Recognition Laws Are (Literally) All Over the Map," *WIRED*, December 16, 2019.

14. D. Gutman, "King County Council Bans Use of Facial Recognition Technology by Sheriff's Office, Other Agencies," *Seattle Times*, June 2, 2021.

15. B. Daley, "Neuroscientists Put the Dubious Theory of 'Phrenology' Through Rigorous Testing for the First Time," *The Conversation*, January 22, 2018.

16. M. Devich-Cyril, "Defund Facial Recognition," *The Atlantic*, July 5, 2020.

17. D. Brand, "New City Law Compels NYPD to Explain Surveillance Tools and Strategies," *Queens Daily Eagle*, July 16, 2020.

18. STOP LAPD Spying Coalition, "Fuck the Police, Trust the People: Surveillance Bureaucracy Expands the Stalker State," June 2020.

19. Quoted in J. Levine and E. Meiners, *The Feminist and the Sex Offender: Confronting Sexual Harm, Ending State Violence* (New York: Verso, 2020), 35.

20. E. Bernstein, "The Sexual Politics of the 'New Abolitionism,'" *Differences* 18, no. 3 (2007): 128–51.

21. Cited in B. Richie, "How Anti-violence Activism Taught Me to Become a Prison Abolitionist," *Feminist Wire*, January 21, 2014.

22. International Association of Chiefs of Police, *Tracking Sex Offenders with Electronic Monitoring Technology*, 2008.

23. B. Richie, *Arrested Justice: Black Women, Violence, and America's Prison Nation* (New York: NYU Press, 2012).

24. INCITE!, "Stop Law Enforcement Violence," n.d.

25. J. Levine and E.R. Meiners, *The Feminist and the Sex Offender: Confronting Sexual Harm, Ending State Violence* (New York: Verso, 2020).

26. K. Zgoba, W.G. Jennings, and L.M. Salerno, "Megan's Law 20 Years Later: An Empirical Analysis and Policy Review," *Criminal Justice and Behavior* 45, no. 7 (2018): 1028–46.

27. J.T. Walker, S. Maddan, and B.E. Vásquez, "The Influence of Sex Offender Registration and Notification Laws in the United States," working paper, Arkansas Crime Information Center, 2007.

28. S. Solomon, "The Sex Offender Registry Leaves Female Sex Offenders Open to Abuse," *Vice*, October 24, 2017.

29. C. Zoukis, "Sex Offender Registries: Common Sense or Nonsense?," *Criminal Legal News*, May 15, 2018.

30. Personal interview, February 15, 2020.

31. Personal interview, October 15, 2020.

32. S. Camacho et al., "The Crisis of Capitalism, Role of Technology and Our Imaginations," *Radical Ecological Democracy*, October 5, 2020.

33. Personal interview with the author, March 13, 2021.

34. L. Miller, "LAPD Will End Controversial Program That Aimed to Predict Where Crimes Would Occur," *Los Angeles Times*, April 21, 2020; T. Ryan Mosley and J. Strong, "The Activist Dismantling Racist Police Algorithms," *MIT Technology Review*, June 5, 2020.

35. T. Petty et al., *Reclaiming Our Data*, Our Data Bodies, June 2018.

36. Our Data Bodies, *Digital Defense Playbook: Community Power Tools for Reclaiming Data*, 2018.

37. Our Data Bodies, *Digital Defense Playbook*.

38. "Safe or Just Surveilled? Tawana Petty and the Fight Against Facial Recognition Surveillance," *Logic*, May 4, 2020.

39. A.R. Levy, "The Incredible Belief That Corporate Ownership Does Not Influence Media Content, *Common Dreams*, September 17, 2019.

40. C. Kumanyika, "Ruth Wilson Gilmore Makes the Case for Abolition," *The Intercept*, June 10, 2020.

41. S. Browne, *Dark Matters: On the Surveillance of Blackness* (Durham, NC: Duke University Press, 2015).

42. J. Kilgore, "A History of Tracking Black Bodies, Policing Boundaries," interview with Simone Browne and Brenda Sanya, *#NoDigitalPrisons* (Medium blog series), June 20, 2018.

INDEX

PUBLISHING IN THE PUBLIC INTEREST

Thank you for reading this book published by The New Press. The New Press is a nonprofit, public interest publisher. New Press books and authors play a crucial role in sparking conversations about the key political and social issues of our day.

We hope you enjoyed this book and that you will stay in touch with The New Press. Here are a few ways to stay up to date with our books, events, and the issues we cover:

- Sign up at www.thenewpress.com/subscribe to receive updates on New Press authors and issues and to be notified about local events
- Like us on Facebook: www.facebook.com/newpressbooks
- Follow us on Twitter: www.twitter.com/thenewpress
- Follow us on Instagram: www.instagram.com/thenewpress

Please consider buying New Press books for yourself; for friends and family; or to donate to schools, libraries, community centers, prison libraries, and other organizations involved with the issues our authors write about.

The New Press is a 501(c)(3) nonprofit organization. You can also support our work with a tax-deductible gift by visiting www.thenewpress.com/donate.